W9-AOY-965

Resourcing Early Learners

Routledge Research in Education

Resourcing Early Learners

New Networks, New Actors

**Sue Nichols, Jennifer Rowsell,
Helen Nixon and Sophia Rainbird**

Routledge
Taylor & Francis Group
NEW YORK   LONDON

First published 2012
by Routledge
711 Third Avenue, New York, NY 10017

Simultaneously published in the UK
by Routledge
2 Park Square, Milton Park, Abingdon, Oxon OX14 4RN

*Routledge is an imprint of the Taylor & Francis Group,
an informa business*

© 2012 Taylor & Francis

The right of Sue Nichols, Jennifer Rowsell, Helen Nixon, and Sophia Rainbird to be identified as the authors of this work has been asserted in accordance with sections 77 and 78 of the Copyright, Designs and Patents Act 1988.

Library of Congress Cataloging-in-Publication Data
Nichols, Sue, 1959–
    Resourcing Early Learners : New Networks, New Actors / Sue Nichols, Jennifer Rowsell, Helen Nixon and Sophia Rainbird.
        p. cm. — (Routledge Research in Education ; 78)
    1. Early childhood education—Information resources.   I. Title.
    LB1139.23.N53 2012
    372.21—dc23
    2011052090

ISBN13: 978-0-415-89759-4 (hbk)
ISBN13: 978-0-203-11293-9 (ebk)

Typeset in Sabon
by IBT Global.

Printed and bound in the United States of America on sustainably sourced paper by IBT Global.

Contents

Figures

Tables

Preface

That young children's learning is important has become a generally accepted view. That those charged with the care of young children need to understand this, and to interact with children in ways that support and develop their capacities as learners, is regularly spoken of as a global imperative. This book is about how caregivers are resourced for this task. At the same time, it casts a critical eye at the concept of early learning. It does this by examining the ways in which knowledge, practice, and goods associated with the young child as learner are circulated through different institutions accessed by parents.

In the prior to school period, the range of organizations and services aiming to resource parents of young children is diverse and proliferating. They include government departments, corporations, community organizations, advocacy groups, and others, at levels from the neighborhood to the international. While they may share an interest in the young child as the subject of a social program, their agendas differ, as do the knowledge bases through which they define the child as learner, and the histories of practice through which they put in place specific programs and activities. The outcome of these differences is that there is no single universally agreed upon definition of early learning or belief concerning what is required to bring it about. Instead, we argue for the importance of understanding this complex, dynamic landscape in terms of these multiple agendas and their impacts on parents and their young children.

This book is the outcome of four years of sustained field work and analysis, carried out across two national and three regional contexts. This project took the research team into many settings from vast shopping malls to family homes, from small country towns to corporate websites. Trained as ethnographic researchers, we added to our repertoires the conceptual resources of actor-network theory and material semiotics to enable us to analyze the processes through which the subject 'early learning' was assembled in different sites and the trajectories through which it was mobilized.

This analysis is organized around four categories of social institution which we found to be significant players in the contemporary field of early learning. Using generic designators—'the mall', 'the clinic', 'the church', and 'the library'—we signal the situated, everyday nature of these institutions (each suburb or town has its own library or shopping strip) and at the same time their social power (The Mall, The Church, etc.). They represent major social institutions with particular reasons for targeting, and intervening in the lives of, young children and their caregivers.

Acknowledgments

The project on which this book is based was funded by the Australian Research Council. Field work in the US was supported by a Rutgers University grant while the University of South Australia funded a pilot study and an honors student scholarship. We are grateful to our excellent team of research assistants comprising Philippa Milroy, Helen Ovsienko, and Helen Sims. Sarah Rose gave stellar administrative support while Imogen Speck provided much appreciated editorial assistance. Thanks to Phil Cormack for critical reading.

Finally our most sincere thanks go to the service providers and the parents who allowed us to spend time with them, ask questions, take photographs of their resources, and generally make nuisances of ourselves. Without your generous participation, this book would not have come into being.

1   The Early Learning Agenda

RAISING EARLY LEARNERS

Debbie is married to a truck driver and the family lives on the outskirts of an Australian country town within reach of the suburban sprawl. With husband Andy, she is raising daughters Morgan (5) and Bonnie (2). Debbie did not complete high school but values education highly for her own children and wants them to attend a private school. She shops around for the cheapest educational toys and activities she can find and uses the Internet to source free materials. Debbie attends a church-run local playgroup and undertook the parenting class run by the state government's health service. She is not a reader and never goes to the town's library: Andy says 'it's called the Internet these days'.

Joanna and her two sons Sam and Alberto live with Sams' father in an American university town. The library is Juliana's favorite place to find materials and activities to support her children's learning. Not only does it have a good selection of children's books and DVDs in both Spanish and English, but it runs Spanish language classes which her eldest attends. Joanna reads parenting books like the 'What to Expect' series, and finds information through Google searches, but if she is ever worried about her children's development she'll talk to the pediatrician at their regular check-up.

Simon is the home-based father to Cassandra (6) and Brian (3), enabling his partner Kristine to work long hours at a well-paying job. Simon wants to ensure that his children's lives are filled with enriching activities. This involves purchasing educational materials but, because Simon doesn't like his children to spend too long in commercial environments, he does quite a bit of research online and goes to stores alone on the weekend. He likes Leapfrog products and educational DVDs which the children can watch in the van while he is driving. Simon has a favorite parenting website and says 'the Internet has been wonderful' in breaking down the isolation of being 'almost a single parent'.

These are some of the parents who told us how and why they invested time, thought, and money in raising their young children to be academically and socially successful in their immediate and future lives. These brief summaries highlight some of the strategies they have used, the services they have accessed and the particular goals which have driven their resourcing practices. They are bringing up children at a time when there has been an upsurge in public interest in the young child as the subject of concern and active shaping. Around the world, there has been significant policy making, funding and service development aimed at bringing the smallest citizens and their carers into the spaces and networks of institutions offering to support them. Along with these initiatives come agendas that privilege particular beliefs about young children and their development and learning, that encourage particular ways of working with and caring for children, and that empower particular agents in the delivery of services aimed at producing early learners.

INVESTING IN EARLY LEARNING: THE SOCIOPOLITICAL CONTEXT

The president of the US office in 2010 released a fact sheet titled *Promoting Early Learning for Success in School and in Life* (US Departments of Education and Health and Human Services). In the statement's opening sentence President Barak Obama is described as 'committed to creating a 21st century workforce' and as viewing early learning programs as 'an integral component to creating an educational system that is internationally competitive'. Among the initiatives detailed in the sheet is an Early Learning Challenge Fund which will be accessed by state governments prepared to 'establish model systems of early learning and development for children from birth to kindergarten'.

In making this commitment, Obama was in part responding to considerable lobbying pressure from a cluster of coalitions representing business, education, and community interests. The role of business leaders in promoting early learning is a notable characteristic of the contemporary scene. An example is Blake Wade, president of the Oklahoma Business Roundtable and a spokesperson for the coalition Oklahoma Champions for Early Opportunities (OCEO). This group provides speakers who attend organizational meetings to speak in favor of increased funding for early childhood education. Wade underlines the economic argument in a quote on the organization's Facebook page:

> This is an economic issue as much as it is an education issue. Businesses need to be able to tap a highly skilled workforce and benefit from the expertise of tomorrow's leaders. Early learning makes good economic sense. (Oklahoma Champions for Early Opportunities 2011)

OCEO supports its campaign with reference to the notion of a critical period in brain development which is assumed to occur in the first four years of life:

About 85 percent of a child's brain architecture is developed by the time he or she is 3 years old, but less than 4 percent of education dollars is typically spent on children by that time. (ibid.)

The Gates Foundation uses the same comparison between brain development and financial investment in its detailed proposal to fund model early learning centers in Washington State (Bill and Melinda Gates Foundation 2005), and indeed versions appear in many places. The rhetorical device can be traced back to Voices for America's Children, an organization which commissioned an analysis comparing public funding for early childhood education with funding for schools and colleges. In the report a graph appears which charts, on one line, brain development over time, and on another, state funding for education over time. The logic of this representation is that funding is being spent on a period where the pay-off is low as presumably the child's brain has virtually stopped growing. This report *Early Learning Left Out* was widely quoted and quickly began appearing as links on the websites of other organizations in the US, such as Texans Care for Children and the Family Policy Center Iowa, and globally, including the Australian Council for Educational Research.

The notion of a critical period of brain development is central to contemporary concerns about the early years of children's lives and the argument that these years ought to be spent in learning (Nadesan 2002). While the idea that children develop rapidly in the early years is not new, its contemporary reemergence owes much to media translations of developments in the field of neuroscience. Like many who write in the field of early childhood education, the authors of this book are not experts in neuroscience. However, it can be seen from the burgeoning of media and consumer products related to claims about infant brain development, that lack of specialist knowledge has not been an impediment to participation in public discourse.

In the process of translating neuroscience into concepts that laypeople can work with, the notion of the critical period has been made to carry a lot of weight. This notion presents the brain as actively growing and thus amenable to influence in the early years but as hard wired and fixed after this period of early growth is over. A structural model of the brain underpins claims such as this from the website of advocacy group First Five Nebraska:

> By the time a child is five years old, the architecture of the brain, the foundation for all future learning, has been built. We can never go back and rewire the foundation. (First Five Nebraska 2011)

The task for those charged with child-rearing is to actively build young children's brain architecture. Older children whose educational achievement is below average are thus positioned as structurally flawed, and their carers are judged as incompetent builders. When looked at retrospectively, given what is known about the composition of the category of 'failing' students, it is possible to see how the argument about brain development impacts differently on families depending on their class and race status. In a review of media and consumer texts, Nadesan has unpacked the class assumptions underpinning the early brain development debate. She notes that:

> Working-class parents, who lack the cultural capital of their middle-class counterparts, are implicitly targeted as lacking the skills to adequately stimulate and prepare their infants. (Nadesan 2002, 422)

The message of neuroscience regarding stimulating young children's brains is not new to middle-class parents who have for generations been consuming advice books and magazines promoting this very idea (Seiter 1993; Woollet and Phoenix 1996; Gram 2004). Thus an established middle-class mode of child-rearing is even more firmly cemented in its privileged position. The class inflection of the debate about early learning is seen even more clearly when considering the underpinning economic arguments. Preventing the next generation of welfare dependent adults from being created is explicitly part of the case presented by business leaders like Blake Wade, referred to earlier as promoting the idea of a critical period:

> [C]hildren who take part in early learning are more likely to succeed in academics, graduate high school and attend college. They are less likely to experience teen pregnancy, have disciplinary problems or be forced to go on welfare programs. (Oklahoma Champions of Early Opportunities 2011 ibid.)

Early learning is thus being framed up, at least in part, as a welfare issue. As such it becomes the business of more than families and the education system.

'Educare'—The Drive to Integration

The *Starting Strong* report, commissioned by the OECD, argued for the global adoption of the term 'Early Childhood Education and Care' to express a new 'systemic and integrated approach for children from birth to 8 years' (OECD 2006, 13). This new approach was described as involving the state and the family in a shared responsibility for young children's socialization, bringing together its social and educational dimensions (Haddad 2001). While several countries had already moved in this direction (for instance Sweden), the drive for integration of education and care became policy in an increasing number of national jurisdictions in the following decade.

The hybridizing of education and care is expressed in the term 'Educare', the modern use of which can be traced back to American professor of pediatrics Bettye Caldwell, who described herself as 'carrying on a one-woman campaign' for its adoption (Caldwell 1991). She would have been delighted to learn that the British government named Educare a key element in its *Five Year Strategy for Children and Learners* (Department of Education and Skills 2004). Early childhood was but one element in this policy which covered infants up to university students and was based on the notion of 'seamless service' both between different agencies and from one stage in a child's life to the next.

As a means to deliver 'seamless' service for young children and their families, the concept of the 'one-stop shop' has gained ground, manifesting in a range of variations in different national and regional contexts. Describing the UK version, government minister Charles Clark stated:

> All parents [are] able to get local one-stop support through Children's Centres that will provide childcare, education, health, employment and parenting support. (Department of Education and Skills 2004, 7)

One-stop shops are generally not new projects but have been created through processes of amalgamation and extension of existing services over which governments have had historical control, such as schools. Inevitably this has meant that the degree to which all the elements claimed to be part of an integrated service actually are present is highly variable. Much of the initial emphasis, by states moving toward integration, has been on the colocation of long-day child care and sessional kindergarten, enabling parents to enroll their children into the one center from infancy to preschool. It is difficult in practice to include substantial health services on sites not designed as clinics; where a health component is present, this has generally taken the form of simple health checks, information provision, and educational programs.

Critics of integration policy point out that the rhetoric of seamlessness draws attention from the tensions and turf-wars between sectors (Cardini 2006). Education has historically greater institutional strength than child care owing to its extensive school sector and more highly educated and paid practitioners. The downward extension of the curriculum, discussed ahead, has met with resistance from some in the care sector. Another tension is between the state, which has a mandate to deliver the public good, and the private sector, which is responsible to its shareholders. The business drive for early childhood resourcing is at the same time a strategy for getting government resources into the hands of private companies.

It does appear, though, that moves to integration have encouraged previously separate agents to increase their awareness of each other's activities and to forge connections and relationships. At the same time, the rhetoric of collaboration and partnership creates openings for a diverse array of players to lobby, mobilize, forge alliances, attempt to influence the agenda, and jostle for resources. The context of integration has contributed to making 'early learning' a space of fuzzy and permeable boundaries, subject to continual redefinition in policy and practice.

The Early Learning Vaccine

Arguments for intervening in the lives and care of young children have gained ground in recent years and have been used to marshal a range of services and stakeholders to the agenda. At the heart of these arguments lie two convictions: that the child contains the seeds of future success and failure, and that the health of a society or nation can be calculated by balancing its successful citizens on one side of the ledger and its failures on the other. Typical of such arguments is the policy statement for the Australian *Stronger Families and Communities Strategy*:

> [E]arly intervention [is] an important strategy for improving the life chances of all children and tackling the root cause of complex social problems'. (Department of Family and Community Services 2005, 3)

Then UK prime minister Tony Blair, interviewed in 2006, said 'we should be intervening far earlier'. The idea that waiting until children are at school is too late is one of the beliefs underpinning early intervention initiatives. Blair based his argument on the assumption that it is possible to tell at an early age the children who will cause trouble for their society when they are older, and by targeted intervention prevent the emergence of full-blown disorder:

> I think if you talk, as I do, to teachers sometimes they will tell you . . . at age 3, 4, 5 they are already noticing the symptoms of a child that when they are 14 or 15 is out on the street causing mayhem. (Quoted in Smeyers 2008, 730)

The school is here understood as the site where preexisting problems are rendered visible, rather than as contributing to the problems. These problems, it is believed, precede the child's entry into formal education. By implication, they are being formed in the settings where young children are raised—their families and communities.

Intervention initiatives take two broad forms: targeted and universal. Interventions targeted at preschool children in disadvantaged populations have been a feature of the landscape for decades; the longest running example is Head Start in the US. Targeted interventions of this kind are specifically designed for problematic subpopulations. States use existing data on social outcomes such as unemployment, high school completion, and juvenile crime rates to identify the communities in which early intervention programs will be located. Programs such as this, which were focused on socializing children of marginalized communities, left the mainstream middle-class population largely untouched.

Universal intervention programs aim to deliver to a whole population some program or treatment which promotes practices believed to improve the life chances of every individual. Universal early childhood interventions are a sign that governments wish to more actively monitor how citizens are raising their children. In achieving this goal they have looked to existing universal services, such as primary health care, which can incorporate new dimensions without greatly altering their mode of delivery. The economic rationale is as attractive to policy makers as it was for vaccinating against polio: a cheap, simple solution administered to a whole population through the medium of universal primary health care.

In the US, where regular well-being checkups with the pediatrician are routine, families are being offered advice on reading to their young children. Reading to children is one practice that has been shown to confer certain advantages on children and has been hailed as an ideal focus for early intervention. Reach Out and Read involves pediatricians talking about reading to children in check-ups, offering advice on techniques, and providing families with free books (Needleman et al. 2005). A similar approach is taken in some Australian states through the nurse home visiting service for parents of infants. In South Australia, parents take their child's 'blue book' (infant health records) to the library to receive their book bag.

Public commentary on these programs frequently uses medical language which represents early learning interventions as a form of vaccination or cure and health practitioners as the go-to people for literacy advice, as in this article from e-magazine *Raising Arizona Kids*:

> Instead of leaving the doctor's office with a prescription for their child's ear infection or strep throat, some Valley parents are taking home Curious George or Madeline. (http://rakschoolsetc.wordpress.com/tag/improving-reading-skills/)

Parents who visit health services in the San Francisco Bay Area are given a Prescription for Reading which is signed by the doctor just like a prescription for medication. This form encourages parents to read with their child for twenty minutes a day.

Universal programs can also be used to identify children who are presumed to be at risk and who then become the subject of more targeted interventions. In order to do this, systems of assessment are needed. In some universal home visiting services the mother's responses to a survey will determine whether she and her child will be offered other services such as specialist playgroups, intensive visits or parent education. Some states are investing in the implementation of a universal screening instrument such as the Early Development Index (Jianghong, D'Angiulli, and Kendall 2007). In Singapore, the online Development Screening Questionnaire aims to 'inform [parents] of their child's developmental status immediately' in the form of a profile giving the child's 'developmental age' in each of five domains (Kwan and Nam 2004, 121). If a child's development is below par, parents are given advice as to the kinds of services they should be accessing.

The From-Birth Curriculum

Not long ago curriculum was a concept applied only to school education. This approach to structuring learning, teaching, and assessment is now in many countries applied to children from birth. In the United Kingdom, the Early Years Foundation Stage was introduced in 2008, providing guidelines for practitioners working with children aged 0 to 5. It specified 69 learning goals to be met before school entry and provided practitioners with a detailed assessment format with which to profile each child (Department for Children Schools and Families 2008). Controversially, the learning goals included literacy skills that previously would not have been taught until formal schooling including writing simple sentences (Curtis 2008).

The introduction of standardized assessment of literacy and numeracy in the first years of formal schooling, and baseline assessment at school entry, has been identified as a major influence in the downward reach of the curriculum (BERA 2003). The prior to school year (variously termed preschool and kindergarten) has become significantly more focused on preparation for schooling with the introduction of explicit teaching of a range of skills. As a result, there is now concern being expressed about the 'transition' to preschool and the question of children's 'readiness' for this environment (Pianta et al. 2001).

Looking after young children, it is no longer sufficient to care for them; adults are required to facilitate learning and to intentionally teach. Governments are setting up processes for monitoring the kind of learning activities that children are exposed to in the prior to school years. The Australian national census for the first time in 2008 added questions for parents about the 'informal learning' of children aged between zero and two years old (Australian Bureau of Statistics 2009).

The change in emphasis has been particularly marked when it comes to babies. Governments, commercial providers, and the profession are equally emphatic that infants are to be viewed as learners. The Australian *Early Years Learning Framework* (EYLF), when referring to the role of practitioners, uses the term 'learning' 220 times and the term 'care' only three times (Ortlipp, Arthur, and Woodrow 2011, 1962). Practitioners, whether working in child care or preschool, are consistently referred to as 'educators' in the document.

Like the concept of development, this view of learning sees it as occurring in different domains such as social, emotional, and linguistic. What is new is an emphasis on the specifically *educational* role of the adult in interaction with the young child and on specific techniques for facilitating and assessing *learning* in each domain. Development is recast as learning. To recognize it as such requires the adult to interpret a young child's behavior in particular ways. For instance, practitioners are given advice on how to:

observe and document the social and emotional learning of infants and toddlers as it presents itself and, through interpretation, make explicit links to the outcomes offered in the EYLF. For example, when six-month-olds stop smiling as an adult's gaze shifts away from them, it could be perceived as evidence of Outcome 4, 'that children resource their own learning through connecting with people'. (Andi 2011, 37)

This approach has been welcomed, overall, by the early childhood profession as marking an elevation in their status and the respect accorded to their work (Ortlipp, Arthur, and Woodrow 2011). Some commentators claim that parenting is becoming technicalized through the transfer of outcomes-based models from professional contexts into the home. Smeyers, for instance, expressing concern about what he sees as government interference in child-rearing, complains that 'being a parent has become a nine-to-five profession' (2008, 737). He argues that the trend toward specifying outcomes for early childhood learning and development encourages parents to adopt a 'means-end framework' and apply 'ready-made answers' to the complex issues involved in raising their children (ibid.). Rather than a completely new phenomenon, though, this is just the latest iteration of a long-standing debate regarding parents' role in their children's educational development. The interesting question is: What form is this now taking and what agents are now assigned with the task of producing the 'good' parent? Our particular focus is on the meaning of 'good' parenting in relation to the goal of producing 'early learners'.

PARENTING EARLY LEARNERS

The trend toward what has been called the 'curricularization' of learning in the home is not new (Seiter 1993, 282). Research conducted decades ago identified school-like language and behavior in the interactions between mothers and preschool children as typical of middle-class homes (Heath 1982). Working-class parents also 'schooled' their children, although their authoritarian instructional approach and focus on the 'basics' was more consistent with the teaching methods they had experienced at school than the progressive child-centered pedagogy of their children's teachers.

The 'invisible pedagogy' (Walkerdine 1988) of progressive teachers and middle-class mothers continues to be promoted in many quarters. Typical of this approach is a study which assessed the educational beliefs and practices of parents of preschoolers (Bennet, Weigel, and Martin 2002). In this study an example of a 'developmentally appropriate belief' is 'My child learns lessons and morals from the stories we read' (ibid., 302). However, a parent who agreed with the statement 'Parents should teach their children to read before school' would be assessed as having a developmentally inappropriate belief. From this perspective, it is acceptable for a book to do the teaching (i.e., by presenting the child with story lines illustrative of proso-cial behavior) but not the parent. The parent's role is in ensuring a supply of books (presumably those with suitable moral 'lessons') and committing to a regular shared reading time.

However this low-key approach is currently under challenge by the drive to measurable standards and associated explicit teaching methods, from the early years on. This is reflected by a shift in the parenting advice literature toward an increasingly 'explicitly pedagogical role' (Hoffman 2009, 19). The force of the standards agenda and its impact on parents is made strik-ingly clear by the action of the International Reading Association (IRA) in producing a pamphlet for parents entitled *Making the Most of Read-ing Tests* (International Reading Association 2008). This peak professional association, which is on the record as critiquing an overreliance on stan-dardized testing, evidently views parents as allies in helping to ameliorate the potentially stressful impact of testing on children. Its advice includes 'do[ing] things each day to help children become better readers', reading 'all sorts of materials . . . with your child as often as possible', encouraging the child to ask questions and 'listen carefully to instructions', and investing in 'educational reading-based computer software programs'.

The inclusion of digital resources in the IRA's advice acknowledges the growing significance of digital technologies to parents' strategies for supporting their children's education. From the time that computers have become small enough to put on a desk, they have been marketed to parents as a tool for improving their children's educational prospects (Nixon 1998). Now that computers have become thoroughly domesticated, research is showing that parents see 'clear links between acquisition of skills, knowl-edge and understanding and new technologies' (Marsh 2006, 34). How-ever, parents do not necessarily see themselves as the ideal mediators of technological learning; rather they report that their children are 'picking up' how to operate devices such as mobile phones, games consoles and DVD players with little or no adult instruction (Plowman, McPake, and Stephen 2008). Parent involvement generally takes the form of ensuring the age-appropriateness of the devices and software (for which they are reliant on manufacturer advice), giving basic operational instructions (e.g., how to turn the device on), and setting limits regarding the duration and timing of children's usage.

The digital realm is also an increasingly significant source of social sup-port and information for parents. Parenting websites have become the 'one-stop shops', for which parents do not even have to leave the house, and their popularity is attested to by a growing body of research. In one study of 'Baby World' parenting website, users ranked the website highest among information sources, slightly above their own mothers and considerably above neighbors (Madge and O'Connor 2006). Swedish site 'The Parenting Network' was visited every day by most surveyed users (Sarkadi and Brem-berg 2005). Women of lower socioeconomic backgrounds ranked the site as their most valued source of advice; they also tended to rank peer advice as more reliable than expert advice. In China, the most popular parenting site 'Yaolan' was seen by young women as providing access to contemporary global views of parenting which an older generation was unable to provide (Wang 2003). This included progressive philosophies of early learning emphasizing creativity, independence, and play. These sites all combine user-generated content (usually in the form of peer-to-peer commentary), access to expert advice, and commercial promotion of goods and services, often in ways that blur the boundaries between these elements.

The Market in Early Learning

Before a child is born, the parents-to-be are already the focus of intensive marketing activity claiming to help them be good parents through the consumption of goods, services, and activities. This is by no means a straightforward task for parents since consumption on behalf of children is the subject of as much moral censure as it is of marketers' persuasion. At issue is the nature of childhood, as a time of innocence to be protected or as the beginning of active engagement in the social world, including the world of consumer culture.

Government and community organizations offering early childhood services rarely directly appeal to young children. The opposite is the case with the sellers of commercial early learning products. From packaging to placement to promotion, manufacturers and marketers do everything in their power to ensure that even the youngest children become aware of, and desire, their products. The use of branded characters with high child recognition (such as the stars of TV and movie animations) links otherwise unrelated objects such as books, clothes, sweets, games, and bed linen into a pervasive 'mediascape' surrounding children (Marsh 2006). In her analysis of toy marketing, Seiter (1993) describes how multisensory features, accessible open packaging, and low placement are specifically designed to enable young children to explore the feel, look, and sound of toys while on shopping trips with their carers, maximizing the likelihood of the child demanding to keep the toy.

Media debates about 'pester power' enjoin parents to take control of their children's consumption in the face of this market pressure (cf. Linn 2005). Parents are well aware that they may be the subject of social censure if they give in to children's demands, particularly for certain kinds of products. Studies of parents' consumption on behalf of children show that they often experience guilt and attempt to regulate their children's consumption, particularly of television, junk food, short-lived fad products, and goods thought to encourage their children to grow up too fast (Brusdal 2005; Chan and McNeal 2007; Seiter 1993). However, they are able to justify consumption if the product is necessary for a child's academic achievement or social standing (Brusdal 2005). Parents also want their child to experience a state of wonder and themselves to relive this experience through the child's consumption (Cross 2002). All this gives plenty of scope for marketers to engage with parents' motives and attract them to products.

The makers of 'edutainment' products hit both the enjoyment and the academic achievement buttons. In purporting to combine learning with fun and childlike wonder, they reassure parents that they can meet their child's needs for social membership and recreation while at the same time painlessly building their academic skills (Scanlon and Buckingham 2004). The range of products in this category includes traditional toy objects, conventional media (television programs, video and audio recordings), print materials (e.g., activity books), and, increasingly, digital devices and software. Edutainment products are deliberately designed into the suite of products associated with any major television series or movie for young children (MacNaughton and Hughes 2005). Because education is not the prime motivation in marketing this material, a rather narrow range of activities is offered and often fairly loosely matched to a child's age and stage, if developmental theory is taken as a guide (Buckingham and Scanlon 2003).

Commercial providers have also been able to create new opportunities as a result of government support for public-private partnerships in the delivery of educational and social services. Compared to public services, those provided by business are believed to deliver 'innovation, effectiveness and efficiency' (Cardini 2006, 398). A case in point is the 'I am your Child' series of DVDs and booklets, produced by Rob Steiner, Hollywood director and neuroscience enthusiast. These products, which feature Steiner and other celebrities giving advice on such subjects as 'how to spark your child's interest in learning', 'establishing reading routines', and 'teaching limits with love' have been purchased by several state jurisdictions in the US for use in both universal and targeted programs.

Public-private partnerships in children's media are, of course, not a new thing. Public broadcasting entities have led the way in the development of children's programming, particularly in the 'edutainment' genre (Scanlon and Buckingham 2003). However, in times of reduced public funding, the private partner gains greater leverage. When the Public Broadcasting Service (PBS) in the United States opened its Kids Pavilion in a Mills shopping mall in St. Louis, it was located opposite a children's clothing store and featured 'a lounge area equipped with 24 plasma-screen televisions broadcasting Mills TV' (Linn 2005, 46). A PBS spokesperson stated that the Mills corporation 'shar[es] our vision of delivering high-quality educational experiences. . . . Kids will learn and play with characters as they watch each day at a place where families already spend time' (ibid.).

All this means that there are few acts of parenting that are not also acts of consumption capable of being interpreted by others as evidence of one's parenting values. Coming out of a fast food restaurant with the plastic toy that was included in the 'meal deal', marks one as a particular kind of parent, even if the main reason for shopping there is poverty. Parents who wish to demonstrate that they are not in thrall to popular or consumer culture, and can afford the price tag of 'quality' 'timeless' toys, can express this through their consumption of products such as those offered in the Waldorf schools' online catalogue (Seiter 1993). There is also a market solution for parents wanting to express their commitment to environmental sustainability by raising a 'green child', in the form of 'green' toys, clothes, and other goods (Nichols 2011).

Engaged Fathers and Double-Shift Mothers

If advertisements for nappies and short-cut 'home cooked' meals are any guide, contemporary fathers are involved in hands-on child care and domestic work to a greater extent than ever before. Of course ads are not mirrors to reality, but what they do show is that, whereas previously this kind of involvement was the domain of a small vanguard of 'new age' men, social expectations for participant fathering have now moved into the mainstream. What we are seeing in the commercial realm is matched in the field of government and community services, many of which now have father engagement written into policy (Berlin, Wise, and Soriano 2008).

One of the main barriers to father involvement has been attachment theory, which has supported the view that infants require a secure attachment to a primary care giver (Tyler 1993). This same theory also mitigated against infants and toddlers being put into paid child care while their mothers undertook paid work. In the last decade, considerable work has gone into extending the concept and practice of attachment to primary caregivers other than the mother. The concept of 'father attachment' is now taken seriously in the child development field (Schneider and Burke 1999; Volliing et al 2002). Partly as a result, men are beginning to experience what mothers have been subjected to for ages—the scrutiny of governments and researchers regarding their parenting behavior. And in this, literacy and particularly reading have assumed prominence. It is now standard for measures of fathering to include reading to children as an item, along with homework assistance (cf. Baxter and Smart 2010; Bulanda 2004).

In this context, reading to children is seen not only as a sign of effective fathering but as the prime means to develop attachment. This is made explicit in education programs for fathers such as *Focus on Fathering*, which was developed initially for fathers in the criminal justice system and has since been mainstreamed (Kaverley and Kostelc 2008). In one of the modules of this course, participating men are asked to consider why it is important to read to children. Second on the list of reasons in the facilitators' notes is 'Reading aloud to children helps fathers form attachments with their children' (ibid., 14). Fathers are encouraged to begin when the child is infancy:

When a father cradles his baby and reads to her with inflection, the child learns to associate reading with love, comfort and pleasure—the beginning of a positive attitude which provides motivation for learning to read. (ibid.)

Fathers are also being instructed as to the right ways to play with their children. Also from the *Focus on Fathers* program, the module on play warns fathers against the attractions of popular culture and electronic toys:

Many toys are derived from television shows or movies. . . . Children may become bored with this type of play because they are not using their creativity and their own experiences to enrich their play. Electronic toys offer some educational benefit, but most encourage rote learning and not creative problem solving. Many electronic toys for infants are overstimulating and frustrating. (ibid., 81)

Here fathers are being directly addressed as consumers in the marketplace for children's products. They are being instructed to choose toys and activities that maximize learning and developmental outcomes.

Participant fathers are perhaps the necessary correlation of career-committed mothers. While middle-class mothers have often curtailed their participation in the paid workforce when their children were small, the high cost of maintaining an affluent lifestyle has seen women's time away from the paid workforce shrinking. Women are also delaying their first pregnancy in order to maximize career gains, changing the profile of clients for 'new parent' programs.

When it comes to mothers' at-home roles, the latest time use studies indicate that they continue to do more of the active parental and domestic work than their male partners, regardless of hours worked outside the home (Baxter and Smart 2010). How to manage the delegation of their preschool educative role is a challenge for middle-class mothers. It enters into the task of arranging child care and articulates with decisions regarding kindergarten and preschool (Ball and Vincent 2005). Private schools' move into early childhood, with the establishment of 'early learning centres' taking children from age two or three, is a response in part to this phenomenon (Caputo 2007). Middle-class mothers in particular also organize children's out-of-school curriculum of activities, even when fathers are delegated to provide transport and attendance (Doucet 2000). In the early years, this may include regular trips to the library, exercise programs, playgroups, and music programs. They also encourage and monitor fathers' reading to children (Nichols 2000).

'Hard-to-reach' Families and Excluding Services

Access to early learning resources is dependent on access to the organizations which produce, promote, and circulate these resources and, in many instances, train parents in their use. Access to commercial resources and services requires economic capital to exchange for goods. Access to government subsidized services may not be financially stressful but still requires means of transport, knowledge of the service, and a positive expectation of the outcome. For all these reasons, families in poverty and challenged by severe disadvantage may not utilize even those services that are specifically targeted at them. The term 'hard-to-reach' is often used in the service sector to designate these families.

Groups underrepresented among service users include families in poverty, sole parents, families where a parent has a mental health or substance use issue, transient and homeless families, and those from indigenous populations surviving the racist policies of prior social regimes (Carbone et al. 2004; Edwards 2004; Roditti 2005; Webber and Boromeo 2005). While knowledge gaps and practical difficulties impede access to services, just getting inside the door does not guarantee a continuing relationship. Clients in these groups describe feelings of being stigmatized and talked down to which discouraged them from returning. Looking into the low rate of participation in Maternal and Child Health services by disadvantaged parents, one researcher notes 'one of the greatest barriers is parents' fear they will be judged by others as "bad" parents' (Carbone et al. 2004, vii).

Intervention programs have been critiqued for assuming a lack of skill and knowledge on the part of carers and failing to capitalize on existing social resources. Following the high attrition rate of a program designed to encourage ethnic 'minority' parents to read to their preschool children, one group of researchers asked participants why it was not more popular (Janes and Kermani 2001). The participating mothers and grandmothers described being required to read approved texts in an approved way as 'castigo' or punishment (ibid., 460). They viewed the children's literature as empty of meaningful messages and the scripted interactions as unnatural. The program became much more successful when based on texts transcribed from participants' oral storytelling with explicit moral messages, as was the usual practice in these communities.

It is often stated that working-class communities are close-knit, making immediate kin an important source of advice and practical support. Parents in very tough circumstances, however, may not be able to rely on the kind of family support that is often regarded as the mainstay of poor communities. A study of solo mothers found that disapproval of their position alienated them their immediate family (Webber and Boromeo 2005). Non-kin friendships and nongovernment organizations operating locally (such as churches) are important resources for marginalized parents. However for some groups, such as the trailer park mothers interviewed by Edwards (2004), almost all social ties have been cut and keeping to oneself is deemed the only way to avoid such dangers as having one's child removed by welfare authorities.

RESOURCING EARLY LEARNING: KEY CONCEPTS

Any investigation into this complex and dynamic field needs some clear reference points. In this section, we discuss some key definitions and concepts which will be used in the analysis of early learning resourcing and resources in each of four key sites: the mall, the clinic, the library, and the church. We will define the early learning resource as a mobile semiotic bundle and the agents who produce and distribute these resources as actor-networks.

What is an early learning resource? The short answer is: Whatever someone thinks can be used to bring about learning in young children. Indeed, understanding how players in the field define a resource is crucial to understanding their priorities and actions in producing, promoting, and distributing particular goods and services. To get a stronger handle on the slippery concept of a resource, turn to the history of literacy instruction, to one of the earliest examples of an educational resource—the hornbook (Monaghan 2005). The hornbook resembled a paddle for playing ping-pong, except that on its face is printed text. This text always included the alphabet and usually also some scripture. It was cheap to produce, easy to store, and had the added advantage, for strict teachers, of being a convenient instrument of punishment.

In these times of multimedia production, the idea that a text can be made out of disparate materials, including language, visual images, and sound, has promoted calls for reading to be reconceptualized. A semiotic approach that views literacy as the simultaneous deployment of multiple modes of meaning-making has been argued for (Cope and Kalantzis 2000). However, it we consider the hornbook, this is not a new thing. It was composed of disparate materials combined into a single object which could be used in teaching and learning.

The Resource as Mobile Semiotic Bundle

The hornbook is a good example of packaging, the process of 'bringing together complex entities into a single object or idea that can be mobilised and circulated like a branded commodity' (Clarke 2001, 7). It demonstrates two of the processes that are inherent to the construction of a resource: packaging and mobilization. The educational resource has been called a 'semiotic bundle' (Arzarello and Paola 2007), a package of meaning-making materials. The hornbook packaged religious messages, reading materials, and disciplinary tool into a mobile bundle.

Understanding the early learning resource as a semiotic bundle draws attention to the actions of resource producers bringing together materials into assemblages. It prompts questions about the constituent elements of resources, the processes by which these bundles are circulated, and the potentials they contain for being unpacked and used in different contexts. To return to an example mentioned earlier, the *I Am Your Child* DVDs bundle commonsense advice about parenting, snippets of scientific 'facts', the personal testament of the parent presenters, and the celebrity backstories of these famous presenters. These DVDs have been created through a process of bringing together these elements and designing them into a unified audiovisual media package. When an *I Am Your Child* DVD is included in the maternity 'show bag' given to all mothers after the birth of a child in hospital, then a new semiotic bundle is produced of which it is an element.

When it comes to unpacking, the DVD and the maternity 'show bag' invite different practices. The bag is a material package designed to give easy access to its contents which usually includes samples of various products (e.g., lotions, disposable nappies), catalogues, pamphlets, and magazines (see Chapter 4, this volume). These contents are separate and do not require each other's presence in order to be used. Indeed they are produced by different agents and carry messages, whether implied or explicit, that may even be in conflict. The bag's user is granted agency to look at or ignore, to use or discard each item. A DVD such as *I Am Your Child*, on the other hand, is designed as a unified media product. This kind of packaging works against the different elements (e.g., stories, 'facts', advice, glimpses of celebrities' domestic lives) being unpacked and separated by consumers.

While packaging involves planning and design, materials can also become combined in ways that are less rational and considered. The term 'aggregate' is a useful one in drawing attention to the ways in which heterogenous materials come to be clumped together without necessarily conscious intention or engineering. Consider the case of a toy marketed as educational, purchased by a parent, and brought home to be used by a child. This toy joins others which have traveled to the home as birthday presents, as hand-me-downs from relatives, or loans from the toy library, and other materials, which are not designated toys but that a child plays with, such as kitchen utensils, discarded boxes, etc. This collection of play objects can be thought of as a 'semiotic aggregate' (Scollon and Scollon 2003). The concept of a 'semiotic aggregate' is scalable; that is, it can apply to small-scale clumps as well as to very large assemblages. A semiotic aggregate is dynamic and changes as elements in it are taken away and new elements are added; human actors are constantly moving elements of large aggregates. Scollon and Scollon apply this term to urban landscape features such as a city intersection or mall concourse (op. cit.). We will be deploying it in a similar manner in analyzing places where early learning resources are found.

The Networking of Resources

The question of how an early learning resource, however constituted, finds its way into the hands of a parent or carer concerns mobility. To be mobilized, a resource has to be passed from point to point, e.g., from manufacturer to warehouse to retail outlet or, in the case of e-shopping, directly to homes in any location. Connectivity is a process of networking. The formal and informal networks which are formed through the connective actions of resource producers and users enable resources to circulate.

It is well established that social networks facilitate the exchange of information, goods, and practices (Baerenholdt and Aarsaether 2002; Saulnier and Rowland 1985). Studies of parents' networks have shown that they are a significant means by which families seek to acquire knowledge, influence, and assistance with the aim of advantaging children (Lareau 1989). Producers and service providers are well aware of this and use strategies to access the social networks of consumers, in order to promote and sell their products. State, as well as commercial, providers utilize these strategies. Indeed, the concepts of 'human capital' and 'partnership', so popular with neoliberal governments, are highly supportive of the appropriation of community-based networks to further government agendas.

The integration of digital networking into virtually all areas of social life means that connections are constantly being made between entities (individuals or collectives) regardless of their geographic proximity. Digital technology has also massively sped up the process of reproduction, whereby copies of a product can be now made with a keystroke. This means that resources that are digitalized can instantly and simultaneously appear in thousands of different locations. Old modes of circulation (e.g., 'snail mail') are being harnessed to the distribution of products bought and sold online.

The places where we live and work can be described as networked activity spaces. In adopting this perspective we draw on the work of geographer Doreen Massey (2000) who has been concerned with the impact of globalization on what happens in people's local places. Her concept of the activity space addresses the way in which local places, while being experienced as immediate and unique to their inhabitants, are at the same time connected to other places outside the local. The social space within which people meet and interact is understood as 'a complexity of social relations stretched out and meeting and intersecting with each other' (Massey 2000, 54). The activity space is 'the spatial network of links and activities, of spatial connections and of locations, within which a particular agent operates' (op. cit.).

The Actor-Network: Heterogenous Engineering

Earlier in this chapter, we sketched out some contemporary developments in the field of what is being called 'early learning'. It is clear from even a brief survey that the field is not unified in terms of underlying theories, political agendas, social goals, or programs. The subject of the preschool child as learner brings together a highly disparate and changing cast of characters, individuals, and collectives.

Bruno Latour begins his book *We Have Never Been Modern* (1993) with a flick through the articles covered in one daily newspaper. He notes that, although the newspaper genre is structured so as to separate subject matter (e.g., into local and international news, current affairs and specialist reporting, facts and editorializing) any one news story actually draws in perspectives from everywhere:

> The horizons, the scales, the time frames, the actors—none of these is commensurable, yet there they are, caught up in the same story. (Latour 1993, 1)

Considering how these incommensurable and disparate actors, events, and representations become and are connected is the business of actor-network theory.

The concept of the actor-network is a hybrid of unity and heterogeneity, of product and process. ANT theorist John Law (1992) explains that the concept of the actor-network is intended to hold in tension forces that pull in different directions. The 'actor' side of the concept is that which appears as a singular agent. We tend to attribute the status of actor to things that, if we think about them, are not singular: institutions like 'the school'; parts of other entities like 'the brain'; sets of practices like 'education'; theories like 'attachment'.

The 'network' part of the concept is where the singularity breaks down, and the boundaries between separate actors become fluid. This is because every entity is able to act in the world only by virtue of being made up of many different kinds of thing, the connections between which make the network. When ANT theorists refer to the constitution of actors, they do not mean just that a whole can be broken down into its components—this would keep intact the idea of the whole. They mean that whatever enables an actor to act becomes part of its network and, more than this, there is no actor without its network.

According to Law, the production of resources is one of the key roles of actor-networks:

> [N]etwork patterns that are widely performed . . . can be counted as resources, resources which may come in a variety of forms: agents, devices, texts, relatively standardised sets of organisational relations, social technologies, boundary protocols, organisational forms—any or all of these. (1992, 5)

ANT is centrally interested in how these resources come to be produced and circulate through networks. This is explained as a process of 'heterogenous engineering', that is, of bringing together disparate kinds of stuff and binding it into a unified package (ibid.) which brings us back to the idea of the resource as a mobile semiotic bundle.

ANT has drawn attention to the process whereby these packages are created, a process also known as 'translation' (Latour 1987a, 1987b). It has tended to be less interested in processes of *unpacking* of resources. However, packing and unpacking are but two aspects of the same process, each integral to mobilizing resources. Toys are often designed to be taken to pieces and assembled; encouraging a child to do this can be interpreted as promoting creativity or manual dexterity. Thus, the very act of unpacking and repacking a resource might be integral to its claimed educational effectiveness.

The process of unpacking though holds risks for the producer as it creates the possibility of parts of the resource being recombined with other things that were not part of the original package. Thus, producers may design into resources constraints on the ways their component parts can fit together. Barbie dolls can be disassembled, as many parents have observed, but their parts are difficult to put together with those of other dolls owing to the distinctive Barbie physique. The Barbie doll is a concrete example of what Latour (1987) calls an 'immutable mobile' something that holds its shape as it moves. Like the term 'actor-network', the term 'immutable mobile' holds in tension opposing forces—identity and transformation. The ability to transform can make something more mobile, but it can also threaten the integrity of the thing. In considering the early learning resource, this raises the question of the strategies that producers use to simultaneously reinforce their identity and enable them to circulate and be put to use.

The Discursive Construction of Early Learning

Specific discourses can be understood as assemblies of meaning which cohere around a particular subject or set of relations, such as 'early learning', and which are expressed by and constructed through representational and social practices. Historical analyses undertaken within a poststructural framework have demonstrated that forms of knowledge are historically variable and contingent (Donzelot 1979; Foucault 1990; Riley 1983; Rose 1990). Conditions contributing to the (re)emergence of discourses include forms of government, political agendas, material conditions, forms of communication, and kinds of social relations. For instance, the knowledge that 'children need their mothers' was produced in the context of social developments emerging out of the industrial revolution, such as the geographical relocation of families from rural to urban habitations and the absorption of men into industry—both of which reduced the child-rearing availability of adults other than mothers (Riley 1983). The authorization of this view of child-rearing was further made possible by the development of scientific modes of enquiry which gave rise to scientifically 'validated' theorizations such as maternal attachment theory.

Discourse analytic studies of early childhood have consistently identified developmental discourse as a pervasive, institutionally embedded form of knowledge which has underpinned professional practice and been heavily endorsed as an appropriate model of parenting (Bloch and Popkewitz 2000, 2005; Howley et al. 1999; Walkerdine 1988). Central themes of the developmental discourse of childhood are that children progress through a series of discrete stages of development; instruments and practices of measurement can be used to gauge what stage a child is at; individual children can be positioned according to the norm for each stage (normal, delayed, or advanced); and it is the responsibility of parents and educators to provide tasks and materials appropriate to the particular stage of the children in their care.

Attachment theory, which developed from studies of institutionalized children and observations of animal behavior undertaken in the 1940s and '50s, became and remains a dominant discourse of childhood. This theory premises that the quality of the relationship between an infant and its primary carer determines the child's ongoing healthy psychological development (Richter 2004). Claims for the importance of mother-child attachment to infant language development (Riley 1983) laid the groundwork for later developments linking attachment to early learning. The concept of 'emergent literacy' saw oral language joined by other skills and dispositions, such as understandings of print, which were seen to develop naturally through immersion in home literacy practices (Sulzby and Teale 1986). Beliefs in the importance of attachment transferred to the development of emergent literacy and more recently to early learning more generally (Smythe 2009).

Under the terms of this discourse, young children are positioned as highly vulnerable to threats to their emotional security. Caregiver story reading is promoted as an activity that produces security, while developing literacy orientations and competencies (Smythe 2006). Literacy is made central to family routines that are crucial to a child's security, which is, in turn, vital for his ability to learn, as in this excerpt from a popular baby care manual:

> Suppose that Thursday afternoon is usually reserved for going to the library; a change of that routine might seem as upsetting to him as the cancellation of Christmas would. When it's necessary to alter a routine, try to prepare him as soon as possible . . . alert him earlier in the day if you have to forgo his bedtime story for one night and explain why. (Leach 1988 in Smythe 2009)

Constructivism, progressivism, and child-centeredness are terms used for a discursive formation that views the child as an active agent engaged in making sense of the world in his own way (Hartley 2009; Nichols 2002; Walkerdine 1998). In this discourse, learning is understood as a process whereby the child actively engages with the environment, and the adult is positioned as facilitator. Value is placed on autonomy, risk-taking, creativity, and imagination for the child and responsiveness, relaxation, and resourcefulness for the adult. Motivation to learn springs from within the child. For example, one family reading advocate cautions parents against teaching their preschool children to read while encouraging them to teach their children to *want* to read (Trelease 2006). Parents and educators are thus tasked with producing desire in the child.

Early learning can be understood as a discursive formation that recombines existing discourses of childhood with other discourses, particularly human capital theory. Under human capital theory, the child is treated as a 'resource, comprising various capacities and potentials' (Peers 2011). Economic arguments underpin calls to invest in the early childhood period in the expectation of returns in the form of a larger pool of skilled workers and diminished welfare burden. The emphasis on productivity under the terms of this discourse creates demand for measurable outcomes in early childhood education and care.

The difference between the contemporary notion of early learning and previous models of early childhood are visible in government policies such as the Early Years Learning Framework in Australia. In a discourse analysis of this document, Ortlipp and colleagues counted usage of the terms 'development', 'care', 'play', and 'learning'. There were 220 references to 'learning', 19 to 'development', and just 2 to 'care'. While 'play' received 68 mentions, the majority were harnessed to 'learning' as in 'play-based learning' and 'learning through play'. This represents a significant discursive shift.

Other discourses of childhood that are less central to contemporary early learning but still part of the broader discursive field of childhood include a nostalgic discourse, which seeks to recapture a golden age of innocence and is often associated with resistance to commercialization, new technologies, and globalization (Scanlon and Buckingham 2003), and a psychoanalytic discourse, which sees early childhood as a period of intense psychic work associated with learning to separate from the mother, dealing with the resultant loss and anger, and forming appropriate gender identity (Hollway 2006).

Networking is integral to Foucault's concept of the discursive field:

> At its very root the statement (énoncée) has a dispersion over an enunciative field in which it has a place and a status, which arranges for it possible relations with the past and opens up possible futures . . . There is no free, neutral, independent statement; a statement always belongs to a series of a whole, plays a role among other statements, is part of a network of statements. (Foucault 1969, 99)

The *Early Years Learning Framework* materializes out of a network of statements. It bundles together disparate discourses, such as constructivism and human capital theory, with practices, such as observation and measurement, and materials, such as professional development resources. Actor-network theory helps us recognize the work that goes into this kind of heterogenous engineering and which enables discursive formations to become mobile and travel to multiple situated sites of practice.

ORGANIZATION OF THE BOOK

In this book, we will be focusing on four categories of stakeholders which each play a distinctive role in resourcing parents of young children. We have designated these agents using generic titles: 'the mall', 'the clinic', 'the library', and 'the church'. These contexts are outside the usual territory of early childhood educational research but, as the foregoing discussion illustrates, this landscape has become extremely diversified. Each of these players also has a history of service provision for families of young children, histories that have tended to be lost in the dominant thrust to looking in the home for the answers to children's successful transition to, and later success in, school. The current policy emphasis on broadening the scope of early childhood provision and on encouraging partnerships with industry, community, and across the professions makes it appropriate to examine the activities of organizations' formal education systems and institutions.

In the same way that 'the school' or 'the home' is often used, these terms cover multiple diverse instances of a phenomenon while indicating something distinctive at the core of the concept. There are many schools, each one different, but 'the school' as an institution has a particular role in society and is the subject of structuring practices that make every instance of a school the same in some ways. The same goes for 'the mall'.

Chapter 2: Tracing Early Learning Resources

The research project is explained. We introduce readers to the social and geographic characteristics of the regions in which we conducted a three-year study of early learning resources, to places we entered, people we met, and the kinds of artifacts we collected. We suggest some principles of practice for actor-network researchers and describe how we addressed the challenges of conducting the project, including recruiting culturally diverse families.

Chapter 3: The Mall

Although commercial spaces and consumer culture have been the subject of academic interest for some time, they have not figured largely in studies of children's early learning. In this chapter we show how commercial spaces like shopping malls are places where early learning, and parents' role in this, is imagined, represented, negotiated, and practiced. We address the questions: What kinds of resources can parents find in commercial spaces? How are these spaces differentiated in terms of their address to parents and the kinds of resources they offer? Ethnographic observations, artifact analysis, and interviews are reinforced by an inventory of an entire shopping mall in one suburban site. In consumer culture, the interpenetration of virtual and actual spaces has progressed more rapidly than in other social domains. We trace network connections from material spaces within our field sites, such as bookstores and supermarkets, to their online counterparts and vice versa. We note how the positioning of parents and children, and the idea of early learning, shifts as users cross between on- and offline spaces.

Chapter 4: The Clinic

Moves toward integrating child and family services in the early years, underpinned by a holistic view of child development, have led to greater overlap between the roles of providers. Health services are expanding into the domain of early learning, particularly in the areas of language, literacy, and social skills. In this chapter we take readers to some of these services and examine the advice, resources, and assistance they offer to parents. We ask: How is parents' role in early learning framed within discourses of health? How do parents view these resources and under what circumstances do they access and use them?

Chapter 5: The Church

Religious organizations have long been significant promoters of education, particularly literacy, yet they have seldom been taken into account in discussions of early childhood education. In this chapter we visit community activities for young children and families run by Christian organizations in each of our three sites. We reveal the important role of these organizations in providing services to families disadvantaged by poverty, geographic isolation, and cultural minority status. Ethnographic research becomes action research as a researcher develops early literacy workshops for African refugee women.

Chapter 6: The Library

The role of libraries in the provision of early learning services has responded to broader imperatives regarding the need to 'hook' young children into literacy as early as possible. Libraries are also becoming networked with other providers, such as health services, at the same time as they are competing with commerce for the child and parent markets. In this chapter, readers will hear librarians' perspectives on their role, observe literacy sessions for babies and toddlers, and hear from parents about what they do and don't find useful when accessing libraries with young children of Green Plains. We ask: What views about early learning and literacy are promoted by libraries? Are their programs reaching those they would most like to engage with early literacy?

Chapter 7: The Networked Discursive Field of Early Learning

Looking across the diverse spaces, players and resources we have encountered, we map the contemporary discursive field of early learning. We identify key alignments and networks that produce strong reinforcement for particular messages about young children's development and the role of parents and other providers and circulate these widely. We also draw out significant tensions between particular agendas and interests aimed at positioning parents, on the one hand, as primarily providers stepping back from their children's encounters with resources and, on the other, as irreplaceable partners in their children's learning. The spatialized and material nature of children's and parents' access to these discourses is made evident by the geosemiotic analysis. We consider how 'geographies of opportunity' create particular localized ecologies within which certain families are more likely to encounter a greater diversity of services and resources, including those which have the advantage of alignment with dominant middle-class educational values. Even with a vast proliferation of producers and promoters we argue that gaps remain where the needs of particular groups are still not met and where the adoption of network and partnership models have not yet fulfilled their promise. We consider implications for policy makers, service providers, and parents, in recognition that the field of early learning has become networked, diversified, differentiated, and contested to the extent that regulation is impossible. We argue for the repositioning of parents and children as knowledge producers and for harnessing of available sponsors and networks to the circulation of even more diverse resources for the support of young children's learning.

2   Tracing Early Learning Resources

INTRODUCTION

This book is in part the story of how four researchers, each with different training and background, together attempted to create a form of researcher life—to become actor-network researchers. The conditions which we have described in Chapter 1 seemed to demand a different approach from educational researchers than conventional ethnography, which tends to involve sustained engagement in a single context. The phenomena which we were interested in were occurring in multiple contexts and modalities simultaneously. Before we even began to determine an approach, it was obvious that the entities that could be called 'early learning resources' were mobile and transformable; they were being packed and unpacked by different agents and used for different purposes; and they were being linked to other entities in ways that constantly changed. In looking for guides on how to produce meaningful knowledge in this world as researchers, we were inspired by those who used the language of complexity and did not seek to reduce phenomena to binaries such as individual–context, public–private, virtual–actual, producer–user. We found this by bringing theories of networking and material semiotics to our existing resources of ethnographic case study and discourse analysis. During the time in which we were embarked on this journey, there were few guidebooks from within the field of education (though see Clarke 2001). Since that time, actor-network theory and geosemiotics have joined the ranks of emerging methodologies in education (Fenwick and Edwards 2010; Hamilton 2010; Mulcahy 2010; Nichols, Nixon, and Rowsell 2011). Here we begin by outlining some key principles of our research practice, following which we describe in detail the design and conduct of the project.

There Is No Outside the Network

The actor-network researcher is always networking. This means that one cannot simply observe a network and analyze it as a product separate from oneself. Quantitative methods of social network analysis do attempt to do this, usually by using surveys to elicit information about individuals' contacts and the kinds of 'goods' which pass from person to person. Statistical analysis of the cohort of individuals then provides a representation of the network and uses concepts like 'strength' and 'density' to measure and make comparisons (Vera and Schupp 2006). Explanations are then sought for these network features. Key theorist of ANT Bruno Latour has emphasized its difference from this kind of quantitative social network analysis:

> One does not jump outside a network to add an explanation—a cause, a factor, a set of factors, a series of co-occurrences; one simply *extends* the network further. (1996, 11)

Ethnographic researchers are already attuned to attending to the consequences of being embedded in a sociocultural context. The actor-network lens adds another layer of awareness; we attend to how our participation in the research process is productive of connections and not just those we actively seek to make. We are also being networked with/into and must notice how other entities extend links, connect, and send goods via us to somewhere else.

Attend to the Nonhuman Actors

If we consider the practicalities of how people manage to circulate resources through social networks, we quickly realize that simply knowing the identities of the players and the nature of their relationships is insufficient. Imagine a mother discovers her friend is pregnant and that this friend became a friend because the two women's husbands work together. Because the family only has one car and it is not easy to visit her friend soon, she gives her husband her favorite baby care guidebook to take to work and pass on to his workmate. The friend reads the book and next time the two talk on the phone, they discuss whether 'controlled crying' is a good method for settling babies.

If we used this example to address the question 'How does knowledge circulate?' then an answer that included only the human actors and their relations to each other would be insufficient. Actor-Network Theory (ANT) conceptualizes networks as 'comprised of diverse materials' (Murdoch 1998) including the human and the nonhuman. This approach is interested in tracing movements and connections between all elements that make up networks (Law 1999). As social researchers, we were used to paying close attention to people—their behavior, interactions, and expressed views. ANT has encouraged us to look at the nonhuman elements in each situation and to ask what is being achieved by and through them. With regard to our example above, ANT would have us include the book, car, home, workplace, and telephone as network elements along with the human actors. These elements are more than just means to an end. The car, for instance, has been a vital element in the production of 'spatially segregated urban neighbourhoods' (Sheller and Urry 2006, 209); it enables middle-class parents to access the massive concentration of goods and services located in malls outside their suburbs.

What we notice when attending to the nonhuman then changes how we view the human dimension. This is because ANT is a material semiotics (Law 2007). It is easier to appreciate the material dimension of the non-human because as humans we are often used to seeing these actors as tools or as elements of our physical environments. The materiality or 'stuffness' of a pram seems self-evident; applied to the baby inside, this perspective may seem strange and even transgressive. And yet the bodies of babies impact how they can be engaged in the kinds of early learning activities being provided by services like libraries, just as the dimensions of their prams can cause practical problems when parked in library aisles (see Chapter 6). Young babies need physical support to maintain a seated position from which to view a book. They are dependent on someone to hold the book. Looked at this way, baby, book, and carer can be understood as an assemblage.

Consider What Is Moving

The research site has often been seen as a 'spatially fixed . . . container for social processes' (Sheller and Urry 2006, 209). In educational research, this view has informed classroom research which examines interactions which occur inside this bounded space. Challenging this, the concept of the 'virtual school bag' (Thomson 2002) has offered a way to consider what students bring to school with them in terms of invisible 'funds of knowledge' (Moll et al. 1992). However, the emphasis on the virtual nature of these 'funds' has not encouraged researchers to look at the *material* dimensions of what is moving in and out of educational spaces. Also, it has tended to focus attention only on certain critical periods of movement such as the transition of the child from home to school.

ANT encourages researchers to be constantly alert to what is mobile, moment by moment as well as on larger timescales (Lemke 2000). In the field work phase, this meant in practice:

- noticing and recording in descriptive notes the movements of people in and through the site
- noticing and recording what people were carrying in and out of sites
- taking note of our own movements in terms of the most obvious/ clearest pathways, decision points and blockages

Considering mobility also means asking where people/objects/practices have come from and where they may be going to. This concern influenced the kinds of questions we asked in interviews and the kinds of categories we applied in analysis. So, for instance if, during a home visit, a parent showed one of the researchers a book, magazine or toy, (s)he would be asked how and where they had acquired it.

Mass production and technologies of reproduction enable multiples of objects to proliferate and to be distributed through networks. For instance, the Leapfrog range of educational toys was mentioned by parents in each of our sites, in both the US and Australia. When an entity, such as Leapfrog, finds its way into widely dispersed sites this is a form of mobility. Latour's (1987a, 227) concept of the 'immutable mobile' alerted us to the need for a certain stability in the form of an object, if it is to be the same thing every where it travels. Branding, for instance, is one of the prime means of achieving stability through producing product recognition across geographically and culturally diverse contexts. Thinking in this way prompted us to ask: What changes and what stays the same when an 'early learning' entity moves from one context to another?

Understand Space as Relational

Three propositions for thinking about space are offered by Massey (2000; 2005). First, recognize space as the product of interrelations and as constituted through relations. Second, understand space as the sphere of possibility of the existence of multiplicity in the sense of 'contemporaneous plurality' (Massey 2005, 10). The concept of multiple layering has helped us to capture the material and immaterial dimensions of spaces. The braiding of discourses and networks within spatial arrangements points to this contemporaneous plurality. The third proposition is that we recognize space as always under construction; 'It is always in the process of being made' (ibid.).

Working across very different regional and national locations, the relationships between these spaces are not always immediately evident. However, the value of being alert to resonances between spaces can be illustrated by a comment made by US-based researcher Jennifer Rowsell on viewing photographs of one of the libraries in the Australian pilot study. She emailed back that it reminded her very much of the library at Greystone and posted photographs on our shared project website to show what she meant. Indeed there were some strong similarities in the ways that these local institutions materialized through such observable elements as architectural design, signage, and furniture. Further reading, discussion, and observation of participation patterns brought to light ways in which a contemporary version of the library, formed partly in response to the challenge of successful commercial bookstores, was materializing in geographically distant locations. Further consideration concerned how, in both sites, a relationship between a university and a community library channelled flows of resources and people to the latter (see also Chapter 6). Marcus has had a similar experience, commenting that 'the global is an emergent dimension of arguing

about the connection among sites in a multi-sited ethnography' (1998, 83).
Or, as Luke and Luke state, regarding their transnational research,

> [O]nly through situated, local and self-critical analyses can we begin to
> see the two-way, mutually constitutive dynamics of local-global flows
> of knowledge, power, and capital, of systematic as well as unsystematic
> and uneven "effects", and of local histories that always embed "the
> new" in existing and generative material-economic and cultural condi-
> tions.' (2000, 276)

Massey's concept of the 'activity space' also informed our analysis of individual parent cases because it encouraged us to consider how each person was located in their immediate social environment but also how their
activities connected them to other places and networks. An example of one
of our case summaries follows. Here, 'Kimberley' could easily have been
understood only in terms of her immediate situation; however her 'activity
space' was more extensive and connected to a global movement.

> *Kimberley had few books in her house and no computer. She had*
> *never used the Internet. She explained that her main sources of*
> *information about child development were family members and*
> *the doctor. Among the artifacts that Kimberley showed us was an*
> *amateur looking magazine called* Mum's the Word, *which was dis-*
> *tributed by the local church of which she was a member. Kimberley*
> *also mentioned that a Christian bookshop sent her catalogues and*
> *she had got her child some books and DVDs from their collection.*
> *From one perspective, Kimberley could be understood in terms*
> *of her embeddedness in immediate social networks of family and*
> *church. However, by tracing the textual and distributive networks*
> *that connected Kimberley to the Christian bookshop, we were able*
> *to see her connectedness with a global Christian network. We visited*
> *the book shop in the capital city, took notes of titles in the parent-*
> *ing and children's sections, and looked at covers and contents. We*
> *went to its online catalogue, noted titles and descriptions of prod-*
> *ucts and the names of main publishers; we went to these publishers'*
> *websites. We then looked again at* Mum's the Word *and the books*
> *and DVDs Kimberley had mentioned purchasing. We considered*
> *all this in relation to an advertisement for a church-run mothers'*
> *group seen on the library noticeboard in Midborough, not far from*
> *where Kimberley lived. This notice had led us to a website which*
> *detailed the curriculum organizing all such groups' activities and*
> *described the movement's spread from the US to many other coun-*
> *tries. Through these rhizomatic moves, we could identify a globally*
> *circulating discourse of Christian motherhood, materialized in mul-*
> *tiple local places through texts and practices. The children's books*

in Kimberley's home were instances of a large market of Christian materials with which parents were encouraged to orient their children to faith and, simultaneously to literacy, numeracy, and other school subjects. Kimberley was part of this network, and as a local distributor for the locally produced church magazine, she was also an actor producing the network.

Become the Resource

Social researchers are often advised to have an unobtrusive presence and avoid acting in such a way as to change the conditions they are observing. However, as actor-networks we expected to be connected with and put into action. This meant in effect that we were open to the possibility of becoming resources. While making clear our interest in the subject of early learning and development, we did not determine in advance what would constitute a resource. This enabled local perceptions of need to drive the definition. If as educational researchers we were considered a means of bringing relevant resources into a community, and this was consistent with ethical research principles and academic workload, then we attempted to assist. Those times when we assumed the role of resource offered privileged insight into how others identified, accessed, and deployed resources.

One example of this occurred in the agricultural community of Geraldine where local migrant workers met to study English. Through a local community worker, one of our researchers gained an invitation to meet this group and, through an interpreter, opened up the topic of 'early learning' to include a wide range of activities including reading, singing, storytelling, conversing, playing, and teaching practical skills. She had brought a poster with images of these activities as well as some examples of resources for parents. Among these was a Little Big Book Club (LBBC) bag, distributed free statewide by the library association.

None of the parents in this group had heard of the LBBC program. They were surprised to learn that the package included a CD with Vietnamese language songs and rhymes and asked how they could get hold of it. However, according to the rules of distribution only parents whose children were currently less than two years old and who could bring the child's authorized health record to a library branch could get access to the package. This group had missed the time window and were further disadvantaged by there being no library branch in the town.

The community members decided that the resource was useful and that the researcher could be a means of bringing it into the community. However, overcoming the regulatory blocks required some networking on the part of the researcher. After leaving the town she later visited a well-equipped library in another of the project field sites. There, she explained the circumstances of the Geraldine parents to a librarian who willingly handed over a set of LLBC bags. On the next research visit to Geraldine, the community members took possession of the resources. The story of the failure of a statewide initiative to reach into this community indicated that resources have to be mobilized in ways that make them accessible. By becoming the resource, the actor-network researcher enabled the resource-fulness of the Geraldine parents to become activated.

RESEARCH DESIGN

Three main strands together helped us to explore the ways in which ideas about early learning—and parents' ideal role in that—are produced, regulated, accessed, and circulated. The separation of the strands is necessarily artificial as they are interrelated; each one informs our approach to, and understanding of, the others.

Strand 1 is a geosemiotic (Scollon and Scollon 2003) study of particular geographic regions in order to examine the affordances they provide for parents to access, produce, and circulate information about children's early learning and development. This was carried out in three distinct geographic areas in two countries. Following an initial reconnaissance of the regions as a whole, we subsequently examined in some detail particular subsites such as shopping areas, libraries, playgroups, and health centers. Our disciplinary grounding in discourse analytic and textual and semiotic studies motivates us to seek ways to study the various *signifying practices* at work in the diverse places that provide early learning resources.

Strand 2 is a study of selected commercial and not-for-profit organizations that are central to the supply and circulation of information for parents about early learning and development. This strand has involved interviews with information workers, observation of the organizations' services and programs, and network tracing of resources and ideas about parenting and children's learning that emanate from the organizations across media, space, and time.

Strand 3 is a study of how parents report that they access, evaluate, and mobilize information about early learning, and how they share their knowledge and participate (or not) in information networks about this topic. During interviews parents have been encouraged to show and speak to material artifacts and resources that they have consulted to support their early years parenting practices, and these have been documented.

Data produced using the methods described above, in conjunction with what we have been told by parents and information workers, has allowed us to build a picture of the potential and actual networks, pathways, and trajectories taken by people, material resources, and ideas about parenting and early learning. When building a picture of these pathways or networks it is possible to begin from several starting points; for example, the study of a specific *locale* such as a mall or main street, or something smaller such as a health clinic or pharmacy, where resources are produced, displayed, and distributed. It is also possible to begin from a spatialized practice observed in the home or reported by parents (Rowsell and Nichols 2009) or from a specific *resource* such as a pamphlet or website that most parents of young children report that they have consulted.

The Sites

Green Plains: A Farming Region

Green Plains is a fertile flood plain district in South Australia, 50 kilometers from the capital city center and the source of much of the vegetable produce that is consumed by the city's citizens. Two towns in close proximity were the focus of our study. Because these towns are so close they are often designated by the one hyphenated name, Deepwater-Geraldine; however they have different histories and social cultures. Geraldine is closer to the river and has been a settling place for successive waves of migrants from rural backgrounds wishing to establish market gardens. Its largest ethnic group is Southeast Asian, but it also has a significant Mediterranean community and a minority of Anglo Australians. Geraldine is part of a council district which includes the furthest fringes of the capital city and has the lowest socioeconomic profile in the state (Australian Bureau of Statistics 2006). Deepwater was established in the mid-1800s to serve a thriving farming community built on grain growing. Its main street has a colonial era feel about it, with the institute building opened in 1877 still its most imposing. Fewer than a thousand reside in or around the town, and the main occupations are truck driving, trades, and animal husbandry (breeding horses and dogs). Compared to neighboring Geraldine, Deepwater is culturally much more homogenous. A resident, noting this, said that being in Geraldine was like playing 'spot the Aussie' (i.e., there were so few Anglo Australians that they could hardly be seen).

Midborough: Urban Sprawl with Centralized Resources

Midborough is one of the largest metropolitan local government districts in the state of South Australia with a population of over 100,000, located ten kilometers northeast of the capital city. Culturally, the district is predominantly Anglo-Australian with a significant minority of older residents of German and Polish extraction. While it is in the median on the Index of Disadvantage (Australian Bureau of Statistics 2006), this masks a considerable disparity between the highest and lowest socioeconomic areas. At one extreme are newer housing developments for young middle- to upper-middle-class families. At the other is a cluster of neighborhoods which contain above-average percentages of adults in lower-paid service and manual occupations and in rental accommodation. The central Midborough Hub is a busy commercial and local government precinct with a very large covered mall on one side of a major highway. This mall's position is virtually an island since it is surrounded by a ring of busy roads. On the other side of this ring is a zone of civic services including a hospital and government welfare offices. A large park occupies a low hill flanking the busy highway on one side of the mall and at the top of this hill is the library, in a large modern complex also including the Midborough Council offices.

Greystone: US Town with High Social Contrast

Greystone is a university town situated an hour outside of a major city, and many of its residents are either commuters or academics. From its early days, Greystone has had a strong working-class black community who lived and worked separately from the established majority upper-middle-class community. In the past ten years, the area has experienced significant growth and change, owing to a Hispanic (primarily Guatemalan and Mexican) community moving into the traditional African American working class area. Spanish is the most common of the 55 languages, other than English, spoken by a diverse community that includes immigrants from 63 countries. In 2003–04, Greystone Regional School's enrollment of 3,275 was 72% White, 11% Asian, 9% African American, and 8% Hispanic. Greystone's historical affluence and its affiliation with well-known academic institutions masks the needs of disadvantaged families who live in public or multifamily rental housing downtown or in the affordable housing units in the surrounding township. Many of the children of these families are eligible for the federal free- and reduced-cost meals program. The disparity between rich and poor plays out in the public schools. While most Greystone families have access to educational resources at home, such as computers and diverse reading materials, over 10 percent of the District's students rely on the resources of schools, churches, or nonprofit organizations to fill the gaps.

Services within Sites

For each site, we set out to identify and access as many as possible of the services which connected in some way with young children's early learning and development from infancy to the preschool period. Depending on the level of access granted, we then undertook data collection. We were successful in negotiating sustained participant observation in at least two kinds of service in each field site and in interviewing key personnel from several contrasting services. A summary of the kinds of service and data collected follows:

Table 2.1 Data Collection from Categories of Service Providers at Three Field Sites

Site/Provident	Commercial	Health service	Religious organization	Library	Other
Midborough	O, P, A, W	I, O, P, A, W	I, O, P, A, W	I, O, P, A	I, P, A
Green Plains	O, P. A	I, P, A	I, O, A	I, P, A	O
Greystone, US	O, P, A, W	I, P, A	I, O, W	I, O, P, A, W	I, P

I = Interview, O = Participant observation, P = Photography, A = Artifact collection, W = Website analysis
NB Green Plains comprises the two adjoining towns of Deepwater and Geraldine

'Other' services included child-care centers, a sporting club, and an agricultural center. The organization of this book according to four main categories of provider means that these services will not be discussed in detail.

In addition to the main field sites, when parents' or community workers' accounts indicated important services within reach of, but outside, our original field site boundaries, we also investigated these locations. These included an outer suburban shopping mall utilized by some Deepwater families, a religious school serving Geraldine's Vietnamese community, and the Blue Sky Club in the county adjoining Greystone (see Chapter 5).

The Reconnaissance Phase

The process of establishing the boundaries of a research site is where the 'groundedness' of traditional ethnography rubs up against the fluidity and ephemerality of mobility, associations, and networks. In the reconnaissance phase, the team engaged in the following research practices:

- collection of existing data, e.g., maps, websites, telephone book entries
- traveling around the site, in car, and on foot taking various trajectories
- photographic documentation and field notes
- drawing of site boundaries using Google Earth
- listing all services
- contacting site managers for permission to gather data and recruit participants
- identifying possible problems for researcher access to sites
- distributing information about the project at sites where permission was granted

While we were focused on issues of access from the parent perspective, we were approaching these sites not as parents but as researchers. This had immediate and significant implications for our own access to sites. Those that were public (like libraries) were the easiest to get into. Community services had coordinating staff with whom it was necessary to establish support for the goals of our research before access was granted.

Government and clinical services often had a public shopfront (such as a waiting room) enabling us to literally get in the door. Receptionists were key gatekeepers in determining whether we could document information available in pamphlet holders or on coffee tables. Access to personnel and activities was not immediate and often required several layers of approval. In the case of a government-run health service for new mothers, this approval process took nearly two years.

The hardest services to access were privately run child-care centers. In a few cases, we were allowed into a reception area, and these indicated that very little information was provided for parents. More usually no entry was permitted to nonclients, and approaches to management did not change this. During the project, one national chain of child-care centers set up in Deepwater; local advertising was heavy with notices placed on nearly every shop window in the main street. Despite this, our attempts to conduct interviews or gather artifactual material in the local center were met with denial.

The Immersion Phase

During our ethnographic study of specific spaces, we examined how and where early learning resources were situated and positioned; where parents congregated and how they acted in these spaces; and how parents were invited to enter into social and textual networks that could be traced into and out of these spaces, even as they went beyond the geographical boundaries of local surrounds including onto the World Wide Web. We analyzed the ways in which organizations operated as sponsors (Brandt 2001) of early learning while encouraging parents to both consume goods and services, and also to participate in and take responsibility for children's early learning and development. Observation and documentation focused on:

- characteristics of public spaces for parent networking and encountering resources
- observable patterns of usage
- displays, i.e., collections of materials on noticeboards, shop windows, etc.
- characteristics of information resources (e.g., type, language, images, portability, location)
- signage identifying services (e.g., legibility, language, accuracy)
- technologies for information provision (e.g., computers, Internet access points, headphones for listening to audio, URLs on printed materials)

For instance, in the case of the Gumtree Plaza shopping mall in Midborough, the research team walked and observed the mall and surrounding area on multiple occasions. We focused on the material pathways parents of young children were invited to take once they arrived at the center on foot or by bus, and how they were directed to find and secure convenient car parking (e.g., in spaces designated as 'Parking for Prams'). We noted how signs and mall layout led parents through the spaces of the mall and highlighted passageways toward the 'Concierge Desks' where they could get help with directions or borrow 'mobility facilities' such as 'kiddy cruisers' and 'fire chief carts' to assist them to traverse the vast spaces of the mall with young children in tow. We also considered where products were placed and identified and followed semiotic pathways that led parents from signs and products located in the mall to spaces and organizations located outside its confines, such as libraries and websites. A case in point was the information booth located in one of the mall's corridors; we collected and examined all the pamphlets housed in this booth, noted their producers, and identified the geographic spaces from which they originated.

In developing our practice, we drew on our previous experience as ethnographers in the classic participant-observer style but consciously attempted to employ methods more sensitive to space, networks, and mobility (Mannion, Ivanic, and LfFE 2007). Partly modeled on the 'ecological survey' (Neuman and Celano 2001), this approach involves a purposive and thorough documentation of a particular space, such as a neighborhood, from a particular perspective. Neuman and Celano paid particular attention to opportunities to participate in literacy practices whereas we were interested in the resourcing of early learning. The approach requires researchers' willingness to spend considerable periods of time in sites, making multiple visits at different times, and employing a range of methods of documentation. Compared to traditional ethnography, particularly in the field of education, researchers have a more mobile orientation both in relation to space and in relation to other participants. They shift from more distanced to more engaged modes of participation depending on the circumstances. Our research looks at a parents' spatial experience of these sites and, by both researcher and parent alike 'trampling' the research site 'underfoot', generates 'internal alterations of the place' (de Certeau 1984, 110). This embodiment of space manifests as place-making and generates potential pathways.

In complex places, such as a mall, there are multiple potential and actual interactions, texts, and pathways. There are also multiple signals about how participants are to interpret signs and spaces. For instance, in a library the arrangement of shelves produces physical paths while signage indicates the location of children's resources; at the same time, the behavior of experienced users models to new participants the kinds of interactions which are acceptable, for instance ways that parents manage young children's movements and voices (see Chapter 6).

Participant Observation

When service providers were agreeable and schedules permitted, we located researchers in services for periods of a week to three months. These observation sessions occurred in the context of specific activities for young children and their carers, such as playgroups and library sessions. These engagements were negotiated on a continuing basis with researchers responding to invitations to converse, participate, and in some cases, as discussed above, to contribute to the service. Formal interviews were conducted with service providers and some clients. Additionally, if the service had a web presence, activity in this domain was investigated.

Parent Interviews

Just fewer than 50 caregivers were interviewed for the project across all sites. As we will describe below, rather than relying on a convenient sample of individuals keen to tell their stories, we went to some trouble to balance our sample for gender and cultural diversity. This no doubt limited the total number of participants, since members of nondominant groups tend to be harder to recruit.

The differences in participant numbers across sites reflect to some extent the pool of potential informants with Deepwater town containing a small number of parents with young children. The addition of a focus group cohort in Midborough was in response to issues of culturally appropriate inclusion for African women at a field site (see below).

Interviews, where possible conducted in the context of home visits with visual documentation and artifact collection, assisted us to investigate:

- parents' priorities for children's learning and development, including any special needs
- resources sought and gathered and the forms these take e.g., books, magazines, educational toys, bookmarked websites
- places where resources were sourced and method of accessing these places;
- social networking in relation to children's learning and development (CLD) information and resources
- practices associated with these resources, e.g., play, reading, behavior management, health care, diagnosis
- how parents manage their economic resources in relation to knowledge resources, e.g., what do they decide to buy rather than borrow and why

Interviews, artifacts, and mapping were combined to develop profiles of parents' activities as they related to resources for supporting children's learning and development. To analyze this data we inventoried all resources mentioned in the interview, listed, and categorized all people, places, and websites

Table 2.2   Caregiver Participants by Site and Role

Sites/Participants	Mothers	Grandmothers	Fathers	Total
Greystone, US	11		5	16
Deepwater Aust	6		0	6
Midborough Aust—individual	11	1	5	17
Midborough—focus groups	7	2	0	9
Totals	35	3	10	48

mentioned as sources of materials, and used Google Map to locate places and note their usage. We also conducted a textual analysis of the interview transcript focusing on priorities for children's learning and development, values associated with resources and their sources, and networking activities.

Networking into 'hard-to-reach' Parents and Families

It was important to us to include the experiences and perspectives of families who, for reasons of ethnic identity, class, gender, or language, may not usually participate in educational research. We know that research purporting to speak about 'parents' as a group more usually attracts mothers of the educated middle-class (David 1993; Nichols 2009). Our efforts to engage with parents from diverse backgrounds met with anticipated mixed success. At times we became acutely aware of our heterogeneity in relation to a network which we wished to join. Our attempts to find different paths show that networking can be an effortful process and is influenced by the individual's identity resources and mobility, both social and physical.

Culturally Diverse Families

Our intentions for this project were to be inclusive of the full range of cultures in the communities within which we researched. Indeed, the site of Green Plains was selected partly because of its cultural diversity in being a place of settlement for immigrants from many different countries of origin. Our efforts to involve these families included locating researchers within services which specifically targeted particular ethnic groups. These included Greystone Baptist Church and Saviour Church Preschool (African American families) and Midborough Uniting Church (African refugee families). Networking into these communities entailed a commitment of time, since as cultural outsiders we needed to learn about the group's values and ways of working, and a willingness to adapt our research agenda to local priorities. For instance, a research assistant attended the Midborough Uniting Church's African Women's day weekly for six months during which time the emphasis was primarily on relationship building rather than research activities.

Language was certainly an issue when attempting to recruit and communicate with parents for whom English was not spoken in the home. Having our recruitment materials and research instruments translated did not, however, turn out to be the sole answer. One can translate words but still research *practices* may not translate. A research interview is a very specific communication genre which researchers understand to have the purpose of producing knowledge without impacting significantly on the research participant. However, for immigrants, refugees, and those on social security, face-to-face questioning brings echoes of other contexts. In the immigration interview, welfare interview, or police interview addressees' answers have direct and material impact on their lives and futures.

A language translator in these circumstances needs also to be a cultural mediator between researchers and participants. This was the role taken by Ayak, a recognized leader for the African community in the region serviced by the Midborough hub. We consulted with Ayak regarding the most relevant and appropriate way to involve African mothers and grandmothers in the project, which resulted in two workshops on early learning (another example of becoming the resource—see above). In keeping with cultural ways, the workshops incorporated oral storytelling, singing, and chanting. As well as translating the presenter's talk into Arabic and Dinka, Ayak modeled and legitimated participation. This was particularly important for the younger mothers present who regarded older women's approval as a necessary element in their own participation.

Individual interviews were not conducted with the African women of Midborough. Responding to their preference for collective activity we ran a series of two focus groups in the weeks following the workshops. Nine women were involved in these focus groups. Most of the women preferred to utilize their English language resources, even though limited, relying on translation mainly to interpret the questions. These focus groups provided genuine and valuable insights into African refugee families' values, priorities, and practices regarding the learning and development of their children, before and during school.

We were not always as successful in our attempts to network into particular cultural communities. The Southeast Asian community of the rural town of Geraldine is a case in point. As mentioned above, we were able to forge a relationship with a community worker operating out of the local agricultural center. However, shortly after our first meeting with the English language group, its funding came to an end, and the community worker ceased operating in the town. Subsequently, we pursued two potential network paths. A telephone contact to the state Vietnamese association revealed the name of a Vietnamese community worker employed by the local council in an outlying suburb's service center which was accessed by some Geraldine families. We also learned that some of the town's children attended a Catholic church and school in another outer suburban area.

The Vietnamese community worker, Tran, was very interested in the project and willing to help us connect with Geraldine families. We developed new bilingual recruitment materials for the Geraldine Primary School specifically targeted at Southeast Asian families. We booked the school hall for a late lunch, following Tran's advice—'You must serve food'—and also hoping to coordinate with the usual mealtime of agricultural workers. We drove out to Geraldine, met with Tran, set up the hall and waited. In vain—not one parent turned up.

Again, at 'Immaculata' Catholic Church, we received a warm welcome from the Vietnamese pastor. It turned out that our project connected with his desire to increase the profile of early learning in the school and its families. We told him about our experience running workshops for the African families of Midborough, and he suggested some specific topics which he felt were relevant to the concerns of the Vietnamese community, including whether television is harmful for children's learning and how to encourage boys to focus on schoolwork. Following another meeting which was attended by the School Council president, a proposal for a series of workshops was written for the council's consideration and translated into Vietnamese for distribution to parents. We did not hear back and after a couple of emails and phone messages felt it would be impolite to keep asking.

Fathers

Research ostensibly focused on 'parents' often succeeds in attracting mainly women as participants. Most often, it appears that researchers frame their invitations to 'parents' or 'the parent' and then accept whoever volunteers to participate. Brantlinger probably represents the prevailing trend in recruitment when she states 'My intent was to include either or both parents' (2003, 32). It is interesting to compare this approach to the construction of cohorts on class lines; it is hard to imagine a researcher interested in class setting out to interview 'either or both' middle- or working-class parents.

We entered communities through the organizations set up to resource early learning such as playgroups, libraries, and health services. The majority of participants in the activities we observed were women (whether mothers, grandmothers, or paid carers), as were those who presented and organized the activities. Recruiting through these avenues. it was not surprising to find that the majority of volunteers for the interview component of our study were mothers.

Attempting to recruit fathers through their female partners was not a successful strategy. This was particularly the case in the rural site, where the researcher was told 'He doesn't know anything. What do you want to talk to him for?' This is similar to the situation faced by Brantlinger who approached potential informants by telephone for her study of middle-class parents' attitudes toward desegregated schooling. She reports that it was mostly women who answered the phone, and 'the few fathers who answered promptly turned the phone over to their wives' (ibid.).

The Greystone site was distinctive in that three of the five fathers who participated were the primary carers of their children. In these families, the mother's superior earning capacity and the father's desire to participate in the children's upbringing had supported a near-complete delegation of daily parenting work to the father. This delegation, it seems, extended to the father's right and obligation to speak for the family on matters related to early learning. This suggests a pattern where the parent with the closest routine responsibility for young children—the 'hands-on parent'—is also the default spokesperson for the parental couple.

Breaking out of this pattern is a challenge for researchers, as it is for service providers. In early childhood, the Pen Green Centre in the United Kingdom has achieved some success through moving from a gender-neutral form of address to parents to one that specifically targets fathers (Whalley and Pen Green Centre Team 2001). Through surveying fathers, they discovered that an emphasis on 'facts' and specific outcomes and a de-emphasis on informal conversation (i.e., coffee and chat) was more conducive to men's participation in activities related to their child's education.

As we did not have the incentive of being the carers of families' children (as did Pen Green), we addressed the issue by identifying community organizations which attracted fathers. Similarly to Whalley, we developed recruitment materials specifically targeting fathers. Then we began contacting sports clubs which catered for children. The majority of the clubs which we contacted did not respond; however the president of 'Valley Dragons', whose headquarters was near Midborough, was receptive. Accordingly, two researchers attended a practice session of the club and mingled with the parents congregated around the sportsground introducing ourselves and talking about our research. Interviews with fathers were subsequently conducted on a game day, while dads attempted to give us their attention while keeping an eye on the state of play. One of them was actually videoing the match at the time.

WORKING WITH DATA

The Inventory of Resources

In their 'ecological survey' of the literacy affordances of four contrasting neighborhoods, Neuman and Celano (2001) systematically documented certain aspects of these environments. These included the outlets where reading materials could be borrowed or bought such as libraries, bookshops, and magazine stands. By quantifying some of these elements, they were able to add a layer of evidence to their contrastive analysis of the literacy affordances of neighborhoods with different demographic profiles.

Like these researchers, we wanted to design an aspect of the project which was a systematic inventory, in this case of resources associated with young children's learning and development. We will leave aside for the moment the question of how we defined these resources and distinguished them from children's and parenting products more generally. The process involved conducting a 'sweep' of a particular site during which we wrote descriptive notes, took photographs, and where possible collected copies, of relevant materials. Following this, the details were entered into a database. These included:

- general location (i.e., library, supermarket, gas station)
- specific location (i.e., noticeboard, shelf, window)
- type of product (i.e., pamphlet, CD, toy)
- title and brand
- producer
- cost
- language (i.e., English or bilingual)

The process was assisted by the supplementary use of web-based resources, such as library and commercial catalogues in which we checked details such as publishers and dates.

The process was complicated by several factors. First, ethics permission was required for photography and was not forthcoming from all sites; in these cases we had to rely on note-taking which was more time consuming. Second, some sites (e.g., department stores) were so large and had so many relevant materials that documentation could not be concluded in a single session; in these cases, we had to return later sometimes to find that displays had changed, and new products had been located in areas previously surveyed. Third, the procedures for electronic data entry evolved as we considered how best to label the diverse materials we were finding. This necessitated a careful clean-up of the database before any statistical analysis could be conducted. While we were able to set up the database without difficulty, we employed a specialist statistician at this stage.

Working with Visual Data

Research practices are responding to the fact that researchers, as well as their subjects, are 'living in an increasingly visually-saturated culture' (Prosser 2008, 36). Much of what we counted as data already had a strong visual dimension, e.g., toy packaging, book covers, and signage. This required visual methods of documentation and data storage as well as attention to how visual codes operated with other symbolic resources, such as print, to signify meanings regarding childhood, learning, parenting, etc. (Kress and van Leeuwen 1996; 2001).

Digital photo manipulation became a standard part of procedure for dealing with data. Copies were made so as to manipulate images making different aspects visible; images were flipped so that titles and signs could be read; enlargements were made so that details (e.g., the print on a leaflet) could be more easily seen; cropping enabled a close focus on a particular aspect. Working in this way increased the speed with which we could document and process some kinds of data. For instance, writing down the names of books displayed spine out on a shelf is time consuming. Photographing the shelf, and flipping the image later in order to read the titles on the spines, made this kind of work more manageable.

At a more interpretive level, being able to manipulate images digitally made it possible for researchers to become aware of aspects of scenes not in focus at the time of capture. Detailed descriptions of photographic images were written with the aim of explicitly articulating spatial qualities. Juxtaposing images taken in different sites or parts of sites made richer comparisons possible. For instance, in Greystone a photo taken of a statue of a man reading a book which was taken in an upmarket shopping square, when placed alongside a banner depicting a man's grey hat hanging outside the library, enabled us to consider how a discourse linking literacy and gender linked commercial and civic sites (these photos have not been included since they may identify the site).

We found PowerPoint a simple and effective way of presenting to each other particular views of sites. The facility of PowerPoint to move images around a slide and to shuffle slides within a sequence, and to add text as headings and commentary, made it a significant, flexible tool of analysis. Sharing presentations via a website made it possible for researchers geographically distant to enter into dialogue about semiotics.

Figure 2.1   Flipped image of library shelf, enabling easier processing of book titles.

The Network Case Study

The case study is at the heart of the ANT approach (Law 2007). This is the case seen through a particular lens, that of the dynamic relations between multiple actor-networks. It is the case networked with other cases, as in the case of Kimberley which became networked with the case of the Christian bookshop which in turn became networked with the case of the Christian mothers' group. We worked up many such cases over the three years of the project, adding layers to them as new dimensions surfaced. These included parent cases, organization cases, activity cases, and place cases.

In working up cases, methods are needed to assist researchers to see, describe, and interpret these connections. In the process, artifacts such as maps, network diagrams, or flow charts may be constructed. The production of these artifacts is not itself the point; the cases still have to be told. However, the process of creating visible traces of networks we have found to be vital in helping us recognize, name, and question the connections we are making. Below is an example of a set of research artifacts. These diagrams depict two different ways of understanding the connections to, in, and through a playgroup. The 'Wave' playgroup was attended by mothers and young children living in and near the small country town of Deepwater.

In each case, we followed the ANT precept of attending equally to the human and nonhuman. This meant thinking about things and particularly how these things were mobilized. We viewed both humans and nonhumans as able to put other things/people into motion, and we asked: What/who is being put into motion and by who/what? Using parents' accounts, and following this up with further tracing of the objects they showed and

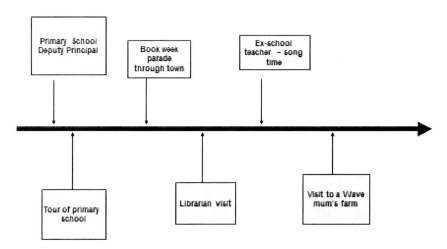

Figure 2.2 Timeline of connections between Wave and Deepwater community over one school term.

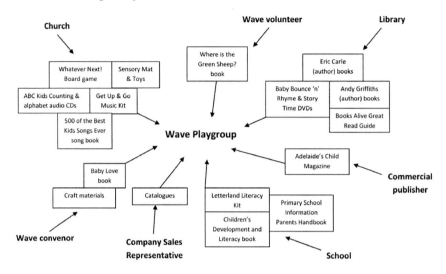

Figure 2.3   Early learning texts and objects coming into Wave from different sources.

talked about, we imaginatively reconstructed the pathways of some of these objects and thought of the parents, in part, as carriers. For example, Paula mentioned a child development book that she had seen at a friend's place. This book exerted a strong attraction on her. It was written by European pediatric biologists and richly illustrated with photographs, some of which simultaneously disturbed and delighted her with their frank graphic quality. The book had come from Germany with the couple who were family friends and university colleagues of Paula's. Paula viewed it as containing authoritative knowledge from a different, more sophisticated, place. In this attraction we could also see signs of its opposite, the repulsion Paula experienced from mass-market products (she told us she would 'not set foot in' Toys R Us). This desirable expensive book could not be borrowed or passed on, unlike some of the other baby books she had acquired from friends whose children had grown. To get this book onto her shelf, Paula had to go online and order it, authorizing an electronic transaction from her bank account to the book distribution company. From a warehouse somewhere in another country, the book that would be hers was packed, driven to an airport, flown, probably first to Sydney then to Adelaide, eventually arriving at her door by postal delivery van. Paula ordered it but, just as truly, the book caused itself to be put into motion.

This approach represents a shift from thinking about things, or even ideas, primarily as possessions of people (seen as the haves and have-nots) to thinking about how these things/ideas came to be taken up. Paula was a 'have'—she could afford expensive imported books—but at the same time she was being 'had' by the book, through her recruitment into its reproduction and distribution.

Time is a dimension of networking often backgrounded in analyses. Partly that is because researchers' tools of representation, such as diagrams, have to be read in the reader's present. On the page a network diagram presents as a time-stripped abstraction. However, ANT views actor-networks as dynamic and constantly in the process of forming connections. This points to the importance of finding a way to incorporate a temporal dimension into network case studies. Actor-networks have histories.

One of our methods to make time visible in our research artifacts was to use a sequence of Powerpoint slides to display an actor-network's changes over time. This was done retrospectively based on field notes and other artifacts. After sustained engagement with a case, we drew the network with all the connections we had been able to make/recognize. This template was then used to reconstruct successive prior versions of the network, by successively removing links. Then the versions were ordered into a sequence which, when the slides were played, presented as an animated changing network. We also at times used the custom animation function within PowerPoint to create movement within a single slide.

Another method, used in analyzing parent cases, was the time/space grid. Constructing this grid involved going through interview transcripts and noting references to space and time. For references to space, we created categories on a continuum from the most immediate personal space (the space of the body) to the most distant (global space). For references to time, the categories ranged from the past of the speaker's childhood to the imagined future of their child with the present time of the interview as the midpoint. During this phase of the analysis, we drew on concepts of narrative time (Ricouer 1980) to better understand how the parents' storying of their lives acted to create connections of meaning linking pasts, presents, and futures, as well as local and distant places (Rowsell and Nichols 2009).

Discourse Analysis

From a discourse theory perspective, our approach draws on Fairclough's (1992; 2003) model of critical discourse analysis (CDA) in which three levels of analysis combine to provide a rich account of the productive workings of discourse: the level of *text*, the level of *interaction* in the specific local (or online) context, and the level of *discourse* or, in other words, knowledge that is circulating through society and reflecting broader cultural and political agendas. Bringing network theory into dialogue with CDA means we consider how networks facilitate the circulation of texts and discourses through direct human interactions and through technological interfaces. Bringing CDA to network analysis means considering networking as a textual practice.

Identifying the discourses circulating through these networks means attending to the ways in which key terms are defined (such as 'learning', 'development'), the kinds of 'ideal parent' and 'ideal child' subjects that are constituted, and the practices which are promoted or discouraged. We saw multiple discourses contesting the field of early learning, offering to parents and children different and even contradictory positions and relationships to the subject.

In this approach, texts are understood as samplings from the field of production within which a range of agents promote and resource early learning and enlist parents and educators into related practices. Post-structural approaches to identity and discursive practice mitigate against researchers making simplistic causal connections between the texts on the one hand and the parents' accounts on the other. For instance, when we compared representations of parenting in texts produced by commercial and government/public institutional interests and the self-representations of individual parents, we recognized that parents negotiate a range of subject positions made available to them (Nichols, Nixon, and Rowsell 2009).

A complex discursive formation such as early learning cannot be characterized in terms of a single set of definitions and subject positions. This is where the concept of assemblage combines with the concept of discourse. The outcome of this analysis was a characterization of the contemporary early learning discourse as an assemblage (see Chapter 1) incorporating elements of prior discourses, such as developmentalism, and bringing them together with new discourses, such as neuroscience.

The interactions between different discursive formations in an assemblage could be observed at the level of a text (such as a Parent Easy Guide, see Chapter 4), a practice (such as Baby Bounce, see Chapter 6), or a site (such as Gumtree Plaza, see Chapter 3). The work of Scollon and Scollon (2003) was helpful in drawing our attention to the different kinds of relations possible between discourses for instance, the merging of discourses by incorporation of features from one into another (e.g., from medical into business) or a kind of 'co-presence' in which discourses 'operate quite independently semiotically, nevertheless, their co-presence produces a kind of dialogicality between them so that each takes part of its meaning from the co-presence of the other' (ibid., 195) An example of this can be seen in our analysis of civic and commercial discourses in the space of Gumtree Plaza (Chapter 3).

CONCLUSION

Data produced using the methods described above has allowed us to build a picture of the potential and actual networks, pathways, and trajectories taken by people, material resources, and ideas about parenting and early learning. When building a picture of these pathways or networks it is possible to begin from several starting points: for example, the study of a specific *locale* such as a mall or main street, or something smaller such as a health

clinic or pharmacy, where resources are produced, displayed, and distributed. It is also possible to begin from a spatialized practice observed or in
the home or reported by parents or specific *resource* such as a pamphlet or
website that parents report that they have consulted.

Whenever we have begun with a specific *locale* in one region, our
method of network tracing has allowed us to build potential pathways.
For instance, starting with public health clinic with an almost universal
reach among new mothers (see Chapter 4), we moved across a road to the
community health service, across a highway into local bookshops in the
mall, and across the mall and over another highway on the other side of the
shopping and transport hub into early literacy programs (0–5 years) run
by the municipal library. From our observations at the clinic, and the texts
it produced, promoted, and circulated, we have been able to see the work
being done by various elements that converged in that place, and how they
set in motion clusters of ideas about why and how parents should engage in
certain early learning practices.

3 The Mall

INTRODUCTION

As one approaches Gumtree Plaza, a sprawling Westfield Mall on the out-skirts of a medium-sized city in Australia, it looks like other malls of its kind. Its car park encircles the mall space, and it has priority parking for handicapped individuals and for parents of small children. If parking in one of these spaces, the nearest entrance of the mall takes the shopper past a children's clothing store on the left and a large bookstore on the right. A sign indicates the direction to a Parents Room ahead. If the destination is one of the variety stores such as Kmart or Target, popular with parents because of their moderately priced children's clothes and household goods, the shopper will enter the 'Playworld' zone. 'Playworld' is an enclosed area equipped with slides, swings, and other equipment for children to play on, flanked with sofas and a café so that parents may watch and socialize with other parents. Toys also figure prominently in the entry displays of the variety stores, creating a seamless recreational path for children from the public to the commercial zone. Beside 'Playworld', there is an information center that contains government-produced pamphlets including some focused on child health, nutrition, childproofing your home, reading to your child, etc. It is clear that Gumtree Plaza caters to parents and actively promotes social, commercial, and informational networks within which parent consumers can encounter various kinds of resources for raising their children.

Other kinds of commercial spaces, such as the traditional high street and the online shop also cater for parents of young children. In different ways and degrees, such commercial spaces may provide opportunities for parents to source information, seek advice, and encounter models of how to care for, socialize, and educate young children. For this reason they are of interest to educators as contexts for educational research in communities; they increasingly function as pedagogic, learning spaces for parents and children.

Although commercial spaces and consumerism have not figured largely in studies of children's early learning and development, they have nonetheless been the subject of academic interest for some time (see Backes 1997;

Goss 1993; Manzo 2005; Salcedo 2003). Shopping malls are derived from department stores dating back to the mid-nineteenth century, with the first enclosed mall constructed in 1956 (Backes 1997, 2). Malls have generally been designed with a focus on the concepts of the 'Gruen Transfer' (the transformation of the 'goal-oriented shopper to the aimless browser') and 'Reilly's Law of Retail Gravitation' (people generally will patronize the largest mall in the area) (Backes 1997, 2). Common features of modern malls include a large covered area, usually on multiple levels, containing an abundance of shops, a food court, and often a cinema complex. Malls are surrounded by car parking space, and there is usually a connection to public transport close by. Inside the mall, shops often include chain stores that can also be found in other shopping locations, state- or nationwide, and across the world.

Several studies explore the notion that commercial spaces serve social and instrumental needs simultaneously. Goss argues that 'the shopping center is a contrived, dominated space that seeks only to resemble a spontaneous, social space' (1993, 30). He identifies various spatial dimensions of the shopping mall that aid in or detract from providing affordances for traveling around the mall and engaging in social interactions. These include configurations of what might be called civic space, transactional space, instrumental space, and so on (19). Salcedo describes such spatial aspects of malls as 'geographically bound expressions' of the tussle between the global logic of developers and contrastive 'local characteristics' of communities that use them (2003, 1084).

We argue that commercial spaces like shopping malls are appropriate sites for study by educational researchers who are interested in how parenting and early learning is imagined, represented, negotiated, and practiced in particular cultural contexts. Some support for this approach is found in studies investigating the participation of children and parents in commercial spaces. Chin argues that shopping may be a 'secondary activity' when mothers visit the mall as an opportunity to meet with other mothers (Chin 1993, 100). Although malls may be described as 'the ultimate manifestation of consumption at its seductive destructive best—or worst', it is more helpful to consider malls as 'complex sites of social reproduction' (Chin 1993, 99). This is particularly relevant when we consider the reproduction of such concepts as 'the good parent' or 'the baby' as a site for educational intervention. Cook refers to commercial sites as aspirational spaces where 'desired and desirable identities and selves' are displayed, but also as proprietary spaces which mark the distinction between child and adult store space (Cook 2003, 161). Spatial interdiction, whereby age and gender are segregated, are also evident in many toy stores, thus applying a 'development sequence' to the layout of the store and people's experience of moving through it (ibid., 163).

Studies focusing on the toy industry are particularly relevant given the blurring between education and entertainment noted by Scanlon and

Buckingham (2004). MacNaughton and Hughes (2005) argue that companies in the toy industry have created a baby 'market' whose objective is to depict babies as 'learners' whose capacity for development can be unleashed through the consumption of their educational toys, DVDs, CDs, books, and so forth (32). The baby's mind therefore becomes the 'temporal/spatial locus for intervention' (Nadesan 2002, 416), while the parent or carer becomes the agent charged with responsibility for that intervention which can be exercised by purchasing the product. Seiter highlights the toy industry's strategy to target parents and children with two main kinds of goods simultaneously: 'mass-marketed promotional toys' that appeal to children, and 'niche-marketed, educational or classic toys' that appeal to parents (Seiter 1993, 232). This view is supported by Nadesan who notes the desire of parents for their children to 'exceed the norm', and the way in which the toy industry, as well as knowledge workers, employ infant 'brain science' to appeal to this desire (Nadesan 2002, 422). Parental attitudes toward such toys largely revolve around 'educational background and cultural capital' (Seiter ibid.), as these toys seduce parents with the 'utopian promise of dissolving class differences, of levelling the playing field for the next generation' (Seiter ibid., 239). This point is developed from Bourdieu's (1984) reference to toy purchasing as based on cultural as distinct from financial reasoning (see also Carrington 2003).

In this chapter 'the mall' is used as a generic category for commercial spaces. These are actual and virtual spaces within which participants are positioned as consumers or sellers involved in the exchange of economic capital for goods. Of course, not every interaction in a commercial space involves purchase, but the other activities (e.g., browsing, socializing, and play) are enabled because of their potential to create opportunities for future commercial transactions. For the three years of our study, we studied commercial spaces in Midborough, Deepwater, Geraldine, Greystone, and further afield as parents' accounts led us into other virtual and actual spaces. As we crossed geographical landscapes we encountered differences in commercial spaces due to such factors as regionality and socioeconomic status of communities which we will discuss further. Types of commercial spaces and networks studied included:

- large malls, e.g., Westfield 'Gumtree Plaza', Midborough
- shops within malls, e.g., book shops, variety stores, toy shops, newsagents
- strip malls (large single outlet shops grouped around a car park), e.g., Babies R Us
- town shopping strips (e.g., Deepwater main street)
- websites linked to specific offline malls or shops (eg Westfield site, Toys R Us site)
- websites linked to producers, e.g., Leapfrog©

- websites operating as directories or portals, linked to a range of commercial services, e.g., Kidspot
- direct selling companies, e.g., Learning Ladder
- promotional packages, e.g., the Bounty Bag

We earlier introduced Massey's (2005) three propositions for thinking about spaces (see Chapter 2): recognize space as the product of interrelations and as constituted through relations; understand space as a layering of multiple possibilities; and recognize space as always under construction. The mall, whatever form it takes, adheres to Massey's proposition as a space that invites, elicits, and maintains interactions; as a space that is multiply embedded, multiply materialized in physical and virtual spaces; and, that is always in flux, never quite complete with a copresence of past and future.

A mall or a high street is not an enclosed system. Even over our three-year study, commercial spaces changed with the removal of a display or with new play areas and with added features for parents such as strollers to rent or borrow and with interactional rhetorical devices such as using a blog or Facebook presence. We tried as much as possible to capture these shifting dynamics as well as the simultaneity of connections between locally situated commercial destinations and their global networks (Brandt and Clinton 2006).

We consider the versions of early learning being defined in commercial products and the practices through which their producers and marketers accessed parents and children as consumers. In this chapter, we take account of commercial sites as spaces of pedagogic practice with multiple opportunities to provide for families' access to resources and information networks about their children's early learning.

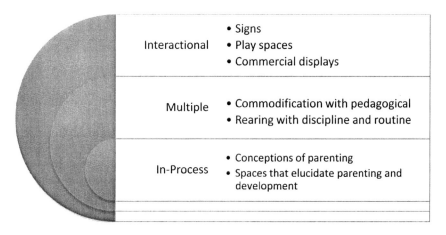

Figure 3.1 Commercial spaces as interactional, multiple, in-process.

LOOKING FOR EARLY LEARNING IN THE MALL

Shopping malls, like Gumtree Plaza, are built by architects and corporations for retailers and for shoppers. While individual retailers pursue their own strategies for marketing to particular shoppers, malls have general strategies to habituate shoppers to the spatial, discursive, material, and immaterial properties of 'the mall.' If they are successful, malls will occupy a taken-for-granted dimension of families' lives, beginning with infancy. Modern malls incorporate many facilities that assist parents and children to visit, browse, and linger: for example, bench and lounge-style seating; freely available baby strollers for loan; parents' rooms that include changing tables, running water, and microwave ovens; child-friendly open-space cafes; play-areas with activities for children, and surrounding seats well located for easy adult supervision.

Five shopping malls were included in the study. In Australia, we examined the large Gumtree Plaza in Midborough and the mini-mall in the town of Geraldine. In the US, we examined one large shopping mall and two strip malls in different parts of Greystone, a medium-sized university town. Both large malls were members of the Westfield chain. The larger the mall, the more design effort had been put into enabling navigation, e.g., through signboards showing floor plans, signage, mobility devices, and specialized staffing (concierges). All larger mall spaces had play areas and parent rooms within restrooms. Across the US and Australian malls there were also some parallels in terms of the kinds of products on display such as LeapFrog© and early readers. However, there were also some key differences in relation to the level of physical, spatial resourcing, and also the kinds of resources available.

GUMTREE PLAZA MALL

Gumtree was one of two Westfield malls we explored for the project, the other being located in the greater Greystone district. Westfield malls are networked commercial spaces described on their website as the 'global brandspace' of the Westfield Group (Westfield Corporation 'http://westfield.com/corporate/property-portfolio/australia/brand-space/). Westfield malls typify the kinds of commercial spaces that architects and corporations construct to speak to regions and communities. Given the predominance of families resident in the regions within which malls are located, it is hardly surprising that on their websites the Westfield group talks about joining the W Family. By promoting a family-integration model, the Westfield Group constructs a network tied materially and discursively to the notion of 'family.' Nixon comments that 'an important aspect of current marketing strategy involves what is known as "interactive" and "cross-channel" marketing which is designed to move potential consumers *from brick to clicks*"; that is from the material space of *bricks* and mortar to the corresponding online space (*clicks*) occupied by each Westfield centre website' (Nixon 2011, 119). A discussion of the online manifestation of the Westfield 'brandspace' occurs later in this chapter. For our field visit to a Westfield mall in a suburban center, our question was how does this commercial mall juggernaut speak to locally situated material commercial spaces?

Westfield Gumtree Plaza is located in Midborough, a suburban region located within a large metropolitan local government district ten miles distant from the center of a capital city, which includes a mix of high and low socioeconomic areas. Designed in the late 1960s, the central Midborough hub is a major commercial and local government precinct and a transport and services hub for the northern suburbs of the city. The commercial zone is spatially distinct and separate from the civic zone. Gumtree Plaza is located inside a ring formed from busy arterial roads, on the other side of which are the sporting, community, and cultural facilities. The commercial hub also includes the greatest concentration of car parking spaces and the safest pedestrian access from a large bus station. This differentiation between the commercial and civic was one of the most significant geosemiotic features of the urban landscape of Midborough, with direct impact on parents' access to services and resources.

The research team walked and observed the Gumtree Plaza and surrounding area on multiple occasions, imagining ourselves as parents accessing this domain accompanied by their young child(ren). We located car spaces designated as 'Parking for Prams', noting that these signaled an intention to smooth the transit of shoppers with infants and toddlers. We also entered the center via the bus transit area. We saw that, once parent shoppers arrived at on foot or by bus, signs and mall layout were designed to lead them through the spaces of the mall, for instance by highlighting passageways toward 'concierge desks'. At these stations, they could get directions or borrow 'mobility facilities' such as 'kiddy cruisers' and 'fire chief carts' to assist them to traverse the vast spaces of the mall with young children in tow.

When our study began there were 237 shops in Gumtree Plaza. We identified 20 stores in Gumtree Plaza (including its adjacent extension Plaza Plus which was under a different roof) which sold products related to early learning and parenting (Table 3.1)

Toys advertised as related to early learning could be sourced from 15 different stores including variety stores, supermarkets, newsagents, and pharmacies. Children's books were available from 12 stores while books related to parenting could be found in 11 locations. Two variety stores sold every category of relevant product, while Toys R Us and the ABC shop stocked all except parenting magazines. Inside variety stores, parents face what are literally walls of products (see Figure 3.2). The visual language employed by designers of toy packaging with its repetition of generic motifs, common colors, and pack constructions produces a distinctive spatial environment

Table 3.1   Gumtree Plaza Outlets and Provision of Products Related to Early Learning and Parenting

Name	Type	Toys	Books Chains	Media Chains	Books Parents	Magazines Parents
Kmart	Variety	❖	❖	❖	❖	❖
Target	Variety	❖	❖	❖	❖	❖
Big W	Variety	❖	❖		❖	
Myer	Dept	❖	❖		❖	
Coles	Supermarket	❖		❖		❖
Woolworths	Supermarket	❖	❖	❖		
Bi-Lo	Supermarket	❖		❖		
Campbells	News	❖	❖		❖	❖
Newsplus	News				❖	❖
Plaza News	News		❖		❖	❖
National	Chemist	❖	❖		❖	
WestPharm	Chemist	❖				
Toys R Us	Specialist	❖	❖	❖	❖	
ABC Shop	Specialist	❖	❖	❖	❖	
Books Plus	Specialist		❖		❖	
Gameworld	Specialist	❖		❖		
Post Office	Service	❖	❖	❖		
Star Craft	Specialist	❖				
Totals		15	12	9	11	6

(see also Seiter 1993). Thus Gumtree Plaza overall, and the variety stores in particular, offered a very considerable stock of products for parents who may be looking for commercial materials related to early learning.

Spatial arrangements, including clustering of outlets and strategies for directing movement, channel parent consumers and bring them into contact with these products. In terms of spatial clustering, the greatest concentration of these products could be found in the area around 'Playworld', the play area for children (see Figure 3.3). This area occupies the concourse between two variety stores and contained a café, lounge, children's play area, ice cream stand, and community information booth.

The children's play area within 'Playworld' is composed of plastic panels incorporating manipulable play materials and simultaneously acting as a fence which contains the area and marks it out for children. If one were to imagine 'Playworld' shrunk in size so that it were small enough to be packed into a box, it would be nearly identical to the plastic 'activity center' kind of toys which have for years been marketed to parents of infants. These kinds of toys are designed to enable children to interact directly with

Figure 3.2   Infant and toddler toy aisle in a variety store (researcher's photograph).

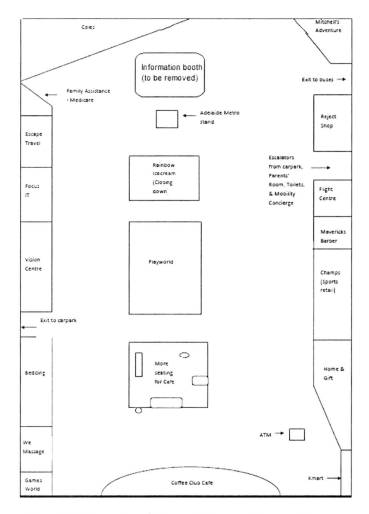

Figure 3.3   Floor plan of 'Playworld' area in Gumtree Plaza.

Figure 3.4 Gumtree Plaza concourse showing cafe seating area looking over 'Playworld' (researcher's photograph).

Figure 3.5 Section of 'Playworld' panel depicting an activity not possible within the play area (researcher's photograph).

objects to cause particular effects such as making parts move, producing sounds, etc. They are a materialization of the Piagetian view of child development which privileges the child's interaction with its environment and the material world (Burman 1994). It is such a view that legitimates the marketing of activity-center toys as providing both 'fun' and 'learning' (Seiter 1993). Indeed, toys of this kind would have until recently filled the shelves of the toy sections in both of the variety stores which flank the concourse. They are now being overtaken by digital and multimedia toys, such as baby computers, which take the fun-learning nexus into the emerging 'wired child' discourse (Nixon 1998).

Signs on the outside of the Playworld panels show photographic images of happy children, suggesting how the space should be emotionally experienced—as enjoyable and carefree. These images show children without adults; this is consistent with images on the packaging of 'educational' toys for children which depict the child-toy pair, devoid of social context. The absence of the parent from such images implies that it is from the toy directly, rather than from human interactions, that the child derives both fun and learning. Such a message aligns nicely with the elements in the adjoining space, such as the comfortable sofas and cafe, which signify the adult leisure which is made possible by children's diversion. Children's play and adult leisure extend parents' time inside the mall, increasing the opportunities for purchases to be made (Manzo 2005).

A little way beyond 'Playworld' was a booth which on all sides displayed pamphlets advertising a range of community, government, and commercial services. In relation to young children, these pamphlet texts made parents central as agents in making decisions about how to cater for their children's various needs (health, education, entertainment). To one side were two computers offering free, though time-limited, online access. The placement of this booth made it likely to be encountered by parents with children during their time in the mall and provided an alternative activity for parents to undertake while their children were occupied in 'Playworld'. Standing inside the booth were volunteers on hand to answer questions about events and facilities in the local community. The distinctive logo of the Gumtree Hills Council gave a clue as to the origin of some of the pamphlets; Council headquarters is located in the service ring area. Others came from government services which also have offices in the ring. Yet others were produced by schools, kindergartens, and other community organizations in the immediate and outlying areas. If the invitations in these texts were taken up, they would send readers to places outside the mall space, particularly to the government and civic services in the ring zone.

Co-consumption in a Variety Store

Kmart is one of the variety stores entered via the 'Playworld' zone and which carries a large stock of relevant products. On a session of focused observation we noted that near to half of all customers entering the store were adults accompanied by children and in the majority of cases the adult was female. Our observations in this store gave insight into how a commercial organization and its clients manage parent-child co-consumption, which is relevant to our specific focus on parents accessing commercial early learning materials. Co-consumption is the term coined to describe the interdependent relationship of a child and parent shopping together (Cook 2008). The young child is unable to act as a fully independent agent in a commercial transaction while the parent's independence is limited by having to care for a child while catering for their own consumption needs. Co-consumption is more demanding than shopping alone and parents have to devise strategies to manage their child's demands. Simon spoke about his strategy of preparing for shopping trips:

> Clara likes to pick her own [clothes] but I am not going to drag her around to five different stores looking for something. What that usually involves is me going to the store ahead of time, seeing if the prices are what I am wanting to pay, whether there's skull and crossbones on any of their shirts that I won't buy, and then I get it down to two stores that qualify that I will take her to, which then I return to those stores with the child.

Kmart employed spatial and semiotic strategies to appeal to both child and adult consumers and keep them circulating within the space. Kmart usually has boxed toys piled up just past the entrance, with early learning toys featured at particular times of year. As noted, these displays in proximity to 'Playworld' produce a seamless 'play pathway' into the store. Once insider shoppers may be directed to clothing, books, or toys by large ceiling hung signs. These sections are at some distance from each other. To get to the toy section it is necessary to walk right through the store.

The music played over the store's PA on this day featured popular children's television character, Hannah Montana, and her image also appeared on clothing and toys. This sound track, which could be heard throughout the store, signaled that the whole space was child oriented.

In the toy section, items for younger children were placed on low shelves or in bins. The most popular attraction during this observation was a large mesh bin of colored balls, cheaply priced and many featuring television characters. A toddler girl spotted something in the crate and pointed, calling 'Iggle!' It was a ball featuring one of the characters from the children's program 'In the Midnight Garden'. Her finding this particular ball was impressive as there were at least ten varieties, all jumbled up, and very few featuring the Iggle brand. Although her mother commented mildly, 'You've got hundreds of balls, Evie', she did not try to take the ball away.

An interaction in the toy section alerted us to another of the store's strategies for empowering child consumers. From the researcher's fieldnotes:

An older and a younger woman, a girl about 7 and a toddler boy in the trolley were in the aisle featuring 'transformer' type toys. The girl looked at a display of Bionicals that was featured at the end of the aisle before selecting one and taking it to her mother. She asked how much it was and her mother said "The scanner is there. Have a look." A scanner is located at child height at the end of this row. The girl swiped the toy and came back to say "Seventeen dollars. Is that good?" Her mum said "Quite good" but shortly after selected a Bionicals toy from the shelf and asked her daughter to take the other one back.

Through placing the scanner at a child's height, the store was training children to take price into consideration when negotiating for toy purchases with their parents. Thus a potential point of adult-child conflict, and a reason for avoiding bringing children shopping, was to some extent defused.

As well as experiencing boredom, young children can find commercial spaces difficult for other reasons, including the presence of strange people and objects. We observed an instance in which a child's anxiety was managed with the promise of visiting the toy section:

One mother with a girl about 3–4 went past the plastic-sheeted entrance to the back storage area just as a staff member emerged pushing a trolley cart. This frightened the girl who then went out of view into an aisle. The mother called to the girl "Are you alright?" and turned the corner to catch up with her. By this time the daughter was crying and repeating "I want to go home". The mother said: "Come on. Let's go and look at the girlie toys. That will make you feel better." They went together to the Barbie aisle where the girl stopped crying and spent several minutes playing with the Barbie Laptop Learner, including activating the voice. The mother eventually said: "Come on, we've got to get going. It's getting late."

Spatial arrangements separating girls' from boys' toys and clothing encouraged parents to identify their child's needs and preferences as aligned to gender (see also Cook 2008). While many of the early learning products, particularly those for infants, presented as gender neutral, makers of gender-oriented products have also entered the early learning market. On this occasion, the child was drawn to the early learner toy, but clearly its educational status was secondary in the parent's mind to its gender alignment and associated value as a distraction. Thus the presence of toys in the store was a means of parents keeping their children compliant while carrying out their own shopping agendas. In this instance and others we observed, allowing the child to play with toys for a while, and sometimes taking the toy through into other departments before putting it back, enabled the parent to manage the child's frustration without the expense of a purchase.

The children's clothing section appeared to be the destination for more extended shopping time by adults in comparison with the toy section, which was treated by parents as a temporary play stop, rather like 'Playworld' in the mall's concourse. The book section was deserted during our observation period. This is despite the fact that Kmart's selection of children's books was more extensive than that of the other two variety stores, Big W and Target. Books clearly were not seen as sufficiently compelling to function as distractions for children that might enable adults to extend their preferred activity of selecting from the racks of moderately priced clothing.

Parents were largely left to navigate the store and glean information about products on their own. Environmental strategies such as signage and product placement seem to have been the store's major means of communicating with its in-store customers. Personnel at Kmart were mainly located at the checkouts and were not observed to approach customers to offer information or advice. Parents used signage and past experience to navigate the space. They also consulted other adult customers, as indicated in field notes:

> In the baby section were two young women, one pushing a pram. The mother was asking the other woman about the suitability of various items for a child aged 4. They walked slowly around the section looking in each aisle.

While Kmart carried early learning products, these did not appear to be a major draw card. What does stand out is the effectiveness of strategies used by it and like companies to train parents and young children in the practice of co-consumption. Even the youngest children are afforded opportunities to practice product recognition, to handle products, to scan prices, and to negotiate with adults about rights to play, with or without purchase. This in itself is a form of early learning.

Early Learning without Children: The ABC Shop

ABC stores have a reputation for quality, high-culture media products associated with the television and radio programs provided by the government-funded Australian Broadcasting Corporation. This reputation builds on a history of being an advertising-free alternative to commercial media provision. These days, merchandise spin-offs and product placement in children's programming is as common on ABC television as it is on its commercial rivals, even though advertising per se is still disallowed. The ABC shops exist to provide a means by which consumers can access this merchandise including books, audiovisual products, and toys.

In Gumtree Plaza, the ABC shop is located in a section between a supermarket and a large variety store. The concourse here is often busy with shoppers pushing trolleys. The shop is well lit, enabling passersby to see right to the back wall. It has an open entrance and aisles wide enough to accommodate shopping trolleys. Although the ABC shop had a smaller quantity of relevant resources compared to stores like Target, early childhood products occupied a more prominent place in its brand. These products were associated with programs and performers targeting toddlers and young children including Play School, The Wiggles, Thomas and Friends, and Charlie and Lola. Window displays commonly featured one of these brands and children were observed to point and comment on these as they walked past.

Despite its enticing window display and ease of access, very few parents with children were seen to enter the store on the three occasions on which we were observing. Indeed, some parents were seen pulling children away when they attempted to enter. Shoppers tended to be older people, often solo. One of the features which set the space apart from its context in the mall was its soundscape. A conservative music selection featured classical music alternating with nostalgic old-style radio shows. While the ABC's music catalogue includes highly popular children's acts (like The Wiggles) that may have attracted children and parents into the store, these were not played. A hushed air reminiscent of a traditional library created a microculture within the noisier environment of the mall, with its soundscape of contemporary soft-rock muzak, cash registers, and conversation. Despite its child-friendly stock lines, the shop as a semiotic aggregate did not signify a welcome to young children and their parents.

At the time of writing, the ABC had just begun a new early literacy promotion linked to the 'Reading Eggs' series. Associated activity books and book packs were displayed in the store. Sue decided to enter into the role of a customer requesting more information about this initiative and approached a staff member. The assistant handed her two leaflets, said 'You can sign up in five weeks', and began to walk away. The researcher asked whether it was possible to buy anything about the Reading Eggs in the store. The assistant led her to a display, and gestured toward it without speaking. Showing more persistence possibly than the average shopper, the researcher attempted to continue an exchange about the Reading Eggs program by asking what age it was suitable for. The assistant did not move away but neither did she answer. When the researcher asked, 'Is it preschool? the assistant pointed to books on a lower shelf saying, 'There's these', indicating books designated for ages 5–7 (i.e., school age).

Thus an outlet with a large selection of products in the early learning category, including a range specifically targeting beginning readers and aiming to involve parents, did not communicate a welcome to consumers in this category. Its brand image as a high-culture broadcaster for older educated viewers and listeners was at odds with the presence of children and parents in the commercial space.

THE STRIP MALLS

Strip malls allow consumers to park and enter specific stores quickly as opposed to walking through larger mall spaces to find particular stores or to moving in a leisurely way through a commercial space. Large warehouse type outlets are arranged around a central car park, and customers attempt to find parking spaces close to the store they wish to visit as distances are too far to walk comfortably. The arrangement of strip malls speaks to the focused consumer, setting up the expectation of a purchase simply by the fact of having chosen to visit the particular outlet. To document the culture, habits, and spatial dimensions of different genres of commercial spaces, two popular strip-mall stores located ten minutes drive from Greystone were observed. Babies R Us and Walmart sit on either side of commercial strips serving notably different clientele, many of them parents and their young children.

Babies R Us is open, expansive, and modern in its feel. Babies R Us materializes its claim that it has anything parents could ever want for their baby and his or her development. 'Quality', 'value', and 'selection' are three descriptors that are reiterated throughout the store, its marketing, and the products. Consumers experience the space as devoted to children in every way. As well as the kinds of toy products also found in variety stores, there are additional services such as a photo studio for family photos, information displays, and an events booth. As Jennifer walked around the store at least three different salespeople asked if they could help her with anything. Information provision is carried out by both human and nonhuman actors. Displays and take-away pamphlets alert parents to noncommercial community services and sales staff proffer detailed product information and more general advice with little prompting. The acceptance of help is normalized in the interaction order (Scollon and Scollon 2003).

Spaces within the store are differentiated by ages and stages. Toys R Us and Babies R Us franchises are spatially laid out so that parents go to certain aisles over others, assisting with focusing their purchases. Walking through the store, shoppers may notice a system of symbolic coding that identifies particular developmental domains which are claimed to be promoted by the child's use of specific products.

The code was initially developed as a response to customers seeking advice on appropriate toys for children with specific needs such as physical or cognitive disabilities. An article on the website Disabled World explains that a Toys R Us partners with Lekotek, a nonprofit organization. This organization 'assesses the play value of hundreds of toys for children with special needs', and the information is used to produce a specialized Toys R Us catalogue for 'differently abled kids' (http://www.disabled-world.com/entertainment/games/toy-guide.php#ixzz1czE5VNYk).

This organizer simultaneously guides parents to products, legitimates their purchase, and constructs a sequence of future needs of their child.

While linked to a campaign of service to children with specific needs, the system of categorizing toys is generalizable. It directly links specific toys with different developmental domains: auditory, fine motor, language, social skills, visual, self esteem, tactile, creativity, gross motor, and thinking. These color-coded categories are placed throughout the store to underscore its commitment to tailoring products to your child's needs. Thus a stock of goods which the company is in any case committed to selling can be made to appear as if there only by virtue of having passed the test of developmental and educational value. With endorsements from well-known personalities such as Maria Shriver, the corporation communicates that they are universally recognized as committed to meeting children's learning and development needs.

Walmart is clearly signposted and sequenced with clothing in the front and toys in the back. It was easy to get assistance with staff readily available to direct shoppers to particular sections of the store, but the resources and materials seemed more paltry than in other outlets. Specialized early childhood and children's development products run second to offering as many affordable, everyday items as possible for consumers. Jennifer observed the following during her fieldwork:

> Moving into the store and walking east along the side you hit: food; drugstore/chemist at the front of the store and on the other side as you walk into the main part of the store you hit: stationery items; housewares; and gardening/landscaping. You walk through aisles and aisles of housewares; sporting goods; electronics; until you hit children's toys in the back of the store. Most of the toys have to do with pure fun, but there is one row dedicated to educational toys.

Of the educational toys on display, Leapfrog© seemed most prominent. This single aisle contained a fraction of the products in that category available in Babies R Us and its counterpart for older children, Toys R Us. Its placement at the back of the store alongside a much larger offering of recreational toys communicates the expectation that only a minority of Walmart customers will be looking to purchase this type of product.

As customers are approaching the cash registers, they may see a display of books and literature on children's development, pregnancy, and child behavior. The selection was more eclectic than at the other outlets and included the popular parenting series *What to Expect* books along with cookbooks, bibles and religious texts, the Twilight series, and Spanish/English dictionaries. These titles speak to the culturally diverse customer base of Walmart which, in the Greystone area, is likely to include families from the growing Latin American immigrant community. These families have to marshal their economic resources carefully and may be attracted by the lower price range of Walmart products. Placing this literature at the front of the store suggests an expectation that customers might browse through before leaving rather than spending significant time considering what books to purchase.

TWO HIGH STREETS

The high street, once the primary location for shopping in many communities, has undergone a massive challenge from the success of undercover and strip malls. It appeared in two guises in our project: as the destination of choice for affluent, educated parents such as the residents of Greystone who are looking for 'quality' alternatives to the mass-market; and as the only local shopping precinct for rural communities such as Deepwater and Geraldine.

Paula, an Australian suburban mother and university professor, was an example of the former trend. She told us, 'I've never set foot inside Toys R Us or Toyworld, just as far as looking for something more educational'. Instead, she regularly visited a network of suburban 'villages' with single-street shopping strips where she accessed independent bookshops and toy suppliers as well as libraries.

An example of a shop approved by Paula was 'Outside the Box' on the high street of the middle-class suburb of 'Cedar', home of many cafes, boutiques, and gourmet food stores. Although Paula did not live in or near Cedar, she made a point to travel there by car for excursions that combined socializing, shopping, and spending time with her young daughter. Shopping for toys at the independently owned 'Outside the Box' was a very different experience from that offered by a strip mall or chain store. Narrow aisles excluding prams, teeming shelves, and single items rather than masses of one product on display all made physical and information processing demands on shoppers. Hand-written comments on particular items were attached to shelves. This communicated that consumers should not rely solely on the manufacturers' own claims for the products and established the authority of the store owners, who personally selected the stock. A large selection of wooden toys imported from Europe also established a material semiotics hinting at the artisanal and historic. The proprietor spoke of the importance of toys being of lasting value ('not throw-away') and claimed that those shopping there understood this:

Table 3.2   Suburbs and Shops Accessed by One Parent Searching for 'Quality' Early Learning Products

Suburbs/Suppliers	Library	Bookshop	Toyshops
'Cedar'	✓	✓	✓
'Acacia'		✓	
'Pine'	✓		✓

'We're preaching to the converted'. This hinted at those other souls, the mass-consuming parents, on whom such a message would be lost.

The high street of Deepwater, a small Australian country town, told a different story. Here were no specialist book or toy stores, as in suburban villages like Greystone and Cedar. Neither was there a large department or variety story as found in Gumtree Plaza or the US strip malls. The implications of this for the resourcing of parents can be seen when we look at two categories of resource—parenting magazines and educational toys for children. This is not to suggest that parents are unable to support early learning without the use of such materials but rather to recognize that they are one of the kinds of resource promoted to, and referred to by, parents.

Four magazines targeted at parents could be found for sale in or near Deepwater. Compare this to the provision of parenting magazines at Gumtree Plaza with a total of fourteen titles available through five outlets. This is not to say that Deepwater residents disliked magazines. Conversely, it would be hard to imagine a more comprehensive offering of titles in the fields of craft, automotive, and animal husbandry. The local newsagent told us that the most popular magazine she stocked was *Horse Deals* which out-sold the long-running Australian women's magazine, the *Women's Weekly* (a monthly).

Magazines were for sale in two locations, the snack bar and the gas station, both owned by the same proprietors. The snack bar stocked *Pregnancy and Birth* and *Pregnancy: Baby and You* while the gas station offered *Little Kids* and *Out and About with Kids*. *Pregnancy and Birth* is an Australian title which focuses on the woman's experience of the physical, emotional, and psychological aspects of the antenatal period and childbirth. As such, its scope does not cover early learning. *Pregnancy: Baby and You,* published in the UK, appeared briefly, advertised as covering pregnancy, birth, and the first two years. *Little Kids* is produced by Australian *National Geographic* and has an explicitly educational tone, emphasizing the practical knowledge and enjoyment that can be gained by families experiencing the natural environment. *Out and About with Kids*, also an Australian publication, is an organ of the travel industry and promotes family holidays and recreational experiences, with learning a minor note. What these magazines shared was Australian content, with advertisements promoting local (in the sense of in-country) goods and services, and an emphasis on practical action.

Toys explicitly labeled as 'educational', 'developmental', or as promoting learning were nowhere to be seen in Deepwater shops. Materials for drawing, writing, and making things (e.g., crayons, pipe cleaners, card and exercise books) could be bought at the grocery store. Basic consumables are not less valuable in promoting learning, and may even be more so, than specially designed 'educational' toys. However, the early learning discourse which is packaged with such designer toys was not materialized on the shelves of local stores as in suburban commercial centers.

When Deepwater parents went out of town to find children's materials, they spoke of accessing large supermarkets like Woolworths and discount stores like the Two Dollar Shop in the nearest outer suburban shopping center. This was also the case for many parents who lived in the Midborough district and those Greystone householders for whom the high-end local stores were outside their interest or price range. Ideas of distinction between 'quality' and junk materials still came into decision making. Belinda believed that playing with puzzles was good for her child's development and spoke about how she selected these:

> We like to buy good-quality ones, not rubbish from the two-dollar shops. We have bought things from a big toyshop called Toys 'R' Us, cause they have everything. Myer also used to have a good toy and game section, not so much David Jones but Myer. Also K-Mart and BigW. They have more than Target.

Hayley placed a high value on outdoor play and had, with her partner, designed a play area in their backyard which was modeled on the playgrounds found in MacDonald's fast food outlets. She was proud that their children had the equal of a professionally built playground and of her ability to provide this without spending a fortune:

> We just sort of get on the phone and source around. I can knock people down pretty good price-wise from place to place, so yeah, you do what you can.

PARTY PLANS, SAMPLERS, AND FREE STUFF

Given the relatively sparse provision of early learning products in local shops, it was not surprising that Deepwater women reported accessing other kinds of commercial networks. Three direct sales companies were mentioned as sources of educational materials for young children: MTA (Modern Teaching Aids), Learning Ladder, and Scholastic. The first two companies had originally been established to service teachers and had more recently begun marketing directly to parents. Scholastic distributed catalogues through kindergartens and schools.

Learning Ladder is an example of a 'party plan' system under which a local distributor employs her or his social network to find buyers. Learning Ladder's description on its website reflects aspects of the contemporary early learning discourse:

> The aim of The Learning Ladder is to help Australian parents instil a love of learning in their children, and to create a home learning environment where learning is easy, effective and fun. (http://www.learningladder.com.au/aboutus.cfm)

Similar to Tupperware, Learning Ladder seeks to recruit women to play the part of hostess and accesses their social networks to create a group with whom the sales representative can interact directly. Selling educational toys in the home is a way of domesticating these products. Belinda described how she had been approached by a friend who was a distributor to 'have a party' but rather than take up the offer personally, she suggested the representative visit the Wave playgroup (see also Chapter 5). In this way, the playgroup benefited from the sales-indexed bonus of 'free' materials.

At the Learning Ladder sales session, Belinda chose to purchase from the 'Stile' range, which the company describes as 'once only available to teachers'. The range offers graded maths and reading cards (called 'books') which the child 'reads' using a system of plastic tiles with letters and numbers. Belinda explains why she was attracted to the product:

> We used to have these in primary school when I was a kid. And then you have your little book, because Damien has always struggled with his reading a little bit, so we got these. And you just shove this under here, and see like number 1 is 'jam', so it's 'j', so number 1 tile goes in there. [. . .] If I told Damien this was homework, he'd never do it, if it was educational, but because it's fun, I just say to him "Oh, you haven't played with your Stiles in a long time".

Knowing how to use the Stiles was important to Belinda as she showed by demonstrating to the researcher how it worked. She was also concerned that her son's reading difficulty be addressed in a way that did not trigger resistance. Being able to present the activity as 'play' supported her attempts to get Damien to spend recreational time on what was a learning task. Childhood memories, tactility, educational legitimacy, the promise of fun, concern about a child's performance, and social networking combined to produce Belinda's decision.

Retailers and manufacturers also access parents directly via product samples and introductory offers. In the domain of early childhood, a prime example of this kind of marketing is the maternity sample bag (see also Chapter 4), a package handed out in hospital to mothers, which contains magazines, catalogues, leaflets, and goods such as baby lotion and disposable nappies (Nichols, Nixon, and Rowsell 2009). Giving parents free stuff is a means by which commercial providers access local households and social networks particularly of those on a tight budget. Linking free services, however loosely, to ideas about early learning and child development increases the value attributable to what are often basic, limited, and cheaply provided goods.

Some of the Deepwater mothers particularly appreciated the 'Bounty' bag as it brought products not available on the high street into their homes. Offers of free or discounted products were particularly appreciated by parents who marshaled their financial resources carefully. Hayley for instance enlisted in a book club but pulled out as soon as she had received the special offer:

> You get a thing [in the Bounty bag], it's a book club, I think it's three books for $16 or something, so I got two free and bought one and said "That's enough, I've had enough". She's too young anyway.

While the Deepwater mothers seemed open to trying samples and investigating offers made attractive by discounting, they were savvy shoppers. Value for money, convenience, relevance, and practicality also determined whether they pursued a commercial offer. Belinda was one who had investigated the contents thoroughly and followed up many of the opportunities offered:

> You'll get your little baby bag of goodies when you're in the hospital, with a nappy sample and bits and pieces. Then you can join the Huggies club. You get emails from Huggies. They used to get a magazine. That was through the stage of the age of your child. [. . .] It was pretty exclusive to Huggies itself and they sent it through your mail. They used to send little samples and vouchers and stuff. It was all connected to Target, yeah, Baby Target, and you get your bits and pieces. There's a thing in there that you fill out and you send it away. It was the Coles Baby. You went to Coles to pick up your box of goodies.

As this account shows, the Bounty Bag not only brought goods into homes, it also mobilized parents to connect with commercial entities by post, online, and by traveling out of town to stores to pursue the opportunities it provided. Through such means, parents were enlisted into a relationship with companies. Huggies is a key player in this domain. We see how the concept of child development was employed by this company to extend this relationship and structure its interactions with parents. Through claims to authoritative knowledge about stages of development, the company created a rationale for regular contact, offering new product ideas to match with the child's current stage. We will see this strategy also used in online commercial sites.

The Virtual Mall and Other Online Marketplaces

Producers of early learning products, as well as those using the promise of early learning to sell other products, are taking advantage of every avenue in their efforts to reach parent consumers. For this project, we focused on the use of websites which were linked to offline outlets or products which we had encountered in our field work or were mentioned by parents in interviews. In this sample were sites specifically focused on early learning, such as Leapfrog, and more general sites within which early learning was an element addressed.

Parents as a distinctive group of Internet users have generally been discussed in relation to the social support offered through online communities, particularly for new mothers (Madge and O'Connor 2006; Wang 2003), working mothers (Wang 2003), and parents of children with disabilities or illness (Scharer 2005). Commercial aspects of digital services for parents are little discussed even when the website in question hosts significant levels of advertising (cf. Wang 2003). A study of Babyworld reports that it represents itself as 'reference source, shopping facility, magazine and extended family rolled into one' (Madge and O'Connor 2006 p. 206). While this study finds that shopping is a minor activity of Babyworld members compared to information seeking and social support, other ways in which participants could be participating in commercial activity are not considered.

Apart from making purchases, there are many online activities through which parents can participate in consumer culture. These include browsing, discussing products, and uploading photos and videos showing products being used and making recommendations. These are means by which what appears to be a noncommercial activity—sharing ideas and experiences—can weave participants into commercial networks. Discussion forums and personal web-pages are termed 'community' strategies in online marketing (Fernback 2007). Users are encouraged to share their experiences and opinions with the promise of making friends, sharing and belonging. Companies 'farm' these areas to learn about trends and preferences in their target market, as well as systematically harvesting and analyzing the data (Fernback ibid.).

In the next section of this chapter, we describe and discuss a number of commercial online spaces within which researchers, or the parent participants in the study, encountered products, activities, or services associated with early learning. We begin with virtual sites that are the direct counterparts of actual sites which we visited. While discussed separately here, it will be seen that the online sites operated integrally with the offline sites, encouraging parents to move between them while staying within a particular company's orbit. The online counterparts of actual stores supplemented the consumer's experience, particularly by providing extended levels of information provision and interactivity. By comparing this provision with the limited provision in most actual stores, it can be seen that presenting themselves as authoritative in fields like early childhood education makes demands on commercial entities which are difficult to satisfy as part of routine in-person shopping transactions. Through their websites, businesses can harness both 'expert' knowledge and the experiential knowledge of parents, the latter provided for no charge.

Online Counterpart Stores

The online spaces of commercial sites accorded to greater and lesser extents with the physical offline spaces. In the case of both Babies R Us and Walmart, the online sites extended, amplified, or modernized the offline provision. In Babies R Us, one of these dimensions of extension was historical. Its home page leads users to the same history page as Toys R Us wherein there is an unfolding of the evolution of the business by its founder, Charles Lazarus, right up to the present with its extensive web-based virtual environment.

The rhetoric of the site continually goes back to the catch line 'THE toy store' as in, the foremost in baby and children's products. The website is sectioned off as follows:

- home
- category
- brand
- collection
- top rated
- top registry items
- what's new
- clearance
- cart

There are subsections that offer advice and guidance for parents and there is a safety overlay on a lot of their online information. On the face of it, the website speaks to parents particularly about their child and their well-being and to popular toy brands.

Walmart's online environment is far more sleek and colorful than its commercial space. The catchphrase for the store featured right below its name on the website is, 'Save money. Live better.' In this way, it underlines that it services the needs of a wide variety of socioeconomic backgrounds. The baby portion of the website has a comprehensive list of product subsections including:

- bedding & décor
- car seats
- clothing
- cribs
- diapering & potty
- feeding
- gear
- gifts for baby
- maternity
- nursery
- strollers
- toddler room
- toys
- travel solutions

In other words, the website has a far more extensive range of products than was available in the particular Walmart that Jennifer visited. In fact, on a sensory level, the website has a different feel than the physical space of Walmart. The website has similar offerings to Babies R Us and is streamlined and designed with high production values, whereas the store is chaotic with low ceilings and darker lighting.

The website for Gumtree Plaza is an example of how the Westfield company locates itself within a hybrid on/offline space. Within this brandspace, the actual malls are described as places with an embodied sensory dimension, offering consumers the opportunity to 'touch, feel, hear, see, try and buy' products (Westfield Corporation, op. cit.). The online stores are constructed as spaces, not just for shopping, but for learning and networking, which operate intertextually with respect to the products physically located in the malls.

A section of Westfield Australia websites is specifically devoted to 'The Family'. Using the slogan "We are Family", this section's main menu on the Gumtree Plaza site includes:

- home
- mum's tips
- special offers
- join our club
- what's on
- center services
- expert advice

Counterpart websites are employed by commercial businesses to expand the connections that consumers have with the brand. Some of the subsections serve to enlist information from parents as a demographic of interest to advertisers and mall clients. Some promote activities and services that might attract parents to visit the mall and to bring their children with them. Other sections, such as 'Mum's Tips' and 'Expert Advice' are, on the face of it, less obviously aimed at the consumption of products that can be purchased in mall stores. Utilizing the organizational and interactive affordances of the online environment means businesses can position users as resource seekers, members, and even knowledge producers, rather than simply as purchasers.

Mum's Tips: Parent as Bricoleur

The provision of advice is one of the ways in which commercial websites position themselves as offering a service to parent consumers. The use of parents themselves as the contributors of this advice accomplishes two goals—by tapping into a pool of free labor, it limits the expenses associated with commissioning professionals and, by building a social network of engaged users, it substantiates Westfield's claims to be a family. 'Mum's

Tips' on the Gumtree Plaza website covers topics apparently related to general health and well-being, inclusive of children and parents:

- eating well
- happy kids
- happy parents
- staying active

Each section provides two kinds of 'tips': 'text tips' are posted by and solicited from parents, while 'video tips' are recorded by 'experts'. Thus mothers are accorded with expertise and positioned as contributors to the knowledge base. Advice and suggestions from mothers are categorized into topics by the website editors. Under the 'Happy Kids' section of 'Mum's Tips', these topics include:

- getting crafty
- readers for life
- knowing nature
- kids and computers
- in the car with kids

This mixture of domestic and garden skills, traditional and newer educational concerns (reading and computers), and ways of adding value to mobile lifestyles combines to create the contemporary mother subject. This parent is thrifty, practical, resourceful, well organized, active in promoting foundational skills for education, and committed to her child's emotional well-being. She efficiently integrates practical and academic learning opportunities into everyday routines, as illustrated by this 'tip' from 'In the Car with Kids':

Story Time

Since my children were young enough to make up stories, we play '3 things'. We play this in the car, in bed . . . anywhere really. Taking it in turns, one person picks 3 things, e.g., a car, a lollypop, grass . . . the other player must try and put these 3 obscure things into a story (obscure because we want to streeeeetch their imagination). *Once upon a time, driving along in mummy's CAR, she surprised me at the lights with a LOLLYPOP! I opened it and we arrived home, when I hopped out, I dropped it on the GRASS! The End.* Then you swap turns, these stories can be very funny! Try this one 1. Shrek 2. Spiderman and 3. a fork! BJ (Mum of 2) Accessed 14th December 2011

This writer's explanation makes her pedagogy visible to other parents. She explains how she uses play to achieve enhanced cognitive performance from her child. Popular culture references are infused into the 'tip' meaning parents do not have to reference 'quality' literary resources, or stretch their own imaginations, to take up the practice.

Another example, from the subsection 'Kids and Computers', shows commercial consumption even more obviously woven into parents' peda-gogic practices:

> I let my kids use the computer to access some very good web sites, such as 'ABC Kids', 'Happy meal', and some colouring website . . . , even 7,9,10 news [Australian commercial TV networks]. I create links that they can easily get on.
>
> Shu-Fen (Mum of 2) [accessed 26 August 2009].

In the 'Mum's Tips'—the advice chosen by Westfield to represent parental knowledge—routine consumption of media and commercial and popular culture has become appropriated into an overarching discourses of the resourceful mother, improvising and making do with the materials to hand. This description of the parent subject has much in common with the figure of the bricoleur who:

> . . . is adept at performing a large number of diverse tasks; but, unlike the engineer, [s]he does not subordinate each of them to the availability of raw materials and tools conceived and procured for the purpose of the project. [Her] universe of instruments is . . . heterogeneous because what it contains bears no relation to the current project, or indeed to any particular project, but is the contingent result of all the occasions there have been to renew or enrich the stock or to maintain it with the remains of previous constructions or destructions. (Levi-Strauss 1966, 19)

The 'stock' of parenting resources is diverse and includes what has been conserved from the past as well as whatever new tools become available. The bricoleur parent is thus disposed to consume while never reliant on a single program.

Reading Eggs Online

On the ABC shop's home page, Reading Eggs is named as one of twelve 'ABC branded stores' or websites devoted to particular themed merchan-dise. Above, we reported a physical encounter with the Reading Eggs prod-uct in the Gumtree branch of the ABC Shop. This encounter was minimally informative, and the shop itself was unwelcoming of children and their carers. It was interesting to contrast this experience with that of entering the online environment which we did via the URL which was printed on the leaflet handed out at the shop.

The entry page of the Reading Eggs online 'store' is largely taken up with an animated display of a virtual world within which animated characters are moving. In another frame, an animated egg directly addresses child users in speech mode: 'Hi and welcome to ABC Reading Eggs. It's great to see you here. My name is Reggie and I'll always be here to help'. The Reading Eggs 'world' is depicted in terms of a green ground on which are a group of disparate buildings, among which are a two-story house, a castle, and a round building with the sign 'Arcade'. In front of this scene, highly stylized cartoon animals, most of them chickens, wander back and forth. These are 'Eggsplorers', avatars for child users. When parents register for the Reading Eggs program, their child adopts an online identity in the form of one of these avatars. In this identity, they participate in various activities (referred to as 'lessons') through which it is claimed they will 'crack the code' of literacy.

Clicking on the 'About' link on the Reading Eggs entry page takes readers to a program description with a sidebar menu that includes a link headed 'Parents'. This contains a brief statement about learning to read, an assurance about Internet safety in the Reading Eggs site, and three dot-points under the heading, 'What can I do?' The advice given amounts to little more than an injunction to buy into the program or, to quote exactly, to 'introduce your child to this exciting experience'.

The Reading Eggs website, which is accessible without subscription, is designed to appeal to a dual audience of potential consumers. Children are appealed to not only as players of the game, but as consumers who can influence a parent's decision to purchase the program. Bright colors, movement, direct address, and the use of cartoon characters all clearly express a welcome and invite children to engage with the game. This is similar to other virtual worlds for young children, such as Club Penguin (Marsh 2008). At the same time, Reggie's promise of being 'always here to help' reassures parents that their child will be able to use the program without recourse to a knowledgeable adult. The implication is that the child can be trained to 'ask Reggie' rather than the parent. The downside of asking a cartoon egg for help is that embodied service workers, such as the shop assistant encountered in Gumtree Plaza, have not been invested with the knowledge necessary to assist embodied parents with their enquiries.

PRODUCER WEBSITES: THE CASE OF LEAPFROG

Developments in the LeapFrog web space over the last decade are evidence of the increasing importance of both online networking, and the parents' educational role, to the marketing of early learning (see also Nixon 2011). In 2003, the company set out to increase parent engagement with its website and saw an 'increased focus on the educational component of LeapFrog and its products' as the way to achieve this goal (Busse Design USA 2000, 9). Providing a 'balance between . . . academic expertise and the creatively playful' was key to this strategy (ibid., 2). The new parent sections of the site were organized in terms of three cross-referenced categories: age of child, specific skill areas, and 'associated developmental and curricular information' (ibid., 3). The four skill areas, signified by color codes, were language and literacy (yellow), mathematics (blue), science (aqua), and 'learning for life' (green). In the 2009 Annual Report, the company's goal was described as 'reinforc[ing] core literacy and math skills as well as introduce[ing] new subjects like science, language skills, and social studies' (Chiasson 2010). Thus the heartland of traditional basics has been maintained while the company moves into broader curriculum areas.

Enabling flows of information between the company's operations and local family uses of its products is a key design element of the Leapfrog brand space. One of the ways this is accomplished is via the 'Leapfrog Learning Path.' Once a child is in possession of a Leapfrog product online connectivity can be enabled, meaning that the child's activities with the device will be recorded in its own online user profile. The ensuing visual representation of a child's 'learning path' is presented as a resource for parents, equipping them with:

- detailed views into your child's learning progress
- insights into the skills your child is exploring
- recommendations to expand the learning
- related articles and learning ideas (Leapfrog Enterprises, 'Leapfrog Learning Path Demo' 2001–2010)

In a published analysis, Nixon comments:

> [T]his set of learning pathways . . . spatialize[s] the online commercial space in particular ways that [has] semiotic and ideological dimensions associated with high-status educational values such as developmental sequencing and measurable progress. (Nixon 2011, 124)

What are the 'learning ideas' provided for parents of young children? A key theme is that learning is best understood as the outcome of working on specific skills. In the area of literacy, the focus is on learning to read, and parents are advised that their child should be working on the component skills of decoding print including phonics (e.g., saying and recognizing vowel sounds or consonant blends), and learning the alphabet and building vocabulary (e.g., creating compound words). The Leapfrog products are designed to train children to work on these decoding skills; once this training has been achieved, the promise to the parent is of minimal intervention.

Leapfrog also draws on sociocultural discourses of literacy which represent reading as a process of shared meaning making (Cook-Gumperz 1987; Dyson 1993). From this perspective the parent, as insider to literate culture, socializes the child into ways of engaging with literature. This is clear from downloadable articles on the subject of reading comprehension:

Learning Tip: Comprehending stories

As you read new books or bedtime stories to your child, periodically stop to ask your child to recount what's happened in the story so far. Start with the main components of the story: beginning, middle and end. Once she is familiar with this, she can try to make more specific recollections, such as: Who was the main character? What problem did the character have? How did the character solve his or her problem? What was the most exciting part of the story?

These are also questions likely to be asked by a teacher once the child is in school. Setting children up for school is important to Leapfrog's claims of educational advantage. The company's effectiveness will be reinforced if the children using its products have a seamless transition to, and success in, school. This requires parents to be inculcated into school-like ways of operating and for these parents to work in explicitly pedagogical ways with their preschool children. Leapfrog's networks connecting its online brand space with families' localized product usage are integral to this strategy.

INFORMATION PORTAL WEBSITES

Many of the sites mentioned by parents were not connected with a single specific commercial entity. They functioned more as portals and networking agents, linking parent users to diverse activities, products, and services. Examples of websites mentioned by parents include www.mybabythisweek. com, http://www.ourlittletreasure.com.au/, http://www.todaysparent.com/, and http://www.kidspot.com.au/. These portal websites operate in a grey area crossing the commercial and the civic. They do this by combining explicit commercial activities such as online shopping and advertising with other functions from which, ostensibly, commercial activity is not solicited. As has been pointed out, these 'community' areas often have back-room operations of data harvesting, such that the opinions, preferences, and experiences discussed are used to shape the marketing activities of commerce (Fernback 2007).

Kidspot, a site which Deepwater mother Belinda referred to for playgroup activities, is typical of this kind of service. The site's technical consultant has described how it was built in 2005 as a 'searchable database of kids' activities, party ideas, events, specials and discounts' (Thompson 2011). Three years later, a social networking dimension was added which means that members can create a profile, start a blog, and join forums. The site also interfaces with Facebook such that, even if a visitor has not signed up to Kidspot, the site will automatically link with their Facebook page (if they have one). As soon as they click on an item, a Facebook window opens and prompts them to comment on or 'like' what they are reading.

(To 'like' online content means to click on a 'thumbs up' icon. This will send a message to the user's Facebook contacts that they approve this item. The number of users 'liking' an item is used as evidence of the effectiveness of a social network marketing strategy.) Another feature of the site's design is wide side borders with advertising material which also function as click zones, meaning that a click anywhere in this zone (not just on an obvious hyperlink) will take the user to a sponsored subsite. Specific parts of the site are sponsored by different companies. In 2009, Kidspot acquired www.birth.com.au, greatly expanding its content and sponsorship base. The site has since been sold to News Corp, reputedly for $A45 million, has added 'apps' (mobile phone applications), and in 2011 was reported to have 53,000 registered users (Thompson ibid).

Searching Kidspot using the term 'early learning' brings users to a specialized portal within the site. A list of links is headed by the statement:

> Find a range of early learning tools and resources for your pre-schooler. There are so many innovative tools to foster literacy, numeracy, a love of reading and developmental play with your child. These specialists offer early learning products and ideas for before kids start school.

The term 'tool' appears regularly on this kind of all-purpose parenting portal. The language here leaves open whether parent or child is the primary user of the tool, enabling several meanings. The parent could be 'finding' the tool and the child 'using it'. The parent could be using the tool to 'foster' various skills and orientations in the child. The parent could be 'play[ing] with' his or her 'child'.

Substituting 'tool' for 'product' also has the advantage for the marketer of avoiding reminding parent users of their consumer status. The 'tools' referred to here are actually products being advertised on company websites, links to which appear on scrolling down the page. These include ABC Reading Eggs (see above), Toyworld, My Busy Day, Intrepica, and many others.

'Parenting' is another key word on this site, with its own tab on the home page. Under this tab is a menu which includes the section 'Mum's School Zone'. This section lists a wide variety of topics, some of them focusing on the early years. The sponsor of 'Mum's School Zone' is Kellogg's, and it is not hard to see the commercial motive being woven into advice on parents' learning support role. For instance, under the heading 'Reading Games', accompanied by a photo of a dismayed looking child surrounded by a large pile of thick books, is a list of strategies to engage children in reading. First on the list is 'Breakfast Bonding':

> Take every opportunity to teach your child to read. Point out letters on the box of cereal at the breakfast table, or ask them to identify letters from their name on the jar of peanut butter.

A tab headed 'Brain food and nutrition' opens a menu, the first item of which is 'Breakfast'. The reference to 'brain' is a gesture towards the neuro-scientific discourse of early learning, a connection that is reiterated in 'Buddy's Bright Ideas', a subsite sponsored by Kellogg's. In this area, the figure of Buddy, an animated cereal square always shown with a light bulb over his head, appears at every turn. The focus here is on school achievement and the content of this page is given authoritative status by being provided by a named education professional, 'Kidspot's resident teacher blogger, Jennifer Barker.' Ms Barker 'offers practical advice on how you can help your child to thrive and enjoy learning' (http://www.kidspot.com.au/sponsor/sultana-bran+30.htm). Her advice, given in a commonsense tone, emphasizes emotional support, a well-organized home, a balance between work and play, and good communication with the teacher. The preschool years are not a focus, but the content gives a clear indication to parents of young children of what will be important in the near future. This is underlined by the use of young children in photographic images, generally shown wearing black-rimmed glasses and surrounded by piles of books. Homework, tests, and examinations are given priority with the parent's role being to provide their children with the right kind of study environment. Not surprisingly this includes nutrition, or rather, breakfast, which is linked to exam success under the heading 'Establishing a routine helps boost learning'.

The Kellogg's subsite is just one of several sponsored areas in the Kidspot website which capitalize on parent's investment in their children's education and learning to expose them to a relentless level of product endorsement.

CONCLUSION

Commercial spaces are particularly naturalized in relation to resources for parenting because they exist in a web of other commodified resources. This chapter has offered a picture of our research in commercial contexts. Within the scope of the book, this analysis of the mall highlights an increasingly powerful network for parents in forming their parental understandings and practices.

In *The Survival of Capitalism* (1976), Lefebvre prompts us to think about commercial infringement of space. Lefebvre claims:

> Capitalism has found itself able to attenuate (if not resolve) its internal contradictions for a century, and consequently, in the hundred years since the writing of *Capital*, it has succeeded in achieving "growth." We cannot calculate at what price, but we do know the means: *by occupying space, by producing a space.* (21)

Edward Soja (2010) writes about the notion of 'seeking spatial justice' as a way forward to critically frame such differentials in space and in the distribution of discourses and ideologies within space. Soja makes a call to readers to revisit Lefebvre's notion of a 'right to the city' as 'a politically charged idea about human rights in an urban context . . . about the consequential geography of urban life and the need for those negatively affected by the urban condition to take greater control over the social production of urbanized space' (ibid., 6). Fighting for the right to the city demands greater control over ways in which we are located in space. In the present chapter and indeed the entire book, we seek to illuminate networks of information, and their differential access by parents of young children in different circumstances.

Spatial (In)Justice in The Mall

Returning to theoretical frameworks referred to earlier in this chapter and throughout the book, the mall takes up its own space and role for parents of small children. Particular commercial spaces embody values, beliefs, social class, and cultures. We expect certain sorts of parents to enter and exit their doors given the cost of merchandise, the choice of signage, language, and rhetoric featured in pamphlets. Books on display speak to target buyers, and these couched discourses and ideologies are inflected with a host of assumptions about how to educate and how to rear.

A central argument in this chapter rests on the powerful role of commercial providers in mall spaces, in stores on main streets, and in strip malls that actively and subtly circulate information and discourses about children's early literacy and development. Implicit to this argument is a differential that exists within commercial spaces to the types and kinds of information that parents take up to educate and rear their children. Returning to Massey's (2005) framework, Gumtree Plaza is a parent-oriented space with signage, play spaces, facilities for nappy changing, and commercial displays speaking to parents. There is not much ambiguity to the messages within the commercial space—it has been designed and marketed, quite actively, to parents and all of their rearing needs. We visited another Westfield Mall in the US to face similar marketing, albeit with fewer of the conveniences and affordances, but with signature items such as a Parents Room and a Play Space. Babies R Us is even more targeted: concepts of child development are infused into its spatial organization and its textual strategies for communicating with consumers. 'Quality' independent suppliers are located on high streets in affluent suburbs, surrounded by cafes and chic boutiques. These outlets cater to parents who have few or no financial constraints and whose higher levels of education make them disdainful of mass consumerism. The independence of the proprietor bestows status on the critical consumer parent and, by association, invests the child user of these high-end products with higher cognitive powers and freedom from imitation.

As we ventured into the two small rural Australian towns, socioeconomics were thrown into relief in the nature of stores and resourcing for parents. That is, in mall spaces such as sprawling shopping malls there are more affordances and resourcing in the form of pamphlets, commercial products, and in spatial facilities, such as parent rooms, provided for parents and caregivers. However, in smaller towns resourcing comes in the form of signage in storefronts or inside stores for local playgroups; in reading circles in the local library; and occasionally, in children's early readers located by the cash register at the local grocery store. Deepwater parents need a car and a spare two hours to access even a large supermarket while Midborough families have twenty outlets within a central commercial hub, served by a bus network, offering a staggering quantity and range of goods related in some way to early learning.

Scholars and practitioners in the early childhood discourse community have been aware of the power of consumer culture in young children's lives. But the reaction has often been one of attempting to channel young children and their parents away from commodified products and practices (Nichols 2011). When we consider the question of how to resource early learning, it is no longer so easy to simply dismiss or avoid the marketplace. Before children arrive at school, they have often been provided with a diverse array of materials with the specific intention, by their caregivers, of supporting their learning and development in various ways. From purchasing learn-to-read games on a party plan to sourcing materials for a backyard play area at the hardware store, all parents in our study, regardless of social position and educational background, engaged in consumption on behalf of their children.

Those who have many choices commonly complain of having too much choice. Back-to-basics traditionalists argue that young children are better off with pots and pans or cardboard boxes to encourage their imaginations to flourish. This very argument was made to one of our researchers by the proprietor of 'Out of the Box', a high-end independent toy store which sold expensive imported educational toys to parents like Paula who would 'not set foot in' Toys R Us. However, many parents wish to take advantage of the information, materials, and practices that are packaged into toys, books, software, and magazines. There is also considerable research and development underpinning some of these products and resources even when this knowledge base is not made visible to consumers. Their beliefs that these goods may support their parenting and their child's development also no doubt have an impact on the products' effectiveness. Caring about availability, access, and cost of these goods, and the ways these differentiate different communities, is of relevance to the question of spatial justice in the resourcing of early learning.

Commercial and Civic Discourses

Market forces are often seen, by critical educators, as separate from and even opposed to public interests (cf. Beder 2009). In this chapter we have seen that disentangling the market from the public is not such an easy thing. This is not just because commercial interests are appropriating the concept of community in order to create and maintain relationships with consumers. It is also because parents and children appropriate commercial spaces for their own purposes.

One way of understanding this relationship is to consider commercial spaces as semiotic aggregates (Scollon and Scollon 2003) within which both civic and commercial discourses are operating. Alternatively we can consider how actor-networks continually create connections as disparate entities seek to access pathways through which knowledge and capital can circulate. Through this heterogenous engineering (Law 1992), the commercial and the civic are inevitably and inextricably drawn into networking with each other. At the same time, it would be naïve to suggest that all players have equal power. The larger the corporation, the more it can expend capital not only in extending its own networks but in creating 'obligatory passage points' (Callon 1986, 205) and other strategies to block or weaken the networking efforts of competitors. It can also invest in design and communication strategies to create seemingly noncommercial dimensions, including appropriating grassroots social movements.

How this struggle/negotiation plays out can be illustrated through three cases described in this chapter. First, the *Toys R Us Guide for Differently Abled Kids* appears to have been initiated as a response to the enquiries of parents whose children were not developing according to the normative sequence. That is, the information provided by toy manufacturers which is based on the age of the child was not adequate to assist them in making purchase decisions. In this case, a commercial corporation recognized a limitation in the standard operating model. By utilizing expertise provided by a not-for-profit service organization and employing a familiar commercial textual device—the catalogue—Toys R Us were able to incorporate an alternative system for categorizing its products, one not tied to age but to developmental skills and domains. It was able to do this without altering its relationships with manufacturers or investing in significant re-skilling of its staff. Civic and commercial discourses are interwoven in the *Guide* and, through incorporating its categorization system into signage, in the space of the store.

Second, the 'Buddy's Bright Ideas' section within the Kidspot website, offered parent participants access to 'teacher tips' as well as the opportunity to initiate topics for discussion. However, unnamed personnel paid by the sponsor Kellogg's were moderating the discussion in ways that foregrounded particular topics. It was notable how often assessment featured in the highlighted discussion topics as well as in the teacher tips. This articulated with the narrative line communicated through the character of Buddy, an animated cereal square, the images of young children 'studying' surrounded by piles of books, and the reiteration of the advice about feeding children breakfast to assist their concentration. Additionally, the whole Kidspot site, like others of its kind, is a data mine which harvests information contributed by parent users.

Finally, the 'Playworld' zone in Gumtree Plaza was a space in which parents and children could spend time engaged in social and play activities, without the requirement of purchase. However its location in the center of a concourse flanked by a large variety of stores, and the stores' strategy of piling boxes of toys near their entrances, made it part of a network of trajectories into commercial spaces. At the same time, parents used the toy sections of these commercial spaces almost like the free play area, as a means of ensuring that their children would have the stamina for an extended period of shopping. The stores were banking on a purchase of some kind and held large inventories of many kinds of products, of which early learning resources were only one kind. Enabling parents and children to meet their leisure and recreational needs was part of their strategy in maximizing the likelihood of a commercial transaction.

Within the 'Playworld' zone, the information booth operated according to a different logic. It was not owned by any business entity but existed in the nature of a guest of the management. With its large collection of pamphlets authored by state, municipal, and community organizations, the information booth set up trajectories to services outside the Plaza, many of them located immediately across the ring of roads and available for free or at a nominal fee. The primary discourse working through the information booth was a discourse of citizenship. In the terms of this discourse, citizens are entitled to services provided by the state and civic entities. They in turn have particular responsibilities to care for themselves, their families, and communities in ways which optimize health and well-being. The booth's volunteer workers were embodied subjects of this discourse, their time and knowledge given freely as an exemplification of civic responsibility.

Sometime in the second year of the project, we returned to Gumtree Plaza to find a space where the information booth had been. Like an alien spacecraft, it had disappeared into another dimension leaving the dominant commercial discourse uncontested. This discourse produces objects and services as commodities which can be acquired by anyone willing to enter into a financial transaction. The responsibility of a consumer is to shop either now or, following a spell of 'window shopping', in the unspecified future. As a spatialized discourse, it operates centrifugally to bring consumers into, and keep them circulating within, the mall for the longest possible time. The discourse of citizenship, materialized by the information booth, opens up other pathways. Noncommercial providers of early learning and parenting resources constitute competition to corporate consumer culture. In the final analysis, they will not be allowed too much power.

4   The Clinic

INTRODUCTION

Moves toward integrating child and family services in the early years, underpinned by a holistic view of child development, have led to greater overlap between the roles of providers. Health services are expanding into the domain of early learning particularly in the areas of language, literacy, and social skills. We are using 'the clinic' as an umbrella term for range of health-oriented institutions, services, and strategies, which have historically been shaped by a medical model of diagnosis, treatment, and prevention. In many contexts, the clinic is now playing a foundational role in shaping parents' understandings of child development, early learning, and even specific strategies for teaching young children skills for school readiness. Applying a normative model of child development which integrates the body, mind, and social self, the clinic provides milestones that chart a child's growth as a learner, linked with optimum parenting practice. This trajectory takes the parent and child from breast-feeding to controlling sleep patterns to early book reading. Services provided by hospitals and clinics are also nodes within a complex, variegated network of concepts, beliefs, discourses, and research on young children's development. In taking on the role of intervening in early learning, health services tap into the social networks parents participate in to circulate knowledge and practice.

In this chapter, we unravel these medicalized discourses, practices, and their implications for parents' resourcing of early learning. We take readers to some of these services and examine the advice, resources, and assistance they offer to parents. We ask: How is the parents' role in early learning framed within discourses of health? How do parents view these resources and under what circumstances do they access and use them? To answer these questions, we present observational, artifactual, and interview data to support our analysis of the clinic and its role in resourcing early learning.

Connecting the Clinic with Early Learning Development

Currently, the move toward integration of early childhood services, underpinned by a philosophy of catering to the whole child, is bringing concerns of health and education into dialogue (Haddad 2001; OECD 2001; Department of Education and Skills 2004). While the notion of integrated services is presented as innovative in creating partnerships between health and education, historical studies present evidence that interpenetration between the fields is not new.

The handbook *The Hygiene of the School Child* is an early example of an argument about schooling that framed its purpose as 'health first, then education' (Terman 1914, 15 cited in Lewis 2009, 489). Its author argued that schools should be judged 'by the contribution they make to preventative mental hygiene in the broad sense' (Terman 1914, 329). Mental hygiene is a concept that brings a medical focus to the subject of social and emotional well-being, with the premise that it is possible to detect, prevent, and treat psychological problems. In relation to young children, parenting and institutional child care have been linked to versions of mental hygiene at various periods. We will see, in later cases, how this view is reemerging in contemporary iterations of the clinic as a service for parents of young children.

A clinical approach to early childhood education underpinned the establishment of model kindergartens such as the Australian Lady Gowrie centers, built during 1939–40, where practitioners and scientific researchers collaborated to shape and produce knowledge about child development (Tyler 1993). These centers 'were explicitly designed to promote behaviours in the child that child psychology held to be part of the child's natural endowment, and to facilitate the production of knowledge about each child and the group' (Tyler ibid., 46). Models in place had been developed in kindergarten laboratories in American universities. Embedded within these spaces was a model of early childhood where children could play and behave as they would if, presumably, left to their own devices, while at the same time being subject to categorization within psychological models of development.

The examination, which is often thought of only in relation to school, also plays an important part in clinic life in setting the benchmarks for a wide range of behaviors, aptitudes, and capacities, from preconception to adulthood (Foucault 1975). The examination is 'one of the most prolific techniques for the production of material inscriptions' (Inda 2005, 10)—that is, for the transformation of abstract ideas about, in this case, childhood into concrete, visible artifacts. Lady Gowrie centers were fitted with one-way mirrors for the purposes of observation. Categories of childhood psychological health were applied in interpreting children's observed behavior as indicating for instance the 'solitary' child or the 'hyperactive' child. Children who fell into categories at either of these extreme ends of a normal continuum were then subject to individualized targeted interventions aimed at bringing their behavior into the middle ground of the well-adapted social child.

Medical experts have at times been highly influential in shaping the nature of early childhood educational provision. An example of this is an American Professor of Pediatrics Bettye Caldwell who in the 1960s established what she called an 'infant care center' for the children of work-ing poor women, describing this as a 'microcosmic health, education and welfare unit' (1991, 199). Caldwell argued against the division of prior–to-school provision into preschool on the one hand and child care on the other, coining the term 'educare' to express the integration of education into all forms of early childhood care setting. Setting out the principles for such a service, Caldwell capitalized the statement 'EDUCARE MUST BE CONCERNED WITH HEALTH' (Caldwell ibid., 21).

She would be pleased with contemporary developments in which it is now not unusual to see preschool education as 'part of the national health ser-vice' (Jalongo et. al. 2004, 145). Current rationales linked this to the basic needs and rights of children and to research on brain development. Inte-grating health and education is being called 'a wise investment' that will reduce the likelihood of later need for intervention and extra service (Jalongo et. al. ibid.). The notion of a healthy brain is creating an analogy with the nutritional needs of a healthy body; developing the former is said to require stimulation through 'a wide range of family settings, child-care practices and pedagogic approaches' to develop a healthy brain (Woodhead 2006, 10).

The concept of school readiness is being reframed from within the health discourse to a 'set of interdependent health and developmental trajectories' (Zuckerman and Halfon 2003, 1434). The promoters of this view point to the importance of 'promoting competent parenting, optimizing children's development, and identifying children with developmental problems'. Par-ents are made central here in working simultaneously on all aspects of their child's healthy development including the physical, social, and cognitive. School readiness is linked to the notion of stimulation by Halfon et al. who argue that health interventions are paramount in identifying and addressing developmental issues that will ensure optimal academic potential (Halfon et al. 2003, vi). This framing of 'school readiness' is seeing health profession-als drawn in to this 'important societal goal' (ibid.), particularly in recruit-ing and skilling parents to the task of ensuring school-ready children.

Within such literature there has been a focus on health networks and clinical contexts as key nodes that establish truths about childhood through the production of knowledge relayed through hierarchical chains of experts. The claim to a scientific epistemology in setting the parameters of good and bad health is a particularly important strategy. The prolifera-tion of often-contradictory claims about what should be done to promote children's good health seems to do little to undermine their epistemological credibility. The production of a 'good' body is taken as an outward sign of the existence of a 'good' self.

Medicalizing Literacy Development in the Early Years

In contemporary times, early literacy has emerged as a new focus for health services working with parents and young children. Community nurses, general practitioners, and pediatricians are being encouraged to take an active role in promoting literacy as part of the parental role. For example, Hewer and Whyatt (2006) describe a home visiting program in Western Australia. Along with taking records of a child's physical health, and discussing issues of care, the nurses' role is to encourage a greater uptake of reading through the provision of reading material and advice. The authors comment that nurses mainly gave 'only a single piece of advice around a single specific behaviour' (ibid., 116). This indicates the central importance that is being granted to the activity of parents reading to their infants and toddlers when health services engage in literacy promotion.

In the US, a literacy intervention program focused on pediatric visits has become widely adopted. This program utilizes volunteers reading to children in waiting rooms, in combination with advice from the pediatrician, to encourage parents, particularly in low-income areas, to read regularly to their preschool children (High et al. 2000; Needleman and Silverstein 2004; Needleman et al. 2005). Popularly known as Reach Out and Read (ROR), the intervention is based on the premise that pediatricians are a vital contact for parents in providing guidance that is likely to influence parental behaviors and child outcomes.

We had the good fortune of interviewing a doctor involved in a well-known reading intervention program, Reach Out and Read. Munsberger (pseudonym) described it as follows: 'We have vaccines against diseases, but is there any vaccine that we could use against language delay or school readiness skills issues or school performance down the line?' Dr. Munsberger went on to describe how research has shown that children who fall behind from the beginning of schooling fall further and further behind without some form of early intervention:

> . . . kids who start behind, tend to stay behind. It is a really big societal issue that children who do poorly in school and continue to do poorly in school tend to have more difficulty in learning to read and don't develop as much skill in reading and are at higher risk for not graduating high school, and for having all kinds of issues as adults. So here, we as pediatricians are kind of on the front lines in a certain kind of way. You know all children have to see us for vaccines and if they don't, they are not allowed to enter school. Therefore, they kind of have to in a captive way.

Thus early intervention in the clinic is seen as a medical response to a social problem. Dr. Munsberger refers to the practice of using vaccination against common diseases as a form of gate-keeping to school entry, maintaining the health of the school population. By analogy, getting parents to administer a dose of book reading also makes the child fit for school and prevents the disease of illiteracy from spreading through the student body. This, however, is a treatment that doctors can only give second-hand. Parents have to be trained to administer the dose. Clinics and doctors who endorse

Reach Out and Read (ROR) often speak of the home environment as the place where a parent can intervene and encourage early literacy. As Dr. Munsberger expressed it:

> . . . it is very clear that the home environment makes a very big differ-ence. . . . Reading aloud fits very nicely into that because reading aloud is a real good opportunity to have verbal interactions between parents and infants. It provides kind of a structured opportunity for parents who might not otherwise know how to do that.

A Child-Centered Literacy Orientation (CCLO) instrument has been devel-oped by pediatric health researchers to be used in conjunction with literacy interventions such as ROR (High et al. 2000). Caregivers are given a score for CCLO based on an aggregate of three factors: whether reading to the child was one of the parent's three favorite activities; whether it was one of the child's three favorite activities, and the number of children's books in the house (High et al. 1999; 2000). Findings from studies have been used, in standard medical research practice, to influence further experiments adjusting the dose for maximum impact. Recently, it has been found that increasing frequency of ROR encounters contributed 5% of the variance explaining a child's home literacy profile (Weitzman et al. 2004). Arguments for maintaining the program rest on its low cost, ability to be administered to whole populations through universal health services, and, in association, likelihood of reaching caregivers with low levels of education. Noting some of the limitations of studies including reliance on convenience samples, reli-ance on self-report, and publication bias researchers have recommended observational studies focusing on the qualitative dimension of parent-child interaction during reading-aloud as a means of testing the efficacy of ROR. None of the evaluations to date has taken this route.

Qualitative research on parents reading to children, and on many other dimensions of children's emergent literacy, is widely available in the early childhood education and literacy research fields. Literacy researchers have tended to work with a broader scope and definition that is inclusive of such emergent literacy activities as drawing (Steward 1995), name writing (Haney 2002), oral storytelling (Anderson et al. 2003; Nord et al. 1999), singing and chanting and, increasingly, computer use (Marsh 2006). How-ever this literature is given little consideration in medical evaluations of literacy interventions. The Centre for Community Child Health, located at a large Australian public hospital, commissioned an evaluation of the local version of ROR, known as *Let's Read*. This review cited forty-nine articles from journals in the fields of pediatrics, psychology, and other health sciences. Only seven papers from literacy journals and six from edu-cation journals were included. This points to the deep divisions that remain between disciplinary fields of knowledge, regardless of the stated value of partnership and dialogue.

What is most prevalent in our research and missing from the research outlined above is the exploration of health services' use of sociocultural avenues and networks. Although health research literature treats interventions as straightforward treatments carried out within the confines of a clinical relationship, what we have found is that services use a range of geographically based, and sociocultural, temporal, and technological methods to recruit, engage with, and influence parents. The discussion outlined here provides the setting for the following case studies of health services in South Australia and the US for parents and their preschool children.

FROM PREBIRTH TO PRESCHOOL: A STATE HEALTH SERVICE NETWORKING INTO PARENTS' LIVES

In the first months after birth, children and their mothers are urged to have check-ups at pediatric clinics (US) or government health clinics (Australia). South Australian parents in our study are directed to clinics run by the state government organization Child, Youth and Women's Health Services (CYWHS). Because of this organisation's wide reach and its frequent mention in interviews with parents, we decided to investigate its mode of operation. Two senior managers and a local practitioner were interviewed, and a researcher attended all the sessions of a class for new mothers in the Midborough district. Photographs were taken of notices referring to its services which we encountered in multiple localities. Its website was scrutinised with a particular emphasis on materials relating to early learning; relevant pamphlets from its series of 'Parent Easy Guides' were downloaded. References to CYWHS services in parent interviews were excerpted and analysed with a focus on messages about early learning and how these services connected parents into social and information networks.

The service employs multiple channels and strategies to access families of infants and young children, beginning at the birth of a baby. New mothers are referred by their family doctor or hospital, and CYWHS nurses make home visits within a few weeks of every child's birth. The service provides a 'blue book' which records all health checkups at 'key milestones' from birth to four years of age and is completed by midwives, family doctor, neonatal home visitors, pediatricians, and specialists. CYWHS also conducts parenting programs, hosts a residential service for at-risk families and provides 24-hour telephone helpline which had been accessed by all the South Australian parents we interviewed. The organisation's own reviews of its website shows it is widely used locally, nationally and internationally with one of the most popular resources being its downloadable Parent Easy Guides (or PEGS). In hard copy form these are distributed widely including in hospitals, clinics, drug stores and local libraries.

This health service's interest in early learning is evident in a number of its activities. Improving educational outcomes has become one of the goals of its home visiting program which in past times had a greater focus on physical and emotional health. The program was inspired by the Olds Model, now the Nurse-Family Partnership in the US (Goodman 2006). Research on this program has found that the children of parents visited by a nurse have better school outcomes (Kitzman et al. 2010). According to CYWHS guidelines it 'enables early identification of family and child development issues, leading to the possibility of earlier intervention and problem prevention' (CYWHS 2005). In the past few years, questions about literacy and learning have been added to the survey which home nurses administer to mothers. A book 'Right from the Start . . . Loving Reading with Your Baby' (2003/2006), distributed free of charge, explicitly teaches parents how to engage infants with reading. A senior manager explained the overall approach was motivated by 'what makes a difference for parents down the track, including educationally'.

Family Home Visiting in Practice

During the first home visit, a community nurse is able to provide mothers with a range of information, as Joanne, the manager of Home Visits, explains:

> We go through the blue book that they've got from the hospital that we've produced, and then we might give them information about the clinic and times, and also all around the area, and then we give them those, and all the information about immunisation, and depending on what are the issues the parent is presenting, then we will give them information on whatever the issues might be as well, but we also give them information about our parent groups as well, particularly the breast-feeding group and the settling groups. We've got flyers for those, not sitting in here but we give them out as part of our package to introduce the parents to the area.

The nurse operates within an organisational network where texts are key resources for making connections. The parent already has a text—the 'blue book'—which the nurse uses as a means of linking her with local services. The nurse brings in other texts such as flyers that potentially link the mother to health-oriented social networks.

Not all parents rely solely on CYWHS nurses to address health problems. Rebecca also used the services of a pediatrician to give her son his 6-week check-up; however the CYWHS nurse was able to provide information about reflux prior to her appointment with the pediatrician:

> Then he was six weeks old, it was a Monday, he screamed from the minute my husband went to work until he got home. [. . .] and I just, I said to him "I can't do this, there's something wrong, you've got to do something to make this different", So he rang the paediatrician, we'd

seen the paediatrician and he said "We need an emergency appointment, this is getting really bad", so we got in the next day and coincidentally the nurse came the same morning, so she saw him and his behaviour, and she's like "No, no, that's acid reflux", so I went to the paediatrician with some sense of confidence about what I was going to tell him.

As Rebecca explained, the support provided to her by the nurse gave her some confidence in the provision of information which supported her as she made contact with other health services.

The initial visit may be followed by regular meetings if the nurse is concerned about the mother's health or coping ability. This seems to have been the case for Olivia:

I have a nurse come see me because [. . .] I was considered an outcast, is that the right word, an outcast, to society, something along those lines, because I'm pretty isolated, I don't know anybody. I moved here, had Ben, lived here [. . .], so I didn't know anybody, and with my family not being here, yeah, she asked whether I'd want to be involved in a program where a nurse would be able to visit me, like monthly, and then any questions I have, I wrote them all down, saved them up for her, and she's fab, she's so great, so yeah.

The nurse became an important resource to Olivia, both alleviating her social isolation and providing information. Writing questions was helpful in itself even though there may be a month's wait for an answer.

GETTING TO KNOW YOUR PARENTING: A CASE STUDY OF BABY CLASSES

Getting to Know Your Baby (GTKYB) classes are the latest iteration of an older model of provision in which community nurses set up walk-in clinic sessions in community centers. These services often offered an informal social dimension as women waited for their babies to be weighed and measured and recorded in the 'Blue Book'. This was in effect a universal service, since being able to provide an up-to-date documentation of a child's progress was an expectation of health delivery.

In South Australia, this practice was discontinued when resources were moved into universal home visiting (as has been described above) and voluntary structured courses. Both of these later developments are much more tightly tied to an explicitly educational role for health providers, encompassing early learning among other dimensions of child development for which parents were deemed responsible.

In one of the community meeting rooms of the Midborough library a number of chairs have been placed around to form a semicircle in readiness for the arrival of mothers and babies attending their first parenting class. Fifteen first-time mothers arrive navigating their prams into the room, arranging their nappy bags, placing their blankets on the ground to shield their newborns from the floor, or nursing their babies in their arms. Some are distracted with their preparations while others greet their peers comparing baby names and birth dates. At the door is Joanne, a community health nurse and convenor of the group to greet the women as they arrive. She is running this six-week Getting to Know Your Baby (GTKYB) class run by the South Australian Government's Child Youth and Women's Health Services (CYWHS). The GTKYB classes are popular in Midborough. Joanne has been running these groups in Midborough as well as having been a home visiting nurse for over twenty-five years. Joanne told our researcher Sophia that middle-class mothers tend to be motivated and keen to attend these groups. She referred to one particular mother in the group who had been phoning around trying to get into a session. She was very happy when she found she could attend this group.

Justine joined the mothers' group after she was approached by a CYWHS nurse:

> After my son was born they contacted us I think and said "Did you want to be in a mothers' group?" and I said "Yes", and then we had to wait a couple of months before they started a new one, but yeah, it started when he was about four months old and, yeah, I still keep in contact with some of them now, which is really lovely, yeah.

For Justine and the other mothers in the group, social isolation had been an issue:

> I found joining the mothers' group useful, support, because we didn't know anybody else with children, so that was good for us.

This class is not the first time that the women have received health intervention outside of the hospital where they gave birth to their babies. The women at the classes have already received a postnatal visit from a community health nurse in their homes. At the home visit women are provided with information about various health interventions and are also invited to attend the classes. These classes represent the way in which health interventions are administered both directly through information given during health check-ups and indirectly through social networks. Health interventions are no longer only confined to the clinic setting that required mothers to approach a health advisor on the needs of their babies.

Like libraries and malls, clinics are repositioning themselves within the landscape of early childhood. Rather than being settings where you go when you are sick or to get immunizations and check-ups, clinics are taking on lifestyle and well-being roles such as providing and offering services for children's development, in particular for this chapter, children's literacy development.

The provision of the GTKYB classes represents a shift in the consideration of how health and development information is best distributed and circulated. The class curriculum is intertextually linked to the other organisational texts such as Parent Easy Guides, parenting books and other information resources. The nurse coordinator strongly promotes social networking between mothers to continue after the series has concluded. Participants are also encouraged to make use of the telephone help service and to consult the website. Thus GTKYB evidences multiple networking strategies.

The geographic location of the classes also facilitates links with other services. GTKYB is are located in the grounds of the local public library in the service ring of Midborough, where many other services are located. The library houses a large collection of parenting books, children's literature, and educational toys. One of the mothers, Rebecca, explained that meeting at the library provided her with the opportunity to interact with library services.

> We met at the library, which is what I think first reintroduced me to the environment.

Now she is a regular library user and considers herself a key influence in her son's literacy development:

> I have always believed that books are so important, and I guess I've been the one that influenced him to love books, because it helps him with his development.

Early Literacy in GTKYB

One of the core modules in the GTKYB course is 'Reading to your baby'. This topic took up half of one week's session and was run by Glenys, a representative from Learning Together, a state-run preschool program for parents and children. Glenys started the session by laying out a colorful patchwork rug and asking all the parents to lay their babies on it and explaining that they should be able to move their arms freely. Some then had to unswaddle their children; swaddling, or close wrapping, being a method of settling babies which had been taught in a previous session.

When all the babies were on the rug, Glenys pulled from her bag a length of parachute silk, tossed it out and asked Joanne to catch the other side. Some of the mothers were rather startled but the babies seemed unperturbed as the cloth billowed above them, moving rhythmically as Glenys sang a simple nursery rhyme.

The presentation followed a developmental logic where exposure to patterned sounds (i.e., music) was seen as preparing the baby for learning speech, and participation in scaffolded verbal interactions was seen as providing the foundation for more advanced literacy skills. This was put to the mothers in simple terms: sing to your babies, talk with your babies, and read to your babies.

Glenys gave clear and detailed advice regarding the kinds of books parents should be selecting for infants and for young children at different ages. She highlighted books that were included in an early literacy campaign, the Little Big Book Club, run jointly by the Libraries Association and a local newspaper publisher. The CYWHS presenter explained to the mothers that they should take their child's 'blue book' (health record) to the library to access free books. Glenys also mentioned garage sales as places to find books without having to spend a fortune.

One of the mothers enacted her understanding of early literacy by surrounding her infant, which was lying on the rug, with open books which she had been carrying in her bag. The child could see a book whichever way it turned its head. One of the other women, noting the baby's eyes resting on a book said, "She's going to be a librarian when she grows up".

In this session we see a health service partnering with an early childhood education provider to promote a particular version of early learning which focuses strongly on the language and literacy domains of child development. The parent's role emphasized is direct verbal interaction with the child mediated through texts such as songs, chants, and storybooks. Potential tension between different agendas was hinted at in the differential treatment of infant bodies. In the practice of settling, taught as necessary to ensure healthy sleep and avoid overstimulation, mothers were taught to wrap their children closely and put them to rest. The early literacy activities, though, were colorful, musical, and accompanied by patterned gestures such as clapping and swaying. Here stimulation was encouraged, albeit with a strong emphasis on rhythm and repetition. There are echoes here with the ways in which library practitioners worked with parents and young children (see Chapter 6).

What is interesting about these classes is the way in which such interventions encourage mothers being networked to ensure that information and services pertaining to the development of their children is accessed and circulated among parents. Indeed, many of the women had specifically attended the sessions as an opportunity to extend their networks. CYWHS and the classes act as a hub that can bring the mothers together and allow them to further expand their networks while ensuring the circulation of approved discourses of parenting associated with the figure of the healthy, optimally developing infant and child.

Changing Provision in a Rural Setting

Economies of scale influence service providers' decisions about what can be offered to parents. In Midborough is a large metropolitan council district and hub, and all its services had high enrollments. In the rural town of Deepwater, however, the GTKYB classes had been discontinued, and all that was available was home visiting and a fortnightly walk-in clinic with a visiting nurse. One of our informants was critical of this change:

> They actually come to you and they have this one-on-one, but I don't think that's as good as in, you know, I think that's pointless, than actually having a load of mums together because other mums ask other questions that might arise for you in a month's time, or three months' time, and you might retain some memory of that which will trigger it later on, where you're just asking questions for now. I mean they've got them there and you can always go down and visit them once a fortnight and ask any questions, because they say "Have you got any questions?" and I just go "No", and then you go home and you go "Oh, I should have asked about that", but you feel silly.

One of the challenges for health providers seeking to network into parents' everyday lives and practices is that the medical discourse is presented and understood as the domain of professionals. For this mother, just finding the language with which to pose a question was daunting. This is one of the major rationales for setting up peer networks via more informal forums, yet in Deepwater, this option had been discontinued.

The gap was filled by a local community run playgroup known as Wave. As an initiative of a local church, we will discuss this playgroup in greater depth in Chapter 5. At this point, what is of interest is how a playgroup in a poorly resourced rural area had networked into health providers. Wave's networking worked to integrate medical, educational, and social discourses into the conversations which took place during sessions. The coordinators, Denise and Amanda, explained how this arose as a result of responding to members' stated needs:

Denise: One mum came up to me and said "Have you thought of, can we do a first aid for children?" Well to me that's looking for information, and that's just like we need to say "We need to look at programming that for next term or something" . . . A lot of the mums do say "Do you have any idea of . . . ?" Like they say immunisation, we've had that discussion for years now, immunisation, so like next week we've got the Child & Youth Health nurse coming in to talk to us, and she's going to talk to us on immunisation.

Amanda: We've had various health, or you know like professionals come in, and we had a chiropractor at the beginning of the year, we had a chiropractor come in just for interest and what not, and the benefits of it and yeah, we've had a dietician-type person.

The Wave coordinators sought out health professionals who were living locally or willing to travel out to the town. They trusted in the expertise of these individuals and did not attempt to apply filters to the advice offered. As we will see in a later chapter, commercial education resource providers also found a welcome as well as traditional knowledge and practices. This was in contrast to the corporate strategy of CYWHS which invested considerable effort in ensuring that only authorized knowledge was disseminated via its website, parent classes, textual resources, and telephone helpline.

Parent Easy Guides (PEGS): Circulating Discourses on Parenting Practices

The most widely available resource provided by CYWHS is a set of A4 double-sided laminated cards on specific topics, collectively known as the *Parent Easy Guides* or colloquially as PEGS. The bringing together of the subject 'parent' with the verb 'guide' constitutes the relationship between the client and the service. It communicates that parenting is to be subject to influence and shaping by an authoritative agency. The adjective 'easy' is reassuring; it suggests that the advice being provided will not require high levels of education, a significant investment of time or putting into practice complicated techniques—all aspects that might be associated with other kinds of authoritative advice to parents.

These PEGS are written by Parenting SA under the umbrella of CYWHS and provide information for parents and professionals under a large number of topics from health to social to behavioral issues. The scope of topics provided by this health service constitutes it as the legitimate source of knowledge on every aspect of child reading and development. Specifically related to early learning are PEGs entitled 'Learning to talk' (PEG 33) and 'Why stories are important' (PEG 57).

The production of these PEGS grew out of the preparation of information for the parent helpline 'so that the parent helpline had sheets of information that they could refer to and send out' (Manager). The parent helpline is a telephone information service for parents in South Australia and provides information on issues such as health, behavior, nutrition, parenting, and parental support (Parenting and Child Health 2011, #647). The PEGS became a resource that could be adapted for use across a variety of services.

Beverly, mother of two, found the PEGS useful and had gathered a large collection over time:

> I've used the service a lot and I like their pamphlets because it's sort of big bold heading and it's exactly the, you know, you go straight to the issue, whereas I guess with a book, yes, you've got to, you know, look through it to find what you want. I do like the brochures a lot I guess. They are straight to the point. They're easy to find. All the information is there and it goes through stages of ages as well, so that's always easy, whereas I guess the books probably focus on a certain period.

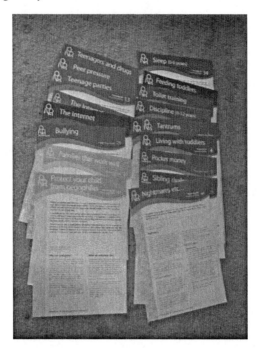

Figure 4.1 Collection of *Parent Easy Guides* owned by a parent informant (researcher photograph) (Parenting SA, various).

Providing the PEGS pamphlets is an expense for the service, and this has been a factor in its attempts to encourage greater utilization of its website. A senior manager told us: 'We were sending a lot [of PEGS] out and it was costing a lot in postage, so we would consolidate them and put them on the website. If you look at the PEGS you will find they are adapted from our website'.

The service also encouraged facilitators of its GTKYB sessions (see above) to refer to the website and encourage parents to download the PEGS, which was noted by a participant:

> They hand out a lot of information and stuff like that through that too, so a lot of that come from off of their website, which I could never get on to, I found it a hard thing to use, but yeah, but they had information that she'd printed off from that, and they said, you know, "If you need anything, you can always get on there and have a look at these things"

In this case, being handed a printout of the web-based material was more acceptable to the parent than accessing it online. She did not feel comfortable or competent in the digital environment.

Nurses conducting home visits also tend to refer parents to the website where the PEGS can be located, but as one nurse pointed out, she will provide a hard copy on some occasions. In this case, the desire to connect with the father, as the parent absent from immediate face-to-face interactions makes the provision of a portable object—a specific PEGS card—strategic:

> I give out PEGS on toddlers on discipline and stuff like that, because men don't, and I don't mean to sort of . . . but in my experience men are work-ing and the mother might be home with the child, so they can't attend and it's all very well for us to talk about issues with the mother, but the father's not hearing that, and it's sometimes easier for the mother if she's got a PEGS there to actually talk about those issues. (Joanne)

In a version of a train-the-trainer model, the nurse first works with the mother as learner and then seeks to enroll her to take the corresponding role for the father. The subject of discipline is more than just an aside. Producing the child as self-regulated, which precludes the parent employ-ing punitive measures, is considered to be key within this health service's program of intervention into the early years.

Discourses of Early Learning in a PEG

To further explore the role of these medically authorized advice texts in circulating notions of early learning, we present a detailed analysis of one PEG which is particularly relevant to our subject. Entitled 'Why stories are important', this text presents an argument for parents engaging their infants and very young children in encounters with read and told narrative. The text is presented in its entirety with key phrases highlighted (Figure 4.2, following page).

A psychotherapeutic discourse is threaded through this text. The young child is viewed as vulnerable to strong feelings, such as fear, and develop-mentally too immature to manage these feelings through cognition. A key task of the parent, in the terms of this discourse, is assisting the child to manage these emotions, and the story, they are advised, is the prime tool by which this can be achieved. The book is represented as communicat-ing directly to the child about the parent's care: 'it can show you under-stand how he feels'. In time, the book can take on some of the qualities of a human attachment enabling the parent to bring the early period of intimate care to a developmentally appropriate close: this 'special sharing time' enables the child to 'learn to love books' and thus, it is suggested, to become a contented, literate self-managing person.

While superficially seeming to take a similar line to early literacy cam-paigns run by other agencies such as libraries and education departments, this advice is less focused on preparing a child for later academic achieve-ment and more on general socioemotional well-being—'security and good

---

Why Stories are Important Parent Easy Guide 57

Stories help children to **cope with a lot of the feelings** and problems that they experience in their day. Story time can be a **special caring time** with you that your children will **remember all their lives**. Whether they are the stories you tell, or stories in books, stories are one of the ways that children **learn to enjoy reading**. Books, and the people they read about in **books, can become their friends**.

Reading and/or story time can be **special time** for both parents and children. If it's a **relaxed and happy time**, it helps build good relationships between you and your child and helps your child develop a sense of **security and good self-esteem**.

You can also **learn to understand how your child feels** when you see him respond to the feelings in the story, e.g. if he really likes a book it may be because it has special meaning for him and is **helping him with his feelings**.

When you read a story to your child it can **show that you understand how he feels**. For example if you are reading a story about another child (or animal) who is frightened of the dark, it **helps your child to know that you understand** that it is easy to be frightened of the dark when you are very young.

Reading and telling stories to your child can become a **very special sharing time** which helps your children to **learn to love books** and to develop a **sense of being a lovable person**. Many children **remember their story times for the rest of their lives**.

Figure 4.2   Text of 'Why stories are important', *Parent Easy Guide 57*, pamphlet collected from parent informant (Parenting SA, revised 2010).

self-esteem'. The problematic future child, which this reading practice is intended to prevent, is not so much the child who struggles with decoding print as the child who is uncontrolled, disruptive, and in line for a diagnosis of one of the many variations of conduct disorder. This is in line with CYWHS' advice about behavior management generally which strongly sanctions against parent coercion and punitive responses, warning that this will exacerbate aggression in children.

This connects the work of this health service with scientific research on child emotional regulation, a strand which Hoffman (2009) has also traced through parent advice in American parenting magazines. A major theme in this research and its popularizations is 'inadequate or improper emotional socialization leading to explosive, impulsive, and destructive behavior' (ibid, 19). Hoffman notes that this advice literature:

> recommends an explicitly pedagogical role of parents in relation to the emotional experiences of their children. Parents need to 'teach children about emotions'; they need to 'monitor' the emotions and 'step in' at

the right moments to 'teach kids suitable responses' before the emotions get out of hand. (ibid.)

Parent magazines are read by a subset of the population. Health services like CYWHS, with their broad reach and state support, are a means by which this therapeutic discourse can be circulated beyond an educated middle-class into the communities from which, it is believed, the next generation of problem children will come.

As has been noted, CYWHS is greatly concerned to ensure that only authorized knowledge regarding child development and parenting is circulated through its many interconnected activities. It polices boundaries between the health domain and the comparatively chaotic and undisciplined field of commercialized early childhood provision. The latter, however, is not as concerned to exclude other players. Quite the reverse: commercial agents are keen to benefit from the legitimacy associated with medical institutions and expertise in order to access parent networks. In the process, a commercialized discourse of parenting and early learning appropriates the capacities of a powerful public health network to circulate its message about the advantage that parents can buy for their youngsters.

THE BOUNTY BAG: BUNDLING
HEALTH AND COMMERCIAL DISCOURSES

Maternity sample bags are vessels that hold texts and objects relating to babies and care of babies. These authorized and authoritative texts are produced for cost-free circulation in the public arena by government health and education agencies; formally recognized and approved services; commercial entities and community organizations.

Bounty Bags, as they are known in the UK and Australia, are made available to expectant and new mothers. Australian mothers receive them at three key points: 1) when they first visit an antenatal clinic or register at a hospital for the birth of a child; 2) when they are in hospital soon after the baby's birth; and 3) when they redeem a voucher from the second sample bag at a Target store. Through this relatively systematic process, Bounty Bags deliver to most mothers a mix of *government produced* public health information and *commercially produced* retail information about children's early health and development. Mothers who do not receive their sample bags from antenatal clinics or when they register at a hospital prior to the child's birth are able to collect one from selected chemists or by ordering online.

According to Emap, the producers of the Bounty Bags, and the books and magazines that the bags contain:

> Our Parenting Division communicates with over 95 per cent of all new mothers and over 82 per cent of pregnant women in Australia through

our parenting magazines, Bounty sample bags and in-hospital antenatal television. (Emap 2007)

The first point to note here is that the company Emap, as well as those who
advertise in the Bounty Bags, are major *sponsors* of the children's learning
and development (CLD) information provided to parents in the very early
stages of their children's lives. We take the term 'sponsors' from Brandt's
(1998) definition: 'any agents, local or distant, concrete or abstract, who
enable, support, teach, model, as well as recruit, regulate, suppress or with-
hold literacy—and gain advantage by it in some way' (166). In this case,
the subject of the sponsorship is early learning, in which literacy plays a
key part.

The second point to note is that Emap, as part of the *global mediascape*
of contemporary life, 'contribute[s] to educating us how to behave and what
to think, feel, believe, fear, and desire—and what not to' (Kellner 1995,
2). The media are sources of stories and other symbolic forms that educate
people about how to buy, consume, negotiate, and value new commodities and services within everyday life (e.g., Kellner 1995; Lury 1996). They
function as one of the 'pedagogies of everyday life' (Luke 1996); they constitute 'new sites of education and potent resources for meaning construction' (Morgan 1993, 39).

Figure 4.3   Bounty Bags and some of the magazines included (ACP Magazines).

The third point is that local *and* global sources of information are both deeply imbricated in this process. Further, both print *and* electronic networks of circulation and dissemination are connected with what Appadurai (1990) has termed the multiple 'landscapes' of the global cultural economy: its mediascapes, technoscapes, finanscapes, and ideoscapes.

A final and related point is that information produced by government agencies and health providers, as well as commercial publishers and advertisers of products for children, is producing and shaping parent information networks right from the earliest antenatal experiences. Further, as many social theorists have noted, in the contemporary world of late capitalism, it is increasingly difficult to separate noncommercial from commercial 'information', just as it is to separate advertising from consumer culture, promotional culture, and media culture more generally (Kellner 1995; Lury 1996).

Along with noncommercially and commercially produced pamphlets providing information about feeding, changing, settling, and immunization, the key print texts in each sample bag are:

- Mother-To-Be Bounty Bag 1: *Bounty Pregnancy Book*
- New Mother Bounty Bag 2: *Bounty Babycare Book*
- New Baby Bounty Bag 3: two parenting magazines *Mother & Baby* and *Little Kids*

Bounty Bag 1: Bounty Pregnancy Book

As might be expected, the *Pregnancy Book* (2007 edition) focuses on mainly medical information the health of the mother-to-be, labor and childbirth, and the health of newborn babies. However, one text in the book—an advert for a series of 'mum to mum' DVD 'how to guides' (68)—illustrates four themes that are repeated throughout the texts in our data set.

- First, it explicitly suggests that sourcing information about how to care for a child is likely to be *serious business* that is complex, time-consuming, and full of conflicting advice, a process that should begin early, and one that will be ongoing for many years.
- Second, it sets up a tension between sourcing information from 'real mums and babies' as compared with 'ploughing through all those books or asking friends millions of questions'.
- Third, it works semiotically to reinforce the importance of 'real mums'—like the real mums who produced the DVDs for other real mums—by including supposedly hand-written testimonials, e.g., as indicated by use of a particular font and simulated letters.
- Fourth, it embodies a *tension* between the value of different *ways* of communicating information in that it privileges as an important source of parenting information not *print* texts, but rather *electronic* DVDs that can be 'viewed in your own home and in your own time'.

Bounty Bag 2: Bounty Babycare Book

Bounty Bag 2 is distributed while mothers are still in hospital. Hayley was one parent who referred specifically to the second Bounty Bag as a means of accessing early learning resources. In this case, she had responded to a promotion by the Scholastic publishing company.

Sophia: So you said you had those Scholastic books.
Hayley: Yeah, I'll grab some out of her room.
Sophia: How did you come across those?
Hayley: There was a thing in there when I had Tamsin I think. In one of the bags, in the second one that you get when you have the baby. That's them, that lot there is Leapfrog, which they've got all the Leapfrog readers and that anyway.

The *Babycare Book* (2007 edition) in the second bag focuses more on products and services for newborns and infants. Here three advertisements—for a sterilizing agent, children's clothing, and a toy—make specific associations with early learning. The first two connect early child care with classic children's literature: germs are analogous to The Big Bad Wolf in the Little Red Riding Hood story (57), and soft baby clothes are presented in a Classic Pooh© design (25). The third advertisement makes connections between certain brands of toys and CLD when it claims that Vtech Baby™ '3-in-1 ride grows with your baby. Teaches the alphabet, colours, shapes, numbers and more' (76). Taken together, this sample bag emphasizes the value of both traditional children's literature and learning experiences promoted by age-appropriate developmental toys that connect active play with language learning and reading.

Bounty Bag 3: Parenting Magazine Mother & Baby

New Baby Bag 3 is the sample bag most frequently mentioned by parents we spoke to who recalled the parenting magazines and Target discount voucher contained in it (see Chapter 3). Taken together, the magazines *Mother & Baby* and *Little Kids* address parents and caregivers of children from birth to six years of age. Here we will focus on the current sample issue of *Mother & Baby* (December/January 2008 expired June 2008) that targets parents of infants. The magazine contains articles about siblings, relationships between new parents, and how to protect children from the summer sun, heat, and exposure to danger when around water. As in all consumer magazines, a high percentage of space is taken up with advertising or editorials that specifically link retail products. Products advertised include medicines, disinfectants, and vaccines; oils and creams for mothers; strollers and baby furniture; nappies, bottles, and food products; children's clothes and toys.

A related theme in our data is that children's education can be facilitated and accelerated through the purchase of 'educational' toys produced by specialized companies, often explicitly described as being in consultation with health and education experts. The Fisher-Price® 'right toys right moments' advertisement in *Mother & Baby* is an example of this. The title of the ad suggests that there are 'right moments' for various stages of development and learning throughout a young child's life, and that this company has 'the right toys' for each one. This is a very language-rich and design-layered ad which has certain *semiotic features* that are typical of the genre to be found in magazines and on toy packaging and which help underscore the theme:

- the use of primary colors in typeface to signal early development (red headings, green subheadings, blue text)
- the incorporation of 'expert' views ('Play is so important—it's the way children learn about the world around them,' Dr. Kathleen Alfano, PhD)
- realistic pictures (with high color definition, saturation, and modality), comprised of actual photographs of children in play scenarios, and engaging in direct eye contact with a mother figure
- a backdrop of an implied common domestic parenting practice (a spiral-bound scrapbook in which the photographs of children at play during various stages of their early life have been loosely stuck on each page and notes have been added in handwriting)
- a language-rich address to parents that adopts a structured and pedagogic approach to information provision: (a) why play is important in general; (b) why play is important at stages: birth+ *sensory stimulation*, 6–12 months *actively exploring*, 12–24 months *role play and interactivity*, 24–36 months *imagination and social play*, and 3–5 years *fantasy play*; (c) specific indicators of development and learning at each stage, e.g., 'introducing animal friends is a great way to help baby learn about sizes, shapes, colours, sounds and more'; 'baby learns academics through interactive activity'.
- a message and company slogan that connects development and learning with fun (play.laugh.grow)

Together, these sample texts from Bounty Bags as generic bags distributed by hospitals and clinics in Australia and the US illustrate how newborn and infant children are now considered ideal subjects for parent-guided socialization and inculcating dispositions toward literacy. This is not merely the case in texts for parents produced by commercial sponsors of literacy, but it is also pervasive in texts and information pathways produced by government-sponsored health organizations.

CONCLUSION: INOCULATION, TREATMENT, AND THERAPY FOR EARLY LEARNING

The metaphor of the 'vaccine' speaks to the penetration of health discourses into the field of early childhood education, particularly in relation to the intervention programs. The inoculation model of early literacy gets much of its support from an epidemiological view of health, which is concerned with population level trends and the economies of large-scale social interventions. This was made clear to us by Dr. Munsberger's statements regarding Reach Out and Read. In this view, finding the simplest and most cost efficient way of reaching the largest possible fraction of the population for the most substantial effect size presents the strongest rationale for an intervention. Promoting parental reading to children is favored as being a straightforward, easily implemented, universal solution to a public health problem.

Debates about the merits of an inoculation model have played out in the scholarly literature. Luke and Luke (2001) have argued that what is being inoculated against is social change that has already exceeded efforts to arrest it; in other words, they see early intervention as a futile nostalgic effort to return to traditional values of print literacy, parental discipline, and docile children in the face of forces which are producing new kinds of social subject such as the globalized techno-citizen. These authors acknowledge their primary focus on young adults who they see as missing out in shifts of resourcing to the early years. Countering this, McNaughton (2002) argues that the field is not overall in the thrall of an inoculation model but rather understands the development and growth of competence in literacy and other areas to be continuous and occurring in diverse sociocultural contexts. This author points out that school entry is a key event in the lives of children, marking the point at which they will be expected to begin attaining competence in formal operations and, for this reason, supporting children well positioned for this event, and assisting those who are not ready to 'catch up', is crucial. McNaughton represents the early childhood education field and perhaps underestimates the extent to which health disciplinary perspectives shape understandings in other service and social settings.

Some researchers are mobilizing an alternative metaphor from the medical discourse to supplement the notion of inoculation. It has been suggested that, beyond the vaccination period, at-risk learners need continuing treatment or 'insulin', to prevent the reemergence of the learning problem (Coyne et al. 2004, 91). This suggestion maintains the concept of a learning problem as a medical disorder, while arguing in effect for continuing doses of treatment, rather than a one-off preventative shot. These authors represent the special education field, where psychological knowledge is dominant. Thus, the extent to which a medical view of early, and later, learning is considered compelling can be understood as linked to the disciplinary framework and training of researchers and practitioners.

In a climate of support for service integration and partnership, it is increasingly the case that medical, psychological, and educational perspectives are coming into contact and interweaving. Indeed, it is this interpenetration that is helping to produce the contemporary discourse of early learning as a hybrid of different knowledge fields, bringing into play rediscovered as well as newer ways of understanding the very young child as a learner and as the subject of the learning and work of its carers.

A Therapeutic Model of Early Learning

The notion of healthy development in early childhood crucially includes the emotional and psychological domains. It is in relation to emotional regulation of the child that a medical discourse of mental health, centered on the notion of prevention and treatment of disorders, enters into the realm of early learning. In our field work, this was seen most clearly in the mission and activities of the Child, Youth and Women's Health Services (CYWHS) in Australia, as they related to working with families of infants and young children. This manifested in the advice to parents regarding managing their child's behavior, settling, language interaction, media participation, and literacy.

The focus on emotional well-being taken by CYWHS and similar agencies leads them to invest as much in supporting mothers (still presumed to be primary carers) as their children, in the assumption that a secure and stable mother will help to ensure a well-adjusted child. This means that the service strongly emphasized peer networking between women, as well as building their self-esteem through messages about trusting one's instinct and being content to be a 'good enough' mother.

This emphasis on psychological health of children and parents was associated with a distinctive contribution to understandings of early literacy development. As we saw in the analysis of a Parent Easy Guide text (above), this de-emphasized socializing the child into print literacy per se. Rather, the emphasis was on the use of a book to mediate the psycho-emotional relationship between the child and its feelings, and between the child and caregiver.

When health services partner with other early childhood providers, the distinctiveness of the therapeutic approach comes into sharper focus. During the GTKYB session in which a representative of the state preschool sector came in to conduct a literacy activity, this contrast was expressed in the different ways that the body of the infant child was treated. While Joanne taught swaddling to produce a simulation of intimate warmth, lulling the child to sleep, the education worker Glenys introduced a curriculum of stimulating multimodal activities. She invoked a developmental trajectory which would lead from participation in physical and auditory actions to language to literacy. The activities were the primary focus, with the adult as enabler and coparticipant, whereas for the child health nurse, the relationship was the primary focus, with the adult as secure base for the child.

Considering this therapeutic emphasis, it is important to acknowledge the broader social context in which such understandings are being mobilized. A representative perspective from the field of public health can be seen in an article in the journal *Child Care Health and Development* (Barlow, Parsons, and Stewart-Brown 2005). The authors begin their review of parenting programs by stating: 'Emotional and behavioural problems

are among the most important causes of functional disability in children'
and that, amongst preschoolers incidence is particularly high (ibid., 33).
In support of this assertion, they cite a study that found that two-thirds of
parents had 'one or more concerns' regarding the behaviour of their three-
year-old children (Stallard 1993 cited in Barlow et al. ibid.) Their argument
for early intervention into parents' management of children's behavior is
grounded on the fear that, without such intervention, children are at risk
of 'externalizing disorders at school entry' (ibid., 34). In citing this category of 'disorder', the authors are clearly referring to the typology used
in the *Diagnostic and Statistical Manual* which categorizes pathologies of
behavior into internalizing (withdrawing) and externalizing (acting out)
disorders, and the latter into a panoply of subcategories such as 'conduct
disorder', 'attention deficit disorder', and 'oppositional defiant disorder'
(American Psychiatric Association 2000). Thus early childhood is understood as the period in which the origins of these disorders can be located
in the unhealthy psycho-emotional environment of (some) families. In this
contemporary version of a mental hygiene model, positioning parents as
learners of how to manage their children's unruly emotions is crucial.

Partnering with education assists health services to circulate this message.
Focusing on activities such as book reading, which are generally recognized
to be linked to future academic achievement, positions health providers as
authoritative in relation to young children's prior-to-school education. This
is in line with the direction, seen in the US, to make pediatricians the first
port of call for concerns about young children's learning, thus encompassing the subject of early learning within an overarching medical model of
healthy development, inclusive of body, mind, and the social self.

5   The Church

INTRODUCTION

Religion has for hundreds of years been integrally connected with the rationale for, and structuring of, formal education in many parts of the world (Graff 1991; Luke 1989). In this chapter we consider how faith institutions and communities are responding to the contemporary early learning agenda, both in terms of how this articulates with their traditional mission and what changes it may be bringing to the ways in which churches network with communities. Following a discussion of the background and published research in this area, we turn to case studies from our own research.

In the Christian tradition, a young child's inculcation into the moral and spiritual beliefs of a faith has long been considered the responsibility of its parents, supported by their own participation in a religious community. Before the age of seven the child was considered unable to reason independently and thus unsuitable for formal instruction though particularly amenable to imitating example, both good and bad (Luke 1989). Describing the prevailing view among Protestants in Puritan New England, Graff writes:

> The very young were to be prepared by oral instruction and moral comments on their actions. The household's piety and morality were to condition the child from the earliest moments of awareness (1991, 170).

Prior to mass schooling, in many contexts, parents and masters continued to be the primary educators of children and servants, integrating religious teaching with basic literacy. In 17th-century Sweden, under the Church Law of 1686, heads of households were required to ensure their dependents were learning to read, and ministers conducted examinations in homes (Lindmark 2003). In such contexts, the church structured and monitored the practices and outcomes of home-based education from the early years and throughout childhood, a phenomenon which continues today in some homeschooling movements.

The notion that parents are a child's first teacher, often voiced by early learning advocates, thus has strong echoes with a strand of religious thinking. However, that all parents will naturally teach the right things in the right way is unlikely to be taken for granted by churches. Luther's argument for compulsory schooling from age seven was in part a response to the perceived shortcomings of parents:

> [T]he majority of parents are unqualified for it, and do not understand how children should be brought up and taught . . . even if parents were qualified and willing . . . they have no time for it, so that necessity requires us to have teachers for public schools. (Luther 1530, in Luke 1989, 105)

This very brief introduction to some aspects of a western religious tradition of childhood education indicates that the home has primarily been considered the site for early learning, focused on moral example and peripheral participation in practices such as Bible reading. The Protestant tradition of promoting reading has also supported home-based literacy instruction to young children, as well as other household dependents.

A Spiritual Curriculum for Early Learners

In these times, a contemporary discourse of early learning is being taken up in some faith settings, reflecting wider social developments. This is manifested in the growing popularity for specialist leadership of spiritual services for children and families, often termed Children's Ministry (Jutila, Wideman, and Verbal 2006), and in the development of curricula and resources for faith-based education targeting preschoolers and younger children. That the move into early learning represents a genuinely new development, as well as maintaining strong strands of continuity with churches' core missions, is indicated in the kinds of arguments made by advocates.

In an article titled 'Ministry to the Sippy-cup Set', one minister, in describing the traditional lack of attention to young children's learning, simultaneously lists the kinds of activities which are being promoted by religious early learning enthusiasts. She complains that the normal effort toward young children's faith learning has been:

> Nothing. No programming, no ministry, no staff person dedicated to early faith formation, no "Here's how to live out your baptism" tips, no parent classes, no Sunday school, no small groups, no playgroups, no Bible storytelling time, no prayer chains, no baptismal birthday celebrations. (Rundman 2009 accessed online)

Thus, a specialized ministry for young children and their parents with dedicated resources and activities is what is being argued for and increasingly being practiced. There is also a pragmatic argument for this investment by churches. Engaging families with young children, particularly in areas where these are a growing percentage of the population, is seen as a means of arresting the trend to dwindling congregations; toddler ministry is held out as a key strategy.

There is much here in common with the way that early learning is viewed in other contexts, though the focus is the specific domain of faith formation. Evidence for churches networking into the discursive field of early learning with its diverse array of theories and practices can be seen in publications and program descriptions. Some early spirituality advocates are drawing on neuroscience, developmental theory, and other conceptual resources in order to argue for and build religious versions of early learning curricula. In a dissertation based on her implementation of the Blessing Based Spiritual Nurture program for toddlers, one minister actively makes connections between theology and early childhood theory, drawing on a very wide range of sources including Wesley, Rousseau, Montessori, Jensen, and Walt Disney (Teel 2007). Developmental theory is applied to stages of early faith development while constructivism and child-centered pedagogy underpin a play-based approach to activities:

> Toddlers play with toys specifically symbolic to the Christian faith and plus common toys used spiritually that enriches the toddler's religious language. . . . This is a place for toddlers to engage in exploring their spiritual journeys through play. (ibid., 34)

As with other manifestations of the early learning discourse, parents are also seen as learners and as needing to be informed about the foundational theories in order to apply appropriate practices. Language interactions are seen as particularly important in ensuring optimum faith development:

> "Parenting is a religious practice in which the theological beliefs and actions that constitute a life of faith are embodied, taught, and tested in parents' relationships with children." [Mercer 2005, 245] . . . Adults model religious language as they relate to the child. . . . This empower[s] the child to feel comfortable and familiar with the language as they grow through each developmental stage in their faith. (Teel, 62)

Brain science is heralded as providing a scientific basis for integrating spiritual rituals and religious symbolic language into young children's daily lives. Parents' role in the early years is linked to the notion of a critical period of brain development. Drawing on the writings of a well-known promoter of 'brain-based' education, Teel argues:

> "The brain is literally customizing itself for your particular lifestyle from the day you're born. Soon after, the brain prunes away unneeded cells and billions of unused connections. . . ." [Jensen, 21]. This author

would encourage parents towards the spiritual customizing of the brain as they nurtured their child. (Teel, 18–20)

To this end, she has devised a parent education program to complement the Blessing Based Spiritual Nurture sessions for young children. Her doctoral research on this program has investigated the impact on families' everyday practices as well as children's behavior in activities. Of course, as the brief historical foray above indicates, there is a tradition of religious institutions seeking to influence and directly monitor parents' work in socializing their young children. However, the contemporary move appears to owe more to theories and practices from within the field of early childhood education, and education more generally, than has been the case in the past. It is probably not coincidental that this coincides with the emergence of officially recognized female religious practitioners in some denominations. Early childhood education and care is a female domain, and women ministers are among its key advocates in the religious field.

Early Learning in Immigrant Faith Communities

So far we have focused on Christian settings in mainstream contexts. However, churches have also been extremely significant in serving immigrant communities around the world. For young children and their families, one of the ways this is experienced is through the provision of early and later education in the languages and practices of the faith community. In the UK, language ethnographer Eve Gregory was first alerted to the key role of faith communities in her study of three generations of families living in East London (Gregory and Williams 2000). She found that community schools operating preschool and out-of-school hours programs offered a combination of language instruction, cultural socialization, and religious teaching. Following this study, Gregory's team has continued to investigate what she terms 'faith literacies' (Gregory 2008; Wallace 2008) or communication and interaction practices for participating in religious life. Case studies of individual children have examined their early and later learning of these literacies.

Ruby (2008) writes about 'Hasanat', six years old, a third-generation British Bengali whose parents enrolled him in an Islamic playgroup at age three. At this playgroup, children learned to memorize a different passage of the sacred text, the Qur'an, each day by repeating it after the teacher until word perfect and were required to recall it the following morning. At home, Hasanat sat on his mother's knee while she read her Qur'an and began to point to letters he recognized. At the age of five, Hasanat graduated to after-school Arabic classes integrating religious instruction with further teaching of Arabic. Here he continued to practice writing and memorizing longer and more complex texts.

In the Samoan Sunday school studied by Dickie and McDonald (2011), integration of mother tongue language learning and religious learning was an important aspect of the educational approach. Photographs taken by children, their diary entries, researcher observation, and interviews with teachers formed the basis of analysis. In this Catholic Sunday school located in a New Zealand township, there was a Samoan alphabet chart on the wall, and the instructor stated that teaching began at about three years old with the sounds of the Samoan alphabet. Once this was mastered, writing was taught, and older children were given Bible verses to take home and learn. Regular examinations were set for recitations from memory, and Samoan Bibles were often presented as prizes. One child said her dad had 'heaps of Bibles' (27), echoing the intergenerational relations found in other studies.

Volk (2008) offers the case of 'Julializ', a Puerto Rican five year old being raised by a devoutly Christian mother. Here the child's presence at community and family worship events is viewed in terms of her literacy learning, even though there are no specific early learning services for children. The family attends church twice weekly, the mother takes a Bible class on another day, and the family engages in home-based Bible study almost daily. Explicit teaching of reading at home is integrated into Bible reading sessions. When she was four, Julializ asked to be allowed to read a Bible passage at a church service, and her mother assisted her to memorize one since she could not yet decode print. Just as many children play at school, Julializ plays at church with her siblings imitating adult ways of Bible reading, praying, singing, and preaching. All these activities can be viewed through the lens of early learning, facilitated by participation in a faith community.

These cases give evidence of traditional ways in which churches have supported young children's learning, in relation to religious participation and also more generally in the acquisition of mother tongue and additional languages. In association with broader moves toward social partnership models, localized faith communities are also being recruited into wider networks which have extended their service provision in child and family support.

Serving the Community: Churches and Early Childhood Provision

Churches serve two communities, the congregation of the faithful and the wider community within which the faithful live and work. For many faiths, the relationship between these two communities is integral to the spiritual mission. The wider community offers believers opportunities to live their faith by demonstrating through their actions in the world the qualities of a godly person. Interactions with the wider community also provide the possibility of bringing new members into the congregation of the faithful. Also, such interactions can bring more practical benefits for religious organizations; as influential outsiders recognize the broader social mission of the church they may be instrumental in channelling resources into churches.

Sunday Schools began, not just to provide religious instruction but often as the only source of formal literacy teaching for poor children and adults prior to the introduction of a state education system (Boylan 1979).

Teaching in Sunday Schools became an approved way for young women to practice religious service. Indeed, the demand for nurseries to be provided for infants and toddlers during worship was often to release their mothers for this kind of work (Boylan ibid.).

A recent study of churches in Detroit found that one-third of congregations were 'engaged in some type of education or childcare and charity work' (Reese 2004). Short-session child care, preschool, feeding, accommodation support, and parent education were among the services provided by churches to families of young children. Teel (op. cit.) describes her own Uniting Church's full-day child-care service, established in the '60s to serve working parents of its city neighborhood, as its 'weekday ministry'. She distinguished this from the Sunday nursery which, prior to her introduction of an early learning curriculum, had been a babysitting service for congregation members.

Under neoliberal governments in some countries, mainstream religious organizations have been repositioned as partners in the provision of social services. Churches were poised to take up this expanded service provision owing to their existing network of local branches with existing concrete infrastructure and human resources. This is particularly true of the US where welfare reform in the '90s removed the necessity for churches to create secular arms in order to secure government funding (Gilman 2007). This move aligned with a critique of the public sector and a drive to privatize and decentralize welfare services. Churches were also seen as more effective at networking into African American communities, from whom the larger proportion of the welfare dependent population was drawn (Hula et al. 2007). The White House Office for Faith-Based and Community Initiatives (OFCBI) was formed on the direction of then President George W. Bush and administered grants to religious, charitable, and other community groups. In Australia, the Salvation Army has been a major beneficiary of government partnership programs (Garland and Darcy 2009). In recent years, under President Obama the direction of the OFBCI has changed to emphasize two main goals—tackling obesity and increasing father participation in child rearing—and there is less focus on explicitly religious motives.

Echoes of earlier approaches to working with the poor can be heard in some of these service directions. A US minister who has opened a chain of low-cost child-care centers describes his goal as being to 'provide a highly structured, stable, Christian learning environment' for infants and children of urban working mothers (Goode 2000). Formal literacy teaching starts at age two using a phonics approach and employing a token system to reinforce good behavior and achievement. Commenting that 'the state has taken the paddle away', the Reverend McIntyre explains how children's participation is regulated:

> During Bible Time, for example, if their hands are together and they're paying attention, they'll get a little ticket put right beside them. They

can't touch the ticket but they can redeem it for a reward. If they don't keep paying attention, you'll see a teacher's aide circulating around and taking the tickets away. (Goode 2000)

This is a very different orientation to early learning than the constructivist, play-based approach promoted by ministers like Teel (2007). However McIntyre is working in poor neighborhoods offering a paid service to the poor whereas Teel is working in a middle-class neighborhood offering a free service once-weekly service to the congregation. She was able to draw on the services of a creative team to transform the drab weekly child-care center into a bright, child-oriented space with comfortable home-like furniture. McIntyre's approach does, however, have points in common with the formal instruction in the Islamic playgroups and community schools (Gregory 2008; Gregory and Williams 2000; Ruby 2008). The emphasis on teacher direction, close attention, memorization, and explicit rewards and sanctions features in both settings. Religious manifestations of early learning represent both continuities and discontinuities with historical traditions of children's socialization into faith communities.

CHURCHES IN THE PARENT NETWORKS PROJECT

The foregoing discussion forms a background to the following case studies of community service provision in early childhood offered by religious organizations. The services we accessed were mainly those provided by churches for the broader community rather than specifically for the faithful. They drew on the commitment to community service as part of a broader spiritual mission with members of the congregation providing the moral and practical support.

In every neighborhood, we found that local churches were significant providers of services for preschool children and their carers. As field work researchers relying on our own ability to network into communities, we found that churches provided opportunities for us to connect with local people. In each site, we were able to place a researcher for sustained field work in at least one church-run service. Sophia joined the Wave playgroup in the Australian country town of Deepwater; Sue attended the Salvation Army playgroups in the suburban hub, Midborough; Jennifer connected with both the Blue Sky preschool run by Saviour Church and a new family literacy initiative offered by First Baptist in Greystone; and the whole Australian team became involved with the weekly African Women's Day provided by the Midborough Uniting Church.

Churches were protective of the activities run solely for members of their own flocks such as worship events. We were not successful in gaining access to all the activities which religious organizations in our field sites were running for parents and young children. For instance, we saw a playgroup advertised on a notice board at Gumtree library and contacted the coordinator. She explained that the playgroup was actually a crèche for children while their mothers participated in a Christian study group. Although motherhood was one of the main topics discussed by the group, the coordinator said she did not think that children's learning or development was a focus. After this, we investigated the group online and found it to be part of a national and international chain of Christian study groups for women. The founders were two American women who each year wrote a book that formed the basis for the study curriculum. So, even though the notice on the library board presented the group as local, it was part of a global network. We purchased a copy of that year's book and read it with some interest for the kinds of ideas about parenting that it circulated. As the coordinator had indicated, children's learning was not central. Rather, the emphasis was on the mother working on her own relationship with God (represented as a kind of self-care) in order to be able to function as the moral compass for her family. Thus we understood that the crèche was provided in order to get mothers away from their children so that they could collectively support each other in this spiritual self-care process. The word 'playgroup', used on the flyer to advertise this activity, suggested a different kind of practice, one where parents and children met collectively with the aim of meeting both groups' needs for social interaction.

The services we observed were of three kinds, dealing differently with the two main targeted groups—young children and their carers. One kind of service was primarily targeted at carers; children were looked after separately, freeing women to participate in other activities. The African Women's Day run by Midborough Uniting Church was this kind of service. While their children were cared for in a crèche, the women were offered sewing, English lessons, and visits from guest speakers as well as a chance to socialize. Inculcating the African women into assumed Western ways of child rearing and schooling was one of the explicit purposes of the church in supporting this service.

The second kind of service was run for carers together with their children in the form of weekly playgroup sessions of two to three hours. The Wave playgroup in Deepwater and the Salvation Army playgroups in Midborough were both examples of this kind of service. Playgroups are a familiar part of the early childhood scene in many countries. One obvious reason for churches to become involved in playgroup provision is that they often have suitable premises in the form of church halls equipped with kitchen and washroom facilities. However, In the case of both the Salvation Army and Wave, the church had proactively established playgroups even when there were existing facilities in their local areas, evidence that religious organizations, in common with other social institutions, see early childhood as an important domain of intervention.

The third kind of service was run solely for children. The Blue Sky preschool run by Saviour Lutheran church was a stand-alone service not connected to any school. We viewed this as an example of a church running a community service in early childhood. Established as a deliberate intervention into the lives of young children living in 'welfare motels', the preschool provided a full educational program five days a week. It is with this case that we begin our exploration of the early learning mission and activities of case study churches.

SAVIOUR CHURCH AND THE BLUE SKY CLUB

Saviour Church came to our notice through its support for a preschool for homeless children, the Blue Sky Club, which was at the time located near to Greystone. Our field work was conducted in this preschool, and we accessed more general information about the church from its well-developed website. Saviour Lutheran church was established in the late 1960s to serve a newly established middle-class suburb. Its current pastor had worked in the church's adult education branch and held a certificate in Digital Cultural Ministry; this educational and technological theme was clear in its website. Statements by the church about its activities strongly reinforced the importance of education as part of its mission, tied to a belief about the mutual nature of the link between faith learning and broader personal, academic, and social enculturation. For instance, a church newsletter cited research in support of the link between church attendance and better behavior at school as well as at home:

> children and youth who attend religious services weekly exhibit fewer at-risk behaviors, are more likely to have high-quality relationships with their parents, and are more likely to exhibit positive social behavior— including showing respect for teachers and neighbors, getting along with others and trying to resolve conflicts with classmates, family or friends. (URL withheld to protect site identity)

Among the explicitly educational activities offered by Saviour Church to its parishioners were Sunday School, Vacation Bible School, Book Group, and Summer Reading Club. Sunday School utilized the new child-friendly Activate program which offers web-based resources for instructors http://www.activatefaith.org/curriculum/. Additionally, a preschool music program was held on the church premises.

The Summer Reading Club was an integral part of the church's Home and Family Ministry, and parishioners were encouraged to contribute to the collective goal of 300 books over the summer vacation. Materials, consisting of a reading log, book report proforma, and coloring-in pages were available from the church or downloadable from its website. Parents were encouraged to adopt the program as a means of fostering goal setting:

Kids can set up their personal reading goals with their family and come up with special rewards like staying up late or choosing the family movie, when the goals are met. (URL withheld to protect site identity)

The Blue Sky Club took the church's educational mission into the community with the aim of changing the lives of young children from impoverished families living in the so-called 'welfare motels' strung along the nearby interstate highway. The Blue Sky preschool had been running about twelve years at the time of the study. Sh'vonn, the preschool director, explained that church members had been concerned at the situation of young children who were often kept in motel rooms all day and did not access any educational service. Sh'vonn told us that even though families could qualify to attend local preschools 'it would take months for them to get the paperwork together' and that some of the preschools were located in 'tough neighbourhoods', making it difficult to provide safe access for children. The need for a specialist preschool facility for the poorest families is illustrated by this testimonial from a parent:

Nate was attending a medical day care, until abruptly in April the school sent a note stating because of insurance guidelines he could no longer attend. My 4 month old was scheduled for his second surgery at [hospital]. I almost had a break down. Nate's father is deceased and his grandmother works full time. Without Blue Sky my baby could not have his surgery.

From small beginnings of one day a week, the Blue Sky club was now operating every weekday and had relocated to larger premises at a Lutheran church some distance from Saviour's district. It had attracted sufficient funds to employ trained teachers and to develop a training program for volunteers. The Club's Mission Statement appears in the volunteer handbook:

The Blue Sky Club provides a loving, nurturing, and safe environment that promotes healthy physical, emotional, social, and intellectual development, with the aim of creating a firm foundation for each child's future academic success. (URL withheld to protect site identity)

A description of activities on one day at Blue Sky illustrates how nurturing and learning were entwined. On this day, twenty children were attending and eight volunteers (all teenagers) were assisting the trained staff. The children were asleep or resting while quiet music played during the scheduled post-lunch nap time. At 2:30 p.m., each child was roused by one of the assistants and was helped to put his or her shoes on. One little girl was inconsolable after being woken so Sh'vonn had a long talk and cuddle with her. A snack was served, and following that was reading and play time. Volunteers offered to read to children and before long all were settled with at least one child. Researcher Jennifer had five children on her lap, clearly comfortable with the contact and familiar with the routine. After twenty minutes, Sh'vonn announced that everyone would be going outside to listen to a story under the tree. There was no compulsion for children to sit still and listen; those who wanted to gathered in the group, while others ran around and played.

During nap time that day, a key point of discussion in the staff meeting was a focus group which had been held with some of the children's parents to discover more about their aspirations for their children and how they saw Blue Sky supporting them as parents. Some parents had spoken of wishing to bring up their children in accordance with their cultural values while still having access to resources and information. Some complained that health professionals and counsellors tried to get them to rear their children 'like white people'. Blue Sky staff were keenly aware of the circumstances of their children's parents and how this impacted on their access to and use of resources and advice. They were very careful not to communicate disrespect and tried to find opportunities for learning and growth in the families' lives.

One of the key focuses in their work with parents was supporting children's language development by encouraging parent-child conversation. A strategy Sh'vonn had tried was 'Food for Thought', a set of cards with conversation starters that she thought could be used at mealtimes. However, many of the families lived in shelters communally with other homeless women and children; mealtimes were 'just too noisy and too chaotic for that kind of a conversation'. Rethinking the approach, Sh'vonn looked for other opportunities for conversation in these families' lives:

> They spend a lot of time waiting for buses. They spend a lot of time waiting, um, in offices for, um, services of, you know, medical, or.[. . .] "While you're waiting for the bus, here's something you can do with your kids."

She had rewritten the cards so that they would be suitable for these occasions. Waiting time was turned into an asset, and parents were encouraged to capitalize on this time to develop their children's oral language skills.

Educating preschool children, and assisting parents to support their children's development, were integral to Blue Sky's philosophy and practice. Direct religious instruction was not undertaken; rather the church's faith mission was expressed through its service to the disadvantaged families in its region.

UNITING CHURCH, MIDBOROUGH: RESOURCING AFRICAN WOMEN

The Uniting Church at Midborough is located directly opposite the Gumtree Municipal Council Chambers and Library and quickly came to our attention as a possible service point for families of young children in the Midborough area. The church had not appointed a specialist children's or family minister, and we did not see or hear evidence that a contemporary early learning discourse was being interwoven with traditional beliefs about socializing children into the faith. The parent organization, the Uniting Church Association, was attempting to encourage this direction. The family ministry section on its website recommended the text *Children's Ministry in the 21st Century* (Jutila, Wideman, and Verbal 2006) for practical ideas including providing 'devotion books' for parent-child sharing, family games nights, picnics, family prayer boxes, playgroups, and parenting seminars.

Midborough Uniting, however, strongly emphasized social inclusion and community service, describing itself on its website as 'an open, caring, welcoming Church' which welcomes 'old and young, married and single, gay and straight, black or white, abled and differently able'. The church's congregation had developed a focus on African families for its community service work. Members raised funds for schools in Sudan which assisted with the provision of computer equipment, books, and uniforms for schools. Closer to home, the church ran a weekly 'African Women's Day' (AWD) for refugee and migrant women and their preschool children. Since our project concluded, a Dinka language school on Saturdays has been added to its services for African families. We sought permission to conduct ethnographic field work in AWD and research assistant Pippa began attending weekly. Eventually, this connection developed into one in which we became resource providers to the church.

A typical AWD starts with around thirty women, and at least as many children, dismounting from the two minibuses which have done the rounds to collect them from their homes. Older children wait by the bus that will take them to a park to play while toddlers and babies are taken to the small crèche where volunteers are waiting to mind them. Each area is staffed by the regular volunteers. Henry is always to be found in the crèche where his gentle humor is particularly popular with the little boys. The children are keen to interact with the researcher, Sue, some poking her tummy to find out if she has a baby in there, others offering to do her hair. Their spoken English is progressing rapidly, as is the pattern for migrant children in multicultural communities.

Inside the main hall, tables are set up with sewing machines and lengths of material for perhaps the most popular activity for women, sewing clothes for their children and themselves. A smaller adjacent room is arranged as a classroom for English lessons led by volunteer Iris, a former teacher, and instruction on how to pass the written driver's license test. A large separate dining hall has chairs arranged along walls and a small corner marked off by freestanding noticeboards. Inside is a bookshelf with a sign 'Library' and a collection of books, most of them on religious themes. We did not see any of the African women enter this area.

At lunch time, adults chat with countrywomen or others who share a common language while children are seated at tables and loosely supervised while they eat. The air is full of many languages in lively conversation. This is in distinct contrast to conversations between the volunteers and the (mainly African) women, which rely on a few words of English aided by nods and smiles. After lunch, Kath the chief organizer gives notices. She thanks volunteers, alerts people to coming events and raises other issues such as requesting women not to barter when purchasing from the church's onsite second-hand goods shop.

After lunch, there may be a guest speaker. Welfare services, the police, the Migrant Resource Centre, Legal Aid, and the local council have all been on the program. A senior community woman, Ayak, who is also one of the few with higher education, often assists as cultural mediator and linguistic translator. Ayak is undertaking training to become a minister in the Uniting Church and is trusted by both church seniors and community members.

Local service providers have often use AWD as their main point of contact for local refugee families. The leaders of AWD were well connected into community services and constantly adding to their networks. This enabled them to respond to issues faced by the refugee families as they arose, accessing information advice and practical help: Kath, one of two organizers, spoke about this approach:

> Well if they've got problems with their bills, with food, also with protection for their children. If they've got a concern that way, they know they can go to Families SA. We have to really assess what their problem is, and often it might take you a few weeks to find out [. . .] We've got a couple of doctors in the area that people can go to. [. . .] We refer them to the dental clinic for adults or for their children; glasses for their eyes; if they've got a pain in their side, yep. Today I have spoken to the people that do the breakfast at Midborough West Primary School, so maybe we need to link with that next year with our Minister's child going there, so that's another thing. As people get to know us, it links us.

AWD had attempted a foray into early learning through the avenue of informal home visiting which was part of the church's role in the settlement of refugee families. Church visitors reported that they had seen few or no children's books in the homes of the families so the congregation decided to purchase some books and donate them to families. On presenting the books, visitors spoke to parents of the importance of reading to children. The provision of books had been an approach suggested by the local librarian as effective; the library itself distributed books as part of the Little Big Book Club program.

Henry had been one of the volunteers involved in this scheme. He told us that parents and carers had accepted books with apparent gratitude. However, on a subsequent visit he observed that the books still looked brand new rather than showing signs of use. They had been put away so as not to be damaged. Henry was puzzled that children's books had been treated as too precious for children to handle.

AWD organizers were clearly still looking for a way to engage parents with their children's literacy learning. They approached one of our researchers to ask if we would like to supply a guest speaker on this subject. A condition of accepting this invitation was that the activity had an adult focus. Bringing parents and children together was seen to be impractical and potentially chaotic. We accepted this challenge and used the insight we had gained into the community to develop what we hoped was a culturally appropriate, interactive series of two workshops.

The Early Literacy Workshops

When we arrived to run the first workshop, Kath directed us to the classroom where we found desks set in straight rows. This indicated an expectation of a formal teacher-directed participation structure, with the African women positioned as listeners. We decided instead to set up a circle of chairs in a corner of the large hall where the women were sewing. Kath was concerned that the sewing machines would be a distraction and addressed this by turning off the power and telling the women to leave their sewing and attend our session. This again acted to reinstate, as much as possible, the 'proper' relations between teacher and student.

We had planned the sessions around multisensory strategies incorporating singing, actions, hands-on activities, storytelling, and information giving. In an attempt to connect with the women on a personal level, Sue told stories from her own experience as a mother and showed books and drawings from her children's preschool time. There were smiles and laughter when Sue showed a squiggle drawing which her three-year-old daughter had stuck on her bedroom door as a 'Keep Out' sign. The presence of some respected elder women was also important in providing leadership. Two of the grandmothers were the first to use the playdough to make letters; their willingness to participate actively and to show enjoyment encouraged younger mothers to join in.

In keeping with the resourcing theme of the project, preparation included sourcing cheap or free materials from around the local area. The women were particularly interested in learning that the magnetic alphabet letters had been bought at a nearby $2 shop. Texts and oral stories were chosen for cultural inclusivity; for instance, a picture book featuring the character 'Grug' (a multicolored nongender-specific mop of hair on legs) showed a simple lifestyle of tending plants.

During both sessions Ayak provided simultaneous interpretation in Arabic and Swahili. Contrary to Kath's fears, the women were more attentive than was usual during a guest speaker session. A volunteer who participated said she could tell the women were very interested because they were so quiet; usually they would talk among themselves, and some might 'wander off'. The provision of translation no doubt assisted the women to absorb the information, removing some of the necessity of checking with each other regarding comprehension of the content. Based on their translated comments, the session was useful precisely for what made it different from the usual guest speaker talk—interactivity, active participation, and practical emphasis. Ayak said emphatically that she would like to see the researchers come back every week.

The contemporary discourse of early learning was not a strong theme at Midborough Uniting. This may have been because the church did not have a specialist minister for children and had not engaged with the parent church's early years faith curriculum. When it came to education, the church's approach was traditional and didactic, positioning parents as receivers of information and advice. While willing to accommodate the interactive workshop approach taken by the researchers, it did not seem likely that this would be repeated. At the same time, through its book donation and home visiting scheme the church did attempt to create change at the sociocultural level by engaging parents in reading to their children. However, this was based on the expectation of a one-to-one parent-to-child interaction which was not consistent with, or reinforced by, practice at AWD.

The Midborough church worked to resource refugee families through information provision, practical assistance, and connecting them with services. By recognizing Ayak as a cultural mediator and by networking with other service providers (including academic researchers) AWD made the church permeable to flows of information, knowledge, and practice. Whether ideas took hold depended on the willingness of their advocates to give time and resources and to build relationships. Ayak was successful in advocating for the Dinka Saturday school to provide combined language and religious instruction to children from the early years up. More extended consultation and commitment would have been needed for an early learning component to be incorporated into AWD on a continuing basis.

PLAYGROUP AT CHURCH

We turn now to two cases of churches providing playgroups for local carers and young children. In each of the communities, one suburban and one rural, the playgroup provided by a church offered an alternative to other local services. In discussing these cases, we consider how the activity of playgroup facilitated an interweaving of a church's moral and spiritual mission with ideas and practices related to child development and learning. We also consider how a focus on social inclusion acted to bring in voices and perspectives different from a dominant middle-class discourse of child rearing.

'Wave' Playgroup, Deepwater

The Uniting church in the Australian country town of Deepwater is located on the outskirts of town. Once a week, a group of women and their children gathered in the church hall to participate in the Wave playgroup. Members did not have to be members of the church congregation; however the impetus to begin Wave, the women who were its leaders, and some of its funding had come from the church. One of the organizers, Denise, explains:

> It was a vision through the church that they needed something in the community for families with young children. . . . The idea was, and still is, to let people know in the community that there is a church here that's open to families.

'Wave' did not respond to a service gap in the town, since there was already a playgroup run out of the local school-based kindergarten. The school-based playgroup was run by a trained educational practitioner and had an explicit learning agenda which involved encouraging parents to engage in learning-focused interactions with their children. Robin, another organizer, referred to the state-run service as the 'real proper playgroup' a designation that signifies legitimacy. 'Proper' can also signal contrived, 'best behaviour', social manners and indeed not all parents felt relaxed in this setting.

Local mother Belinda explains why she stopped attending the school-based playgroup; she compares the school-based playgroup with the church-based Wave playgroup:

> Playgroup was, to me the Deepwater playgroup anyway, was more focused on "These are my children, they're your children", and there was a lot of trying to outdo, like "My Johnny is doing this, and my Johnny was doing that", and trying to outdo, whereas at Wave it's "Yep, these are your kids, these are my kids, but we're all looking after everyone's kids here."

Belinda creates two parent characters in this statement, one of whom is unable to see beyond her own child, and the other who, while recognizing that each child is owned by its parent, accepts a part of the collective responsibility. The repetition of 'trying to outdo' suggests that the child-centered learning focus of the school-based playgroup was being interpreted by some parents as encouraging a competitive climate.

A culture of shared responsibility was integral to the purpose for Wave, as explained by its coordinators:

Amanda: [The children] do look to anyone, and if they're hurt they don't just go running to their own mum, they will go to whoever is closest, which is a nice feeling.

Denise: That was the idea of Wave, like families learning and growing
. . . to give the mums a break from the everyday stuff and giving somebody else, like somebody . . . they'll [children] listen to
somebody else, not just listen to your own [mother].

Thus social learning was a focus of Wave and was understood as needing
a community to reinforce its lessons. From this perspective, young children
should not just listen to their own parents but should be aware that their
behavior impacted on others. Belinda made this explicit:

If yours is doing something wrong we tell them off. If mine is doing something wrong we tell them off. If they're doing good then we praise them.

This way of thinking about children's social learning, and the parental role, was
at odds with the individualistic approach promoted at the state playgroup.

In other ways the approaches were similar. A mix of free play and organized activities happened at each Wave playgroup session as it did at the
state-run playgroup. For the craft activity, one of the Wave organizers
would create the prototype, e.g., a caterpillar made from an old stocking
stuffed with shredded magazine pages and tied with rubber bands. Children
were instructed in techniques for making these objects, and their mothers
assisted them to copy the prototype. The popularity of craft reflected the
women's personal interests. The town librarian told us that the craft section
was popular with the 'Wave mothers', and the local grocery store also had
a large selection of craft magazines.

Story reading was a regular feature, as was singing. These activities were
often led by a volunteer church member who was also a retired teacher, Ray.
For singing she would take the group into the church where there was a
piano. Denise had bought a *Get Up and Go Music Kit* full of easy-to-use
musical instruments (e.g., tapping sticks, castanets), colorful scarves, and big
song cards. These instruments were handed round to the children while Ray
took her place at the piano, introducing each song and encouraging children
and mothers to sing along, play their instruments, and do any actions.

Ideas about child development and learning informed planning for activities. Denise explained:

I've got a childcare background. I have thought about those sort of
things previously. When I first started we would go through and say
"Right, well this is really good for their coordination, thinking skills,
problem solving." I'm a strong believer in you don't put all the toys out,
because then the kids are going to get so confused they don't learn to
sit down and play, they just go from one thing to the other.

So it was intended that children would not simply amuse themselves but
would, through play, develop specific skills. This included the skill of

concentrating on and persisting with a specific play activity—'learn[ing] to sit down and play'.

Preparing children for school was clearly among the aims of Wave. One of the activities aimed at making this transition smoother was a tour of the school. We were fortunate that this visit took place on an occasion when Sophia, our field work researcher, was present. The absence of the scheduled tour host meant that one of the Wave organizers, Belinda, actually led the tour. It was interesting to hear her particular perspective on what was important for mothers to know. Belinda emphasized routines and procedures. She pointed out which sections of the school yard were 'out of bounds' to the younger children and how to tell by looking at the colored lines marked on the ground. She explained that young children ate their lunch in their classrooms so that their lunch would not get stolen—'It happens'—and that the close monitoring of lunch orders prevented theft of money. On the academic side, Belinda reassured mothers that whether a child was finding work 'too easy' or was 'struggling', they would get appropriate support.

In Wave, a collective approach to child rearing and the explicit teaching of social norms coexisted with educationally informed ideas about child development and the importance of play in building skills. The Uniting Church facilitated this endeavor by providing space, personnel, and funding. This enabled a group of women, who did not feel comfortable in a more formal educational space and sought respite from the pressure of individual responsibility for their children, to experience a supportive community.

Playgroup at the Salvation Army Midborough

The Salvation Army Centre, a low-lying modern building, is located on a major arterial road heading into Midborough's main commercial hub, Gumtree Plaza. The center's weekly playgroup for children under age five is advertised on a huge bright banner, highly visible to passing traffic. Playgroups are a common element in the Australian Salvation Army's suite of programs. They can be run either as part of, or separate from, the Children's Ministry. As part of ministry, playgroups run the 'First Steps' program. This is a relatively new initiative which is representative of the more general shift in thinking about the role of the church in young children's development (discussed earlier). First Steps is described as centered on 'making a positive difference in the spiritual development of children, and supporting and resourcing parents during this journey' (http://www.salvationarmy.org.au/children/first-steps.html). The program is structured around 'key milestones' including welcoming, dedication, and thanksgiving. Its name represents not only a child's first steps but also 'the first steps for many parents into a Christian church'. This reflects the integration between the organization's spiritual and social missions. It is hoped that families who are not currently members of the faithful can be brought into the fold via the Army's outreach work.

While First Steps is for those already in, or considering joining, the corps, playgroups are also run by the Army as part of its community service work.

The participants they seek to attract are families disadvantaged by poverty, substance abuse, mental illness, severe family breakdown, or disability. Playgroups attract parents who may then be recruited into concurrent programs such as Parenting Partners Promoting Positive Parenting (http://www.salvationarmy.org.au/e-connect-issue-17.html). The Army in Australia has been successful in attracting federal government funding for these and other early childhood support activities. It also networks with other community organizations such as The Pyjama Foundation, which provides volunteer literacy mentors for children in care (http://www.thepyjamafoundation.com/about_us.htm).

Writing about a playgroup run in an area noted for high welfare dependency and social disorder, an Army leader explains:

> We target that group not because we deem them more impressionable, but simply because we have the skills and a lifestyle that meets their needs. . . . For many of these children, safety and stability is not a given in life; creating safe spaces of fun and learning is one way we build into their lives. . . . They are following us; we are following Jesus. The process of discipleship above all is one of following, learning and then becoming. (Peterson 2011)

Midborough offered two weekly playgroups which were held in the Worship Centre.

Through an informal arrangement, the membership of these two groups roughly reflected the two kinds of target audiences for the Army's mission. One session attracted more Army members, and the other had more non-members including welfare clients and others.

At the time of the study, the center's leaders were Majors Doreen and Reg, a married couple in the Army tradition and fairly new to this center, having moved from the country. Doreen was coordinator of the playgroups, a role which she was struggling to reconcile with her principal commitment to 'Women's Ministry'. She told a researcher that she really wanted to set up two Bible classes, including one for the mums with a crèche, but it was hard to find the time when she had to 'do all this'. However, she was supportive of the idea of the Army offering playgroups which she explained were a way of:

> coming onside with the mums and trying to er form a relationship . . . but also to give the opportunity, without pushing it onto them, that if they wish to come to church there's always that option and they've walked into a church by having to come to playgroup.

Multiple use of the Worship Centre space is made possible because of the absence of fixed furniture; chairs are cleared away each playgroup morning to make room for large plastic indoor playground equipment, mats, low tables, and wheeled toys (see Figure 5.1). When set up for playgroup, this

Figure 5.1   Worship Centre set up for playgroup (researcher's photograph).

contemporary child's play space is as well equipped as a private child-care center for which parents would pay considerably higher fees.

The Army's spiritual mission is signified by large bright banners bearing uplifting messages. The lectern with a cross and flower arrangements on pedestals signals the sacred area of the room where the minister will lead worship.

Playgroup activities followed a routine which began with free play for children while the mothers watched and chatted, followed by 'craft time', 'snack time', and 'song time'. Of all these activities, the two which had the most importance for Doreen were craft and music which she viewed as providing opportunities for parents and children to interact:

> I think what's an integral part of the whole thing is to be able to encourage interaction between the mother and the child, and to be able to, for instance, with the craft or the playdough, any of the activities including

the singing, to encourage that the mother participates with the child, and continue their bonding relationship.

This view aligns with the emphasis on attachment which is a key element in contemporary early learning discourse. Shared activities are seen as producing attachment which in turn produces developmental benefits for the child.

Not having run a playgroup before, Doreen felt ill equipped to lead either craft or music activities. Taking the responsibility very seriously she looked at the existing resources on site, consulted her daughter, a child-care worker, and browsed several books:

> With a mixture of those we set up a syllabus. And once I had a syllabus established in my own mind that helped clarify a lot of things for me as well.

The idea of a syllabus linked Doreen's playgroup coordination with her experience of running Women's Ministry. The structure of this practice was indicated by a notice headed 'Syllabus' on the noticeboard in the corridor leading to the Worship Centre. This listed a program of monthly sessions, each with a guest speaker, an activity, and a 'devotion'. Dale realized that working with children would be different—'You don't have everybody sitting there and giving attention'—so she utilized themes she believed would be engaging for children, such as pirates, nursery rhymes, animals, and popular media characters.

Referencing popular media is a standard strategy in the Salvation Army's engagement with children. It puts out a children's magazine, *Kidzone*, which strongly features characters from contemporary children's movies and adapts the story lines to communicate spiritual and moral messages. For instance, in the Ratatouille issue, the feature story was 'Bad Rat-titude' and concerned a rat Felix who would 'take more than he should.' The commentary explicates the religious theme:

> There is a story in the Bible (Luke chapter 19) similar to Bad Rat-titude. Zacchaeus is the name of the little guy and Jesus is the name of the king. In this story [describes Bible story and similarities with magazine story]. Jesus knows your name and wants to be your friend too!

Doreen looked for craft activities featuring popular culture characters she considered would be attractive to young children, such as Elmo from Sesame Street.

> I think part of the, not only the educational process with playgroup, is important obviously, but it's also to keep people inspired and excited, and if we can provide a little bit more fun and also we don't seem to have to educate a lot of the children on Elmo, they already know him before we do . . . it also adds that little bit of an excitement to the whole thing.

The perceived benefit of not having to educate the children suggests that Doreen did not take an explicitly pedagogic approach to craft, and this was in fact the case. While she prepared and supplied materials, she did not provide an example of the finished product or give any instruction as to how to it should be produced. Field work notes describe one session where the theme was 'Elmo's birthday':

> The craft activity consisted of making an Elmo puppet. There were also Elmo colouring sheets and these were mainly what the children did for craft. The adults made the Elmo puppets which required a lot of detailed cutting and sticking all the limbs on the right way. Some of the women were saying that they had no idea what to do. One punned 'Grandma's not cut out for this'.

Music time was limited to singing a small group of familiar songs, some with lyrics adapted to Christian themes ('If you're happy and you know it say Amen. Amen!'). Doreen again wanted to see more fun and excitement being injected into playgroup. This seems in keeping with the Army's orientation to worship which integrates traditional and contemporary Christian music performance to encourage enthusiastic devotion. She researched music programs for preschoolers and had found one which integrated movement and singing, utilizing props such as a ball and a length of parachute silk. The program was expensive to purchase so she was considering how to replicate it by buying the materials and assembling a kit. Doreen asked one of the church members, a talented singer, if she would be willing to take the lead in introducing this new approach. However, this individual 'made it clear that she is doing enough'. Doreen commented that it was 'good of her to come to playgroup' as 'she doesn't really have to'. This made it clear that playgroup had different purposes for the faithful than it had for the outsider community participants.

One of the impacts of the Army's acceptance of popular culture was that middle-class taste was not the only influence on the social scene, particularly in Friday playgroup. This was evident in the kinds of movies, television programs, child behavior. and food discussed in playgroup. For instance, during one song time, when participants were thinking about what to sing next, [Amanda] broke into a song which began 'Big Macs, Pizza Hut and Kentucky Fried' and encouraged her son to show how he could do the Hungry Jacks hamburger hand sign (imitating a TV advertisement). Some of the other mothers looked nonplussed. She looked surprised in turn and said, 'Don't you know that one?'

Overt parental discipline, such as talking sharply to children and threatening them with a smack, which is seen as unacceptable in a middle-class approach to parenting (Walkerdine and Lucey 1989), seemed to be accepted. Overt displays of affection were even more common. Doreen told me she thought that all the parents interacted very well with their children: 'They all seem to come alongside with their children and be playing with them, which is really great'. This open and nonjudgmental attitude to different parenting styles was a factor in Midborough Centre's ability to attract and maintain a connection with parents and young children from diverse backgrounds.

FIRST BAPTIST, GREYSTONE: INTRODUCING FAMILY LITERACY

We finally present a case in which individuals within a congregation introduced an innovation in the domain of early learning that was directed at members of the congregation rather than a target group of disadvantaged others. This initiative brought parents and children together for a series of literacy workshops held after service. It was innovative for addressing the adult-child pair as its subject rather than, as in traditional religious education, working with age-segregated groups. It was also a departure by presenting the parent's role as pedagogic within a constructivist model of learning.

First Baptist has served the African American community of Greystone since the 19th century and today its socially diverse congregation continues to worship from the church which was built in 1885. Its mission states:

> We take pride in our African-American heritage, as we embrace persons from diverse backgrounds, cultures, lifestyles and experiences. We are committed to the Christian ministry of word, sacrament, and service, through worship, discipleship, fellowship, evangelism, and advocacy for social justice. (URL withheld to protect site identity)

First Baptist Greystone is a member of the Progressive National Baptist Convention, an alliance of churches which was formed in the 1960s to work for African American communities within the broader Baptist church movement and challenge obstacles to black progress more generally. Education is considered a vital means toward this aim:

> Progressives believe that there can be no liberation without education. The truth will make us free! (www.pnbc.org)

In common with other Baptist churches, First Greystone offered Sunday school for children and Bible study for adults. Older children and youth were engaged through the arts with a choir and a dance group among activities provided. In contrast to the Lutheran church, and its umbrella organization, First Baptist was not involved with preschool education and did not explicitly single out very young children for a specialized ministry.

The means by which the church came into the orbit of our early learning project is an example of social networking in a close-knit small town context. During the course of investigating community resources for families with young children, researcher Jennifer made the acquaintance of Thelma, organizer with 'Greystone Youth Aspire' (GYA), a program for 'low to moderate income' students, particularly from 'minorities'. GYA provided after-school homework support, tutoring, mentoring, and enrichment activities. Its leaders hoped to involve students and academics from the town's university in its mission and, with this aim, had developed some possible research questions. Thelma and Jennifer recognized the possibility of collaboration. They agreed there was a gap in the local area for services advocating and resourcing family literacy for members of minority communities.

It transpired that Thelma was a member of First Baptist Church and that another church member was Patsy, the Children's Librarian at Greystone Library. The two women took a proposal for a family literacy program to the council of First Baptist Church. Among those who discussed it, a local pediatrican was particularly supportive. It connected with the drive for health professionals to actively promote parents reading to children (see also Chapter 2). Thus a small group of church members with high levels of formal education and positions of responsibility in the wider community networked with an academic researcher to create an advocacy coalition in support of a church-based early learning program. Their shared aim was to change parent practices and ultimately improve children's educational outcomes. This was not a religious program. It did not seek to bring new members into the church or to give congregation members a chance to express their faith through service to disadvantaged others. Rather it relied on the congregation seeing a need in itself and one which could not be met through traditional spiritual practices.

The program was planned by Jennifer with Patsy and was held on five consecutive Sundays after service in the church basement. It included sessions on shared reading, an introduction to the library, and strategies that parents could adopt when doing literacy 'work' at home. The sessions had a small regular attendance of three or four parents and two or three grandparents and their preschool children. At the first session, Thelma and Jennifer put each parent/grandparent-child into clusters around the room with a book for each pair. Thelma began each session with a reading from a picture book, after which Jennifer discussed its themes and led the group in discussing how the themes related to their own lives. Patsy talked about books and key events at the library and encouraged families to attend (African American families were underrepresented among members of the library—see Chapter 6).

Each session targeted different skills such as sound–letter patterns. After the focal skill had been introduced, adult–child pairs had time to share books together as Jennifer, Patsy, and Thelma circulated to each cluster and worked one-on-one with them. Jennifer reported that it took 'coaxing' to get some caregivers involved and that some 'seemed insecure about their own literacy'. This was followed by after-reading activities, and suggestions were made for activities to be undertaken at home. Finally, participants ate a shared meal where the atmosphere was described by Jennifer as 'much livelier' and with a 'strong sense of community spirit'.

This activity connected with many of the ideas about early learning which were circulating in the wider community. It positioned parents/carers as colearners with their children and made book-sharing a central focus. It also connected with traditional views of teaching and learning by providing explicit instruction in skills and setting homework tasks. Thus it attempted to provide continuity with current understandings of literacy learning while representing an innovation for First Baptist. Church members who actively promoted this activity were linked to other community institutions with roles in literacy and education such as the library, pediatric clinic, and Youth Aspire. They were open to networking with a literacy researcher, to using her as a resource, and to themselves become resources. However, small attendance suggests that their vision for promoting early learning as part of the church's role had yet to gain broad acceptance. The following year, the researcher was no longer in the neighborhood, and we understand the program was not repeated.

CONCLUSION: BUILDING ON THE LEGACY

From deep historical traditions of educating communities, contemporary religious organizations are extending their community engagement as opportunities open up in relation to the early learning agenda. There are two main reasons for churches being positioned to do this work. The first relates to the inextricable links between literacy and religious practice and the second to the emplacement of churches within communities.

Literacy is a key element of early learning, as it is currently understood. Engaging infants and young children with the written word has been strongly emphasized in the programs of social institutions pursuing early childhood outcomes (Nichols, Nixon, and Rowsell 2009). Whether it was preparing parents as sponsors for their children's literacy (Brandt 2001) in Midborough at African Women's Day School, or preparing young children and their parents for school in the Wave playgroup, or focusing on disenfranchised, economically disadvantaged children at Blue Sky in Greystone—each faith setting that we entered leveraged literacy development as paving a road to future success.

Religion and literacy have been tied since time immemorial. Reading and writing script by rote have been part and parcel of religious life, and these strongly rooted rites and ideologies of religious script and literate competence have been extended to teaching young children literacy. During an interview, Deborah Brandt avowed the church's continuing role as a sponsor of literacy: 'The great big sponsors of literacy throughout history have always been religions, states (including schools and military), and commerce and I don't really see that changing. These are the big catalysts for literacy learning and the agents of change and appropriation' (March 25, 2010). Literacy has been an important means by which religion has been able to build and extend its networks and influence social practice. As Graff articulates it:

> Literacy and print acted in concert with personal and institutional contacts and exchanges to spread the Reformation. . . . From this basis, we begin to grasp the fuller nature of communications linkages and the mixture of media in sixteenth-century society. . . . Personal relations, printing and writing, oral communications, institutions: each played a part, separately and interactively. The meaning of literacy to the reform effort, and its opposition, lies precisely in the nature of these relationships.' (Graff 1991, 134–135)

The church has also played a role in the history of research in literacy education. Think back to Shirley Brice Heath's well-known ethnography in the Piedmont Carolinas when she offered two-year-old Lem's oral response to church and church bells as an example of how literacy practices meshed with the everyday lives of children from their early years:

> *Way Far*
> *Now*
> *It a Church bell*
> *Ringin'*
> *Dey singin'*
> *Ringin'*
> *You hear it?*
> *I hear it*
> *Far*
> *Now*
> (Heath 1983, 170)

Throughout her ten-year ethnography, Heath observed the pivotal role of religion in teaching children literacy through the word of God. She reiterates the importance of the church in setting the rules and practices for being literate which are then reflected in home literacy practices:

> The religious experience at church and in church-related affairs thus reinforces the home emphasis on the teaching of fixed and memorisable statements and labels. Recitation in both church activities and the home calls for bounded knowledge which is exhibited in the memorization of words exactly as they have been taught. (ibid., 140–141)

The pedagogy through which churches seek to teach young children and their caregivers has changed since those times as new specialist practitioners

—Children's Ministers—draw on models from mainstream early childhood education, as well as creatively transmuting theories of brain development to apply to spirituality. At the same time, older practices survive as with the Reverend McIntyre's use of 'tickets' in regulating the participation of children in his child-care centers (Goode 2000), a practice that dates from the times of the monitorial schools (cf. Lancaster 1816/1994). We were struck by the way in which churches keep alive older models of learning while at the same time appropriating contemporary discourses such as the notion of early learning. In doing so, faith settings are able to serve, and renew, two kinds of membership for the faithful and the needy.

Regardless of the particular participation structures set up for young children, religious organizations actively seek to spark, and maintain, religious commitment on behalf of their parents. In furthering this end, churches have a powerful resource in their community infrastructure. Churches are situated and own valuable places within communities. In each community in which we conducted fieldwork, the church held community capital: material, economic, and social. They could offer physical spaces and facilities for parents of young children and in so doing bring them literally into the church.

A key tension for religious organizations, in relation to young children and their caregivers, is between a commitment on behalf of some faith settings to build the mother as the spiritual heart of the family, or instead, focus on the needs of the child and develop their capacity so that they have the intellectual resources and wherewithal to succeed. The first model rests on a contention that a mother–child bond elucidates a child's development and primes the mother for such active teaching and learning for their child. The second model rests on a contention that a child living in poverty and under arduous conditions such as a homeless, nomadic life needs to be separated from parents and caregivers to foster learning and development. Where one model relies on the logic of separating a mother from her child to fully equip her to develop her own capacity to learn, the other depends on maintaining the bond between mother and child to heighten the child's development. Across the four case studies featured in this chapter we see traces of these tensions playing out, particularly in African Women's Day School and Greystone's Blue Sky preschool.

When compared to other community agencies, there is some basis for claiming that, despite (or perhaps, because of) their conservatism, churches are less influenced by the dominant middle-class discourse of early learning. Clients of the Salvation Army playgroup do not face censure for referring to junk food or reprimanding their children; rather their affection is noted, and they are praised for being 'alongside' their children. In a similar vein, Blue Sky parents are listened to respectfully when they state their wishes not to be 'made over' into white people. As we go on to examine another historic community institution—the library—differences will be evident in the ways that cultural capital is valued and mobilized toward early learning.

6 The Library

INTRODUCTION

Libraries are repositioning themselves within the landscape of early childhood education. While there is a long tradition of libraries having children's collections and offering children's activities such as story reading, the focus has shifted to a younger age group. As part of the more general drive to inculcate young children into literacy prior to preschool, libraries have developed programs targeted at parents of infants, toddlers, and kindergartners. Rather than being left at home while adults and older children go out to borrow books (as in the past when libraries required quiet and stillness) this youngest generation is now being welcomed and specifically catered for. Sessions for lap-sitting youngsters combining story reading with songs and actions are common in libraries around the world.

Experienced librarians have generally not been taught to work with babies as part of their initial training. In order to run activity sessions for infants and their carers, they are attending professional development on early child development. Librarians are adopting the language of developmental theory, attachment, and neuroscience to explain the benefits of these activities. An example is the Saginaw Public Library in Michigan which in 1999 started running 'child development-based toddler story times' (Oser 2006). As part of their training:

> [l]ibrarians discovered how and when babies learn and were able to incorporate this knowledge in programming and collection development. . . . Children's librarians are daily placed in the position of a child-development expert and parenting expert. What we have done in Saginaw is simply acknowledge that our staff is being asked to play these roles, and we have taken the necessary steps to provide new models and training. (ibid.)

While libraries have long had collections of books on child development and care, the idea that librarians can be considered experts in child development and the first port of call on early learning is new. One factor is a broader trend of libraries redesigning their mission to meet the challenges of digitalization and open sourcing (Karas 2011). The fight for survival is real. Local governments in many regions worldwide are currently in the process of closing, particularly smaller, libraries (Wynne-Jones 2011). Keeping up to date with social trends and selling the library's ability to provide relevant information and resources is one of the means by which libraries are working to stay relevant: one director advises colleagues to use 'trend tracking' services to accomplish this (Doucet 2010). Early learning and baby brain stimulation are trends a keen trend-watching library director could not fail to note.

Libraries, unlike schools and preschools, do not have to comply with an early childhood curriculum, and this can produce some interesting initiatives. The creativity with which some libraries network their early childhood practices with that of other agents and institutions is evident from the case of *Mother Goose on the Loose* (MGOL). This program, which combines nursery-rhyme focused activity sessions for babies with parent education, emerged as a hybrid of Canadian music education and Israeli storytelling sessions (Diamant-Cohen 2004). A retired opera singer developed in the 1980s an approach to teaching music to babies and toddlers and gave a series of workshops in Israel which were attended by staff of the Youth Wing Library of the Israel Museum. The blended program was eventually noticed by visiting American librarians and found its way to the US. From its new home in the Enoch Pratt Free Library in Maryland it was the focus of training for librarians statewide and expanded into Early Head Start Daycare Centers. Then, developments in brain research came to the attention of the program's presenters:

> It was instantly clear that the structure and activities in MGOL provided an optimal learning environment for the growth and development of babies' brains. (ibid., 42)

Eventually, the library wanted to ensure that parents did not just bring their babies to the sessions but understood the (new) rationale. A parent training program was added in which participants

> had the opportunity to explore brain anatomy and development, to review specific groups of skills that their child is developing through MGOL, and to learn exercises that support brain development. (ibid.)

The curriculum included exercises in which a librarian would recite a nursery rhyme and parents would be challenged to call out specific developmental goals which that rhyme could promote.

Regardless of the rationale, attending library activity sessions is becoming an accepted part of socializing young children into literacy and researchers have been paying attention. One study noted the use of multiple modalities in sessions where the presentation of books is interwoven with singing, gestures, dramatization and the crafting of materials (Ward and Wason-Elam 2005). Thus, early literacy in the library can be seen in relation to a broader trend in multimodality, or the blending of print, visual, audio, and gestural signs to create and interpret texts (Bearne 2009; Kress 2000b). This multimodal orientation to literacy was also seen in parents' borrowing habits for their children, with DVDs as often taken as books (Ward and Wason-Elam 2005.)

At the same time, these researchers noted that sessions for preschoolers reinforced traditional 'school-like' behaviors such as sitting on the floor and attending to the adult facilitator. They concluded that contemporary libraries are operating according to two discourses, the 'dominant/academic/hierarchical literacy model' and an alternative 'informal literacies [model] more closely allied to popular culture' (ibid., 206). For each of these models, they saw the library acting to create 'communities of practice' through modelling, supporting, and explicitly teaching to children and their carers the modes of participation. Children's activity sessions in the library brought both these communities of practice together, which can be seen to align libraries with the concept of 'edutainment', a hybrid combining formal education and popular culture entertainment, typical of commercial early learning resources (Buckingham and Scanlon 2001).

The design of library spaces is one of the ways in which different models or discourses of literacy are expressed and, by shaping behavior in libraries, constitute discursive practices. Traditionally, libraries order books, and thus spaces, in terms of a 'compartmentalised and hierarchical universe' (Manguel 2007, 138); numbering systems, straight lines, and rows produce ordered pathways through knowledge made material. However, the library has had to respond to market forces and to compete in the market for the consumers of texts. The 'aesthetics of libraries' have been borrowed by bookstores which began in the 90s 'including seating areas so that patrons could read books in comfort' even without purchase; libraries responded by redesigning their spaces to include cafes (Goodall 2003, 1).

The library has been called 'a paradox, a building set aside for an essentially private craft (reading) which . . . take[s] place communally' (Manguel 2007, 31). The 'private-in-public' nature of this space (Viseu et al. 2006) is itself a resource for families, enabling parents to do some of their parenting in an unobtrusively supportive communal environment. Homeless mothers have reported that in the library they can demonstrate values about literacy and education through guiding their book selection, sharing books, and modeling personal reading (MacGillivray, Ardell, and Curwen 2009). For these families in poverty, the chance to exercise choice and take books home offered some of the agency and experience of possession otherwise only available through commercial consumption.

In our project, the libraries in each region were significant resources for parents of young children. In this chapter, we look at how they related to their communities, how the information workers within libraries saw their role in resourcing parents of young children and the nature of the experience offered. We show how the geographic, social, and cultural context of communities impacted on libraries' resources, goals, and strategies. At the same time, libraries were being recruited into broader agendas regarding the socialization of young children.

GUMTREE MUNICIPAL LIBRARY: MAKING ROOM FOR PARENTS

The suburb of Midborough is dominated by Gumtree Plaza, but its library has the topological advantage. It occupies the high ground atop a hill, overlooking a large green expanse of park, downhill from which is the busy highway, and on the other side, Gumtree Plaza mall. Gumtree Library is in the service ring which runs right around the island of the mall. It occupies the ground floor of a large modern complex, above which are local government offices. A café with large windows offering a view of the park serves patrons and staff of both services and also provides a serving hatch into the library so that coffee can be consumed while reading or using the computer.

The library had two years previously appointed a Children's Officer with responsibility for all children's programs. This signaled an intention to take on a specifically educational role in the community. The Children's Officer was tasked with working collaboratively with local schools to integrate library-based activities into school curriculum and to have oversight of library activities for preschool children. Prior to this, the library's main service for parents of young children had been a weekly storytelling session. Now, in keeping with the general focus on the early years, the Children's Officer introduced a structured activity for infants—Baby Bounce and Rhyme. At the same time, Story Time was renovated to become more explicitly educational.

Baby Bounce was described by the chief librarian Megan as aimed at 'developing children's literacy skills, as well as the social interaction opportunities for new mums, as well as trying to build their confidence'. Baby Bounce, in common with similar library-hosted early learning sessions (see Mother Goose, above), comprised a sequence of nursery rhymes, accompanied with actions, interleaved with book readings. Infants and toddlers were seated on their carers' laps in a circle with the presenter on a low chair at the front and were assisted to accomplish actions such as clapping and waving. Presenters each week followed a sequence that had been programmed by the coordinator and was linked to a theme such as 'At the beach'. Books were selected with an ear to the sounds of language with rhyming, alliteration, and repetition common features. Narratives were simple with minimal character development and often episodic.

In just a few years, Baby Bounce at Gumtree had become extremely popular, and group sizes were at a maximum. Presenters began to complain about having to raise their voices to be heard. The Children's Librarian began to consider reducing the number of preschool story times to enable an increase in the number of Baby Bounce sessions. Baby Bounce was bringing unprecedented numbers of infants into the library and their prams were blocking aisles, impeding the access of older children to the children's section. This problem helped to prompt a major reorganization of space in the library in which the shelving was rearranged to create a wide path from the front desk to the children's section.

The Parenting Section

Another way in which Gumtree Library positioned itself as an important resource for parents of young children was also related to space. When we began observation, the parenting resources were located in the general nonfiction area. Parents with young children generally headed straight to the children's section on entry, a pathway which did not even take them past nonfiction. This had been noted by the librarians:

> They [parents] tend not to borrow books for themselves because when they're here with a child for Story Time, or the Baby Bounce, pushing a pram, and they're carrying a bag, and they're also trying to hang onto their kid at the same time, but they want to get some books, they're not going to wander over to the non-fiction shelves.

In response, the library management decided to move the parenting books from nonfiction to a dedicated section adjacent to the children's section and the toy library. At the same time, they released a generous allocation of funding to upgrade books in this section. Listening to the chief librarian explaining how selections were made, it was clear that the library was involved in considerable networking activity around this task:

> A person who has a particular interest in that area did some research, and spent a lot of time in the bookshops going through books [. . .] And we also get suggestions from parents as well, from people generally, and we try and purchase what they request, as well as being aware of what's coming out through publication magazines, and we get notified prior to their books being published through online selection that we do throughout the state.

The librarians told us that local parents preferred 'Australian-based' material. They made particular efforts to find titles which clearly signaled local content, such as *Having a Great Birth in Australia* (Vernon 2005) and *A Commonsense Guide for Australian Parents* (Fallows and Collier 2004) as well as those by well-known Australian authors such as Kaz Cooke (*Kid Wrangling: A Guide to Caring for 0–5s*, 2005). Materials sourced from the UK were considered more acceptable than those from the US, leading to a

Table 6.1   Top Five Categories of Parenting Resources in Gumtree Library

Category	No. of titles	Example book titles
Baby care	56	Your Happy Baby; What to Expect the First Year; Baby Gym: Brain and body gym for babies
Health and Nutrition	32	Positive Food for Kids; First Aid for Babies and Children; Natural Children's Health
Behaviour and Emotion Management	30	Nurturing Good Children Now; Parenting for Character; Ask Supernanny
Exceptional Children	21	Gifted Children; Understanding Children with Language Problems; The Everything Parents Guide to Children with Bipolar Disorder
Education/literacy	18	Smart Start for Your Baby; Parenting a Struggling Reader; You are Your Child's First Teacher; Baby Read-Aloud Basics

predominance of British parenting manuals. This policy, which was strikingly different from that adopted in the library's adult fiction section, perhaps reflects broader Australian fears about the Americanization of culture which manifests, for instance, in resistance to terms such as 'mom' rather than the Anglo-Australian 'mum' for mother (Bartlett and Gray 2009).

A fraction of the total parenting collection was on display at any one time. To get a sense of what was typically available to a parent with a few minutes to spare for browsing while their child was occupied in the children's section, we inventoried the displayed collection on one visit. There were 278 titles on display that day, mainly books, but also DVDs, videos, and CDs. There were also sets of three magazines: *Practically Parenting, Parents,* and *Mother & Baby.* As Table 6.1 shows, the largest number of displayed resources was in the category of baby care, followed by health and nutrition.

It is interesting that the third largest set of titles was in the category of behavior and emotion management, reflecting broader societal concerns about the perceived need for parent regulation of children (see Chapter 1). The category of exceptional children shows the library attempting to cater for the information requirements of parents whose children have special needs. Many of these titles had an educational focus with an emphasis on supporting children to successfully participate in school. There were also numbers of titles targeted to particular kinds of parents or carers including fathers, working mothers, grandparents, divorced parents and adoptive parents.

Across the collection, parents could find support for a range of parenting approaches from the directive to the laissez-faire. However, the notion of 'smart' babies and their necessarily 'smart' parents was a recurrent motif. Those wanting to take an interventionist approach to fostering early learning could conceivably resource a complete home-based curriculum from birth to school entry, perhaps beginning with *Baby Gym: Brain and Body Gym for Babies* ('26 physical movements that enhance learning and performance'), moving on to *The Very Best Games Ever: 365 Games Smart Toddlers Play* ('opportunities for you to teach, share and grow closer'), and continuing with *Tiny Talk* (a 'three-level communicative listening and speaking series for 3 to 6 year-olds').

The Gumtree Parent User

Olivia was a library regular. As well as bringing her son to Baby Bounce weekly, she used it as a place to spend time with him:

> It's my favourite place . . . we go there three times a week, especially because of the Civic Park, we go feed the ducks first and then we have a wander around the park and then go up to the library. We love it. . . . And then we do swimming on a Tuesday morning, and then other than that we do our own thing, don't we little man?

Olivia believed her son was benefiting from his regular participation in Baby Bounce; compared to children who rarely attended she judged he was 'a lot more confident and involved'. She also borrowed CDs and DVDs for his use at home, mentioning the Baby Einstein series and In the Night Garden. However, she did not make much use of the library's parenting resources, preferring to ask the women she worked with for advice:

> I'd ask a million questions, I used to bombard them, but like there's no one else to ask, is there?

When her work friends recommended books, she would buy them rather than borrow from the library. Examples she gave were books related to baby diet and nutrition.

As a part-time working mother in a dual-income family, Olivia had both time to use the free library resources and the income to purchase those goods she wanted to keep using. Her social network of workmates was a trusted source of advice and recommendations and, as her son was so far developing normally, she had not looked outside this circle for specialist knowledge. She viewed the world of information as open, 'I think everything is so easily accessible nowadays, especially with the Internet', and did not rely on library personnel for assistance with her information requirements.

Beverley had tried bringing her young daughter to Gumtree Library but didn't find it a rewarding experience:

> I did go to Baby Bounce once, that didn't really work that well. She didn't really want to sit still for that long.

This points to the fact that, even though the sessions were designed to be active, they still required a considerable degree of regulation of children's behavior. Beverley preferred to take her daughter to swimming lessons where the coach was in charge, and she could simply observe. She avoided the library even as a place to access books for children. Beverley sourced books through a commercial catalogue which was distributed through her daughter's child-care center. Looking at the catalogue together was an easy way of giving her daughter a say in selecting books as well as ensuring that there was sufficient variety in the home library. She was committed to a nightly routine of reading together:

> It's the one thing that we can do together, there's never any fights about it, so we'll sit for 40 minutes at night and have stories together, and that's fantastic.

Perhaps the reference to 'fights' is another clue as to the lack of appeal of Baby Bounce, an activity in which parent–child interactions were on public display. Certainly, our field notes record several instances of parents censoring and subtly excluding those whose children persistently misbehaved.

Beverley did not mention acquiring books for her own use. Rather, she described herself as responding to her daughter's desire: 'I buy a lot of books just because she does like them so much'. Beverley was currently studying for a trade certificate at a technical college. Students of these educational institutions have generally followed a nonacademic stream at high school so it may be that she herself was not a keen reader.

Midborough hub served a diverse population. Just down the road, the Salvation Army Centre offered employment, financial, and social support for clients in poverty, and further around the ring, the state welfare services had their district headquarters. It was not far to the neighboring suburb of Falcon Rise, where families lived in state welfare housing, and the highway was lined with pawn shops, bargain stores, and car yards. Yet Gumtree Library client records showed that few of its borrowers came from Falcon Rise or other nearby suburbs with similar demographics.

As, unlike other council districts, Gumtree did not have branch libraries, residents who wished to use a library had to travel to Midborough hub. For those without a car, or who needed to ration petrol use, public transport access was vital. The children's librarian acknowledged that the public transport option was not attractive to everyone:

> We are fortunate that public transport is reasonable in terms of its proximity to the busway. There can, as you would know, there can be some issues sometimes in people's heads around using some of that [. . .] Particularly with quite young children, people are reluctant to travel, or sometimes they're reluctant to travel distances.

The nearest bus station was actually on the other side of the large Gumtree Plaza mall meaning that most direct pathway to the library was through the mall and then across a six lane main road and up a steep hill. Thus those on low incomes who would benefit most from the free resources of the library had to manage their children's passage through a busy shopping center, filled with enticements for which they would have to pay, as well as the physical challenge of getting child, bags, and pram up the hill. Under the circumstances it would be understandable if they got no further than the mall.

Deepwater Library: Creating the New Third Space

Deepwater Library was among the first social institutions to service the small rural town. In the early years of white settlement, the library service took the form of a horseback rider with a saddlebag of books delivered from the nascent capital city. Once the townspeople had built their church, they established an institute on the main street to house a book collection and meeting room.

Balancing the costs of services with rates income is a constant challenge for local government serving scattered small communities. Added to this the demand for a technology upgrade of the library, the Council decided in the previous year to take the town's library collection out of the institute building and move it into the primary school to be colocated with the school collection. They reckoned without the clash of wills between school and town librarians. The town collection was crowded in much less space than before, and town librarians regularly complained about working conditions.

Eventually a new librarian, Ashleigh, was appointed to manage the town collection. With a professional background in a large regional center, she believed that a library should serve as an information hub. She found that the school and the town were united in their dissatisfaction with the current state of the library.

> They invited all the councillors over and they worked out quite good because the councillors were actually able to see what the library was. Our councillors, some of them, had never been into the library.

The Council was convinced to move the town library back to the main street and to spend their limited upgrade budget on the old institute building.

"We're not really library lovers."

The council members who had never been into the library were not alone. While the service was greatly appreciated by the keen readers in the community, another view prevailed that saw 'book learning' as different from, and less valuable than, practical know-how. The lack of a shared value for reading, and by extension libraries, was indicated by Belinda, a mother and one of the keen readers, feeling the need to explain her unusual orientation:

> I go to the library and I . . . but see I like to, you know, do the . . . I don't know, everyone is different, like some people say "Oh, you just go along and you just talk . . . hands-on experience is better than . . .", but I like reading books.

Practical know-how could only be learned through experience (or by tapping into the experience of others); by definition, it was an adult form of knowledge. Reading was seen as an unproductive activity, which could become appropriate on retirement; as evidence, most of the library's regular users were over the age of 60. Learning how to read was a task of childhood and the responsibility of school. Thus reading, for many in the community, was relegated to either side of a productive adult life.

These community values meant that the idea of 'early learning', as a task for parents to achieve with their children before school, had not really taken off here as it had in the suburbs. Parenting was, rather, seen as a matter of practical experience, quite different from the task of the schoolteacher, which was understood to require an academic background. In a similar way, children's minor ailments could be treated at home but, if serious, would be referred to a doctor. Indeed, health services were viewed as more useful for parents than any educational service, in which category the library was included.

Debbie was representative of Deepwater parents in this respect. Her reading of print material took the form of the local newspaper and pamphlets picked up at health services and shops. Debbie, speaking for her family, said 'We're not really library lovers'. Even the concept of a personal library was unappealing as she wryly implied, with reference to a commercial product:

> Once you have your baby, too, they somehow get hold of your address and they will send you stuff. "Here's *Cat in the Hat*. Let's start your library". So next thing you're inundated with all this *Cat in the Hat* stuff.

The only books that came into the house were others' presents for her children or school library books. On the other hand, Debbie loved digital products; she was always online and had bought both her young children their own Playstations. As a keen web surfer and pamphlet collector, Debbie might have been receptive to the idea of the library as an information hub, but to her it was just a building filled with books.

Parents and Children in the 'Third Space' Library

With a budget for upgrading, Ashleigh's priority was to make Deepwater relevant to the lives of residents. An important part of the mission was to bring a new generation of users into the library—parents with young children. This required changes to the library's environment and its collection. Ashleigh found that she was part of a more general transformational trend:

> I did do research to find out what the current trends are and libraries are, as you know, becoming more of a place for recreation. They're also becoming a third space people are using—it's not their workplace—it's not their home but it's another third place where they feel comfortable spending time. And also libraries are very much looking at the shop front type system.

The limited budget made upgrading a challenge; Ashleigh was relieved when a local organization donated a desk. The face-out shelves required by a 'shopfront' system were expensive and could accommodate fewer books than conventional shelves. However, the new parenting and health books which Ashleigh had purchased were highly visible and the new clear pamphlet holder located near the entrance improved access to information about services. The strategy was starting to work:

> New parents are definitely starting to come here asking for normal books and so on, on pregnancy and child birth and health related matters. [. . .] We're a logical place to come to and I actually think that word is spreading because I know I've had more enquiries about different parenting topics.

The 'country grapevine' (as one parent termed it) had begun to work in the library's favor. Parents were also combining their information searching strategies, using the library in conjunction with the Internet:

> They've been searching on the Internet themselves and they've decided that these are books related to parenting that they've wanted to borrow and, out of those, some of them actually have purchased.

New parents were also bringing in their baby's health records to get the free books that were distributed through the state wide Little Big Book Club scheme.

However, it seems that children were not so easy to accommodate in this 'third space'. There were no plans for a regular story time and, although [Kimberley] was aware of programs like Baby Bounce, she did not see it as a likely addition to local services. Her description of Baby Bounce emphasized its difference from the usual practices of interacting with library resources:

> It's more an active program I think, dancing, and still exposing them to books, but not the sit down listen to the story, yeah, a bit more action.

Too much action was not on the agenda. Children were still expected to behave in a sedate manner in the library. Interestingly, it was in relation to disciplining children that Ashleigh had forged a relationship with one father:

> We had one parent here, his two young boys were quite badly behaved in the library and I had to have a quiet word to him. And that was quite good because it got us into a discussion about [how] he would appreciate some help and I was able to show him what books we had.

Ashleigh preferred to connect with young children through occasional visits to playgroups such as Wave (see Chapter 5) where she would read a couple of storybooks. When it came to the library premises, the only kind of activity she could imagine for parents and children presupposed that the family was already engaged with literacy:

> It may be that we have a children's book group. I know that sounds really technical but maybe it's a time for parents to have a playgroup but with a story but also an opportunity for them to discus books that they've read to their kids.

Here Ashleigh was clearly improvising, trying to imagine a way of bringing children into the library, and to make reading the focus, but in a way that fit with her vision of the kind of 'third space' that adults like herself would want to spend time in.

GREYSTONE: THE LIBRARY AS POWERHOUSE

The university town of Greystone is bisected by two main roads coming together in a T-junction. On one side of the main shopping strip, with an imposing entrance opposite the junction, is Greystone University with its many stately buildings. The other main road bisects the town. The two largest nonuniversity buildings in town are located on one side of this long street; Greystone Library is one and Greystone Hospital the other.

Greystone Library is, in the words of its children's librarian, Patsy, 'a destination'. The modern building is designed in a contemporary neoclassical style with rows of three-story columns on the two street sides. The library is entered through a high light-filled lobby with a striking large artwork along one wall, and past a cafe, indistinguishable in style from a high street business. Patsy explained that the building was deliberately designed with a more commercial aesthetic than its smaller and more traditional predecessor:

> One of the concepts was to have it be more like Barnes and Noble— that was always put out there, that we were competing with the big box book stores, and so hence the café, hence the store that is now closed, hence the layout. . . . The first floor is very much laid out like a book store [more] than what you would traditionally think of as a library.

The library has a secure funding base from local taxes as well as being the recipient of many bequests. Its situation in a university town also enabled it to draw on the expertise and prestige of the academic community, both symbolically and practically. Patsy was aware that this placed it in an advantageous position relative to libraries in neighboring communities, including some that served disadvantaged populations:

> People like to be associated with success and affluence and stuff, so we get given books, and people want to come and do programs here and they either don't charge, or they charge less, because they want to have the name Greystone attached to it. So, it's ironic—they are much less likely to go to Smallton Public Library and offer their . . . (laughing) but in some ways Smallton needs it more, you could say.

Owing to its superior collections and facilities, the library attracted large numbers of visitors from neighboring communities. Patsy described the out-of-towners as suffering from 'library envy' because, as nonlocals, they had no borrowing rights. This was confirmed by one of our parent informants, Cassandra, who had recently moved from a housing estate to the Greystone township. She described her former local library as 'a lot less inviting and really small', although she had still used it as 'a place to go' with her young son 'especially in the winter when it's cold and dark and wet'. Even before the move, she was coming into Greystone purposively to access the library. Comparing the two libraries, she said:

> It's a bit akin to a one-room schoolhouse versus a multi-level vast new school that's been built. [. . .] I remember thinking, "I'm so thrilled that we're moving to a place where THIS is the library versus that other place that seems so rinky-dinky." . . . Maybe if there was nothing else around but to have that little, tiny place next to this incredible, nationally recognized library and it just seems to me that it's one of the best things about Greystone. That library means more to me than the University for me as a parent.

Cassandra's description explicitly frames the library as an educational institution and applies a set of values that privilege scale, modernity, and national standing. She has identified access to a superior library as a vital part of her parenting strategy to maximize advantage for her young son.

Early Learning at Greystone Library

The entire third floor of the library building was given over to the children's collection. It included reading areas, a toy library, a computer area, and a striking womb-like circular room, which was the setting for storytelling. The library ran a regular weekly Mother Goose session for babies and toddlers, as well as Story Time for preschoolers. In addition to on-site activities, the library also offered the Every Child Ready to Read program in outreach mode, at preschools, playgroups, and child-care centers.

Similar to Baby Bounce in Australia, the Mother Goose sessions interwove storytelling from books with nursery rhymes, sung with actions. Carers were expected to sing the rhymes and physically assist their young charges to do the actions, for instance by taking their hands and clapping them together. Patsy referred to brain science in explaining the benefit of these activities to young children's development:

> There is a full body of research that had used MRI's and PET scans that show what happens to a baby's brain when you sing to them, or talk to them or whatever, and it helped to confirm what we have always known that what we as librarians do in storytime from birth is we're getting children ready to read . . . we are preparing them, laying the ground work, in terms of their brain development, language development and so on.

The sessions kept to a snappy pace which seemed intended to prevent children from being distracted. However, this required much low-key coaxing and directing by the adult carers of the participating youngsters. Examples from field notes bear this out:

> Boy in front of me tries to get his mum to come up the front with him. This time she shakes her index finger at him to say no and points ahead to the librarian again.

> The grandma is now holding her grandchild on the floor trying to keep hold but the child is focussed on another baby.

Some adults faced an additional challenge. Between one-third and one-half of carers at any session were paid nannies, and many of these did not have English as a first language. Patsy explained that she had been asked to provide printed words to the songs so that these carers could have a chance to become familiar with them.

While the group was culturally diverse, it was not fully representative of the town's population. Patsy acknowledged that there had been scarcely ever any participation by African American families, saying, 'I hardly have black kids in the space'. Crossway Street bisected the town, not just geographically but along class and cultural lines; it was the recognized boundary of the long-standing African American neighborhood. While Greystone Library was not located far from any part of the compact town, crossing the street to use it was clearly more than just a matter of facing the traffic.

Educating Parent Teachers

Patsy believed that parents are not only a child's first teachers but could be the best teachers. In this she was drawing on personal commitment and history. A trained teacher, she had quit her job to homeschool her children, a role in which she had regularly used the facilities and resources of Greystone Library. While still a community user, she initiated a homeschooling discussion group which met at the library and was an effective platform for influencing the library's resourcing of homeschooling parents. It proved to be a career move for Patsy; she was approached by management to train as a librarian and had her educational costs paid. This in itself is strong evidence of Greystone Library's interest in the educating and educated parent client.

The homeschooling movement covers a range of orientations from progressive to conservative, as with orientations to parenting more generally. In the former camp, the 'unschoolers' adopt a child-centered, discovery learning approach in which direct teaching is discouraged (Holt and Farenga 2003); Patsy was of this persuasion. In the latter, parents are enjoined to use highly structured methods often with the rationale that schools are insufficiently rigorous. The Greystone parent resource collection covered the whole spectrum.

On the one hand, parents could pick up a book entitled *Ready to Learn: How to Help Your Preschooler Succeed* with an encouraging cover image showing a smiling mother helping her son to tie his shoelaces (Goldberg 2005). Inside they would be directed to 'teach children as young as two years skills that will ready them for kindergarten and the rest of their life' and provided with protocols and techniques such as 'model advance organizer statements' and 'multiple reinforcement schedule' (Goldberg ibid., xiii). They would be warned to follow the sequence and structure of the approach consistently: 'You can't do it by "leap-frogging" from one section to the next' (ibid.).

On the other hand, they might be attracted by the disturbing image of a small naked baby wearing a grey wig and floating in a black space on the cover of *Einstein Never Used Flashcards: How Our Children Really Learn and Why They Need to Play More and Memorize Less* (Hirsh-Pask, Golinkoff, and Eyer 2003). Here they will be informed that 'PLAY = LEARNING' and that they should take advantage of 'teachable moments' as they arise, resisting the temptation to 'push learning along at a rapid pace' (ibid., xvii).

Regardless of the theories of learning underlying these different arguments, one thing was consistent in the books found in Greystone's collections: the authors were all highly educated experts with prestigious academic credentials, and this was made clear in the first pages:

> Every suggestion in this book is based on my 25 years as a university professor, researcher, clinician, and parent. (Goldberg 2005, from Preface)

> The last 4 decades have witnessed an unparalleled burst of scientific study on infants and toddlers, and we have been privileged to be a part of this revolution with our colleagues around the world. (Hirsh-Pask, Golinkoff, and Eyer 2003, from Preface)

Having attained a postgraduate qualification was evidence, not only of specialist knowledge, but of the success of the author's own upbringing. In the introduction to *How Asian Parents Raise High Achievers and You Can Too,* the authors introduce themselves:

> Soo is a board-certified surgeon and an assistant professor at the University of Pennsylvania; Jane is an attorney and immigration specialist at The Children's hospital of Philadelphia. We are first-generation Korean-Americans . . . (Abboud and Kim 2006, 2)

These authors stress the importance of 'instilling a love of learning' from the earliest years ('early childhood is the best time to start') and warn of the consequences should parents fail to do so:

> Not surprisingly, years later these parents find themselves wondering why their son or daughter has no interest in going to college, much less to graduate school. (op. cit. 5).

Thus through its collection, as well as through its funding and location, Greystone Library allied itself with an educated elite. The ultimate goal of parenting for this community was for their children to take up positions as leading professionals and knowledge producers; the library was doing its best to ensure that the early years of children's lives set them on this trajectory.

LIBRARIES, DISCOURSES, AND NETWORKS

Libraries are clearly significant nodes in networks which relay information, resources, and practices through social worlds. The networking activities of libraries, and the individuals who work in and use them, forge connections with the networks of other institutions, collectivities, and individuals. While this is so in a more general sense, we are interested in how this operates in relation to the focal subject of early learning. What ideas and practices do libraries assist in mobilizing?

At the same time, to speak of 'the library' as a generic institution is to ignore the specificities of how libraries in particular geographic and social locations connect with local community networks and how the material affordances of the hardware (buildings, furniture) produce differences in libraries' resourcing capabilities.

Mother Goose as Neuroscientist

Libraries are appropriating elements of contemporary early learning discourse to position themselves as important providers of services to young children and their carers. In doing so, they are able to draw on their long-standing mission of literacy promotion in communities which has traditionally involved inculcating children into the culture of reading for pleasure through such practices as group story reading. However, libraries' move into the early years is a significant new development. While libraries publicly represent programs such as 'Baby Bounce' as a natural extension of their work, they have come about as a result of considerable lobbying and advocacy within the library profession. One such advocate wrote in a library journal:

> Babies are not welcome in theatres. They are not welcome in restaurants. And they are not welcome in libraries. [. . .] There seems to be a discrimination issue happening right before our eyes and no one seems to care. Let's call it underageism. (Oser 2006)

This advocate goes on to argue on the basis of neuroscience for libraries promoting literacy as part of infant care.

However, neuroscience alone does not rationalize libraries taking up an early learning mission. It seems important to libraries that their role as cultural custodians remains central. It could be argued that libraries are mobilizing 'brain science' in the service of an inherently conservative goal, to continue to circulate a canon of authorized early childhood texts—traditional rhymes and stories that have been on the reading lists of library story times for decades. 'Conservative' here is meant literally rather than pejoratively. In a retrospective argument, librarians are discovering that they had all along been practicing brain stimulation by conducting storytelling and sing-alongs with young children. This provides a modern and scientific rationale for the use of early childhood texts with which librarians are familiar and comfortable. Reflecting this, a review of *Every Child Ready to Read* kit (used by Greystone librarians in talks to community groups) recommends that librarians 'Rename some of the skills to be better aligned with current research' (Neuman and Celano 2010, online). Since librarians do not usually have an extensive training in child development, their adoption of neuroscience and cognitive psychology as theoretical bases for their work provides a more compelling legitimacy for their work.

An agenda of inculcating a new generation into the traditions and values of literate middle-class culture underlies the choice of traditional nursery rhymes as the centrepiece of early learning activities in libraries. This was made clear by a librarian in the pilot study of this project who said about the young parents in her community:

> They don't know the nursery rhymes, the stories that we all used to have in common like 'I'm a little teapot'. It's quite a challenge to ask young parents what nursery rhymes they know. We can help because we have got the books, we've also got CDs with traditional rhymes and modern rhymes. We've got books on parenting.

Parenting young children is presented as a practice of social conservation and libraries as the grandparents of the community, responsible for passing on cultural traditions which have been threatened by cultural diversity and globalization. Brain science brings an aura of modernity and legitimacy to this role.

Information Seeking as Parenting Work

All the libraries had recently prioritized upgrading resources on parenting and librarians expressed concern that these resources were accessible and valued by parent clients. Gumtree had moved the parenting collection next to the children's collection and had physically moved library furniture to facilitate access by pram-pushing parents; Deepwater had invested in face-out shelves and new parenting titles; Greystone had trained and employed a homeschooling parent to run its early childhood program. They were united in seeing reading about parenting as an essential part of being a successful parent and books as the source of solutions to the problems of parenting. Along with adolescence, the preschool years were seen as a time of confusion and worry for parents, when authoritative advice would be welcome.

In this emphasis, libraries were connecting with a broader discursive network that circulates the notion that parenting is knowledge work, with parents as lifelong learners. Human capital discourse, which sees the child as resource, positions the parent as resource for the child (Peers 2011). In order for children's potential to be maximized, society must ensure that parents have the knowledge and skills to support development across all domains—social, cognitive, and physical.

Taking advantage of libraries' parenting collections requires a certain level of literacy and, in the case of some of the more technical and scientific child development manuals, an advanced level of education. These parenting collections can be seen as the middle-class alternative to the pamphlet holder at a community health or welfare center, in the sense that they are take-away resources which aim to transform parenting practices in the home. Going to the library does not carry the stigma of sitting in a waiting room to see a social worker: the reverse, it signifies cultural capital.

At the same time, libraries along with other community information providers are fighting the challenge of an expanded digital universe of information which parents are accessing unmediated by information or other professionals. As one of the Deepwater fathers said when asked about the library, 'It's called the Internet these days' (see Chapter 1). Parents who are not 'book lovers', and do not identify with the library as a cultural institution, are nonetheless aligning themselves with the information move in parenting. While Google is becoming the ubiquitous entry point to information about everything, books remain the primary currency of libraries. Online catalogues operate as a means of identifying what is on the shelves. It appears that socializing children into storybook reading is accepted by a much wider demographic than parents' own reading of advice in book form.

Responding to Localized Cultures of Child-Rearing

Libraries' histories as community-based institutions made them sensitive to what was local. While broader social themes connected libraries' work, their approaches to resourcing parents played out differently in different contexts. At the same time, only some kinds of difference counted. For instance, breast-feeding is a cultural practice strongly promoted in some countries while downplayed in others. In Australia, the movement in support of breast-feeding is particularly strong, and so it was not surprising that the Gumtree librarians' commitment to Australian content was reflected in titles which promoted breast-feeding. This linked the library with other local initiatives supporting the practice. The nurse running the new mothers' group which met in a library meeting room was very keen to encourage women to breast-feed, and the Gumtree council supported breastfeeding with a promotional display in the library foyer.

In Greystone, the library was associated with prestigious local institutions, particularly the town's notable university. This university represents the height of American families' educational aspirations for their children. The themes of higher education and academic scholarship were prominent in the library's resources for parents, reinforcing the link between the literate culture of the library and the elite futures of the town's children. The local homeschooling movement created a demand for library resources that emphasized the parents' role in children's education. This may also have been intensified by the local phenomenon of a small, but larger than average, group of highly educated primary caregiving fathers. At the same time, fears about the dangers of parents' aspirations for children's healthy development found a place in the books on its shelves. The 'unschooling' movement, represented by librarian Patsy, operated in the contradictory space created by parent desires to control children's education together with a belief in children's unfettered development which would be harmed by institutionalised schooling. Greystone library played a significant role in supporting this movement through its parenting resources and training of a homeschooling parent.

Deepwater Library was reinventing itself to gain relevance with a new generation of townspeople. Recognizing the practical values of many rural families, its new librarian was emphasizing information provision, rather than promoting literary culture, as the key role of the library. This strategy seemed to be succeeding in bringing in young parents, including fathers. The local enthusiasm for the Internet was working in the library's favor as parents combined home-based web-searching with accessing the library to borrow resources already identified online. However, the discourse of early learning was not in the forefront here. This was partly due to the physical constraints of a space too small to easily accommodate mobile toddlers and babies in prams and partly because too few local parents had embraced the concept. Rather, many parents waited for their children to be taught to read at which point they were able to access their school library. The town librarian's policing of children's behavior also reinforced that the library was an institution for mature, well-regulated individuals.

Local cultural diversity was not strongly represented in any of the libraries. Resources in languages other than English were rarely seen except in Greystone's Spanish language materials and classes. The nannies of Greystone often did not speak English; yet the content of children's activities was not translated. Rather, these paid carers had to learn the songs and rhymes in English so as to participate. The immigrant families of Geraldine did not have access to a local library. The nearest outer-suburban library had a book bus which visited Geraldine fortnightly, but this service ceased during the time of our study. Deepwater was not too far to drive, if you had a car, but in practice Geraldine residents did not venture there. If they had, they would have found very few resources in their home languages and no bilingual staff. Gumtree Library accessed a local church program for African families (see Chapter 5) to provide an occasional guest speaker promoting the library's children's collection and activities such as Baby Bounce. The presence of African mothers in the library was evidenced by a sign, depicting a dark-skinned woman, and warning against changing children in any area but the toilets. This suggests a degree of discomfort with child-rearing practices different from the cultural norm.

The content of activities such as Baby Bounce and Mother Goose reflects a Western traditional culture of childhood. In some cases, librarians explicitly embraced a role in teaching a new generation this canon. However, the contemporary neuroscientific rationale enables this practice to be presented as culture-free. Brain science operates to universalize practices and draw attention away from their cultural specificity. Since every baby has a brain and stimulation is assumed to work in the same way for all, then the content of stories and rhymes is not questioned.

7   The Networked Discursive Field of Early Learning

Why is it that neither the multicultural women's group at the small country town of Geraldine or the church-run playgroup in the suburb of Midborough had heard of the Little Big Book Club? This campaign offering free books to encourage parents to read to babies and toddlers was promoted by all libraries in that state and supported by a leading newspaper and a child health service. Granted, the Geraldine group's members all spoke either Vietnamese or Khmer as a first language. Yet inside every Little Big Book Club bag was a DVD of songs and rhymes for children which included a Vietnamese language section. Perhaps the nearest library was not conveniently located? Maybe so for the rural women of Geraldine, but a large well-equipped library was located just across the road from the church playgroup. These are some of the questions which set us on our quest to investigate the circulation of knowledge and practice relating to young children's learning and development.

Resources used by families to support children's literacy are located in geographic space. Many of these spaces may seem quite obvious including schools and libraries; others are less so, such as doctors' waiting rooms and supermarkets. Even Internet access points (including wireless hotspots) are physically located. Based on their comparative study of four neighborhoods in terms of literacy opportunities for children and families, Neuman and Celano argued that 'learning and development cannot be considered apart from the individual's social environment, the ecological niche' (2001, 8). They recognized that this 'niche' incorporates a diversity of public and private spaces with greater and lesser constraints on participation.

In this book, we have taken readers to three different neighborhoods across two countries and, in each of these neighborhoods, into four kinds of spaces. We have referred to these spaces generically as 'the mall', 'the clinic', 'the library', and 'the church' in order to highlight how commercial, medical, literary, and religious institutions are offering particular kinds of opportunities to parents of young children. Encompassed by these generic terms have been a diversity of actual sites from the roadside gas station (a major commercial site for one country town) to the mega concentration of commercial outlets that is Gumtree Plaza; from the three-story library in the US university town of Greystone to the mobile book bus serving the Australian rural fringe in which the town of Geraldine is located.

Virtual places, in the form of online sites, have also been included in our investigation of locations for early learning resources. We have found that our generic typology of mall, clinic, library, and church can be extended to the virtual realm. We have described how institutions offering early learning resources are moving online and taking institutional agendas and discourses along in the process. At the same time, differences are appearing between on- and off-line manifestations of these places, with consequences for the participation of young children and their parents.

This chapter brings together what was learned from an examination of each of these kinds of spaces into an overarching description of the complex contemporary landscape within which circulates knowledge and practice about children's early learning. First, however, we return to some key ideas which have shaped our analysis to remind readers of the ways in which these have been defined and mobilized.

IRONING OUT TERMS

A *semiotic view* has informed our analysis, meaning that we understand early learning in terms of practices inclusive of a range of modalities rather than as being limited to the reading and writing of print texts (Cope and Kalantzis 2000). This inclusive view is particularly relevant in early childhood where a child's first understandings of communication are formed through interactions using oral language, sound, movement, and visual images (Hill and Nichols 2006: Lawhon and Cobb 2002; Trushell 1998). It follows that we define parental beliefs and practices relating to their children's early learning inclusively, as well as the resources parents use to undertake these practices. Texts, objects, and practices which purport to foster young children's development in ways which impact on their learning (whether or not these claims can be substantiated)—including books, toys, websites, magazines, TV programs, playgroups, diets, speech assessments, behavioral training—all have been encompassed in this study.

Networks and networking thread arguments in the book as concepts that signal an active seeking out of information through a variety of sources that can be tied to local spaces, their resources, and affordances as well as being tied to global spaces and their flows of information online and further afield (Law 2003; Sheller and Urry 2006). Massey's idea of the 'activity space' as 'the spatial network of links and activities, of spatial connections and of locations, within which a particular agent operates' (2000, 54) has underpinned how we understand players in the field of early learning connecting with institutions, with each other and with families. The terms 'network' and 'networking' elucidate a simultaneous movement and convergence of ideas and discourses in parental practices. We found that parents move physically and virtually into and out of a range of places in their local neighborhoods, and also travel further afield outside the region and into cyberspace in order to access the resources they seek. Parents themselves, as well as the available conceptual and material resources, are at one and the same time located *in place*, and also *mobile, connected,* and *networked* across local and global spaces or contexts.

Discourse, as a term and concept, recurs in the book to describe ways of representing elements of the physical, social, and psychological world of children's early learning and development. Discourse theory has always been concerned with the circulation of ideas; Foucault explains that every statement is part of 'an enunciative network that extends beyond it' (1969, 99). To trace the circulation of ideas about early learning we have brought the concept of a discursive network to the analysis of texts and artifacts collected in the diverse spaces into which we have ventured (Nichols 2006). Geosemiotics has contributed the notion of *discourses in place* (Scollon and Scollon 2003). Taking this perspective has enabled us to see how discourses of early learning are contextualized in particular spaces, and recontextualized as they move through different local spaces—our three neighborhoods and four kinds of sites. Specific discursive formations have been identified by bringing together clusters of definitions, prescriptions, problem statements, implications, and recommendations that cohere around particular views of the young child as learner. Examples of significant formations are the 'baby literacy' and the 'edutainment' discourses of early learning (Buckingham and Scanlon 2001).

The concept of *capital* acknowledges that the field of early learning, as with education more generally, is also a marketplace and that the goods it provides can only be acquired through exchange (Reay 1998). Families' material and sociocultural resources—their capital—influence not only what they can afford to acquire and their access to these goods but also what they understand as significant to resourcing children's early learning (Holloway 1998). Economic capital plays a major part in families' locations, and we have seen that this in turn impacts heavily on their awareness of, and ability to enter, places in which recognized early learning resources are to be found. In our study, the interplay of families' economic, social, and cultural capital with the structure of the early learning marketplace has been made evident. For example, Midborough municipal council has been influenced by the location of the massive Gumtree Plaza mall to create a corporate headquarters adjacent to this hub, incorporating a large library building. The decision not to provide neighborhood branches, together with the difficulty of reaching the library on public transport, can help to explain the absence of residents of the poor neighborhood Falcon Rise on the library's borrowing register.

By mobilizing these concepts, we have developed detailed analyses of the production and circulation of discourses and practices of early learning through domestic, commercial, and civic spaces. The specific character that early learning takes in the four zones of mall, clinic, library, and church has been the subject of the preceding chapters. Through the book, we have analyzed a wide range of texts associated with the key sites of the clinic, the church, the mall, and the library. These texts have included pamphlets, magazines, books, signage, packaging, and websites. We have examined how participants in each of the four sites speak about subjects such as 'early learning', 'reading to babies', and 'language development' both during interviews and in the course of observed activities. We have also considered how participants respond to the texts and associated activities produced by the various agencies which operate in the sites. Here, we move between these zones, and through places, texts, artifacts, and narratives to draw out important features of the discursive landscape of early learning and consider their implications.

THE NETWORKED DISCURSIVE FIELD OF EARLY LEARNING

The field of early learning is one in which networking is both officially sanctioned and promoted and at the same time informal and opportunistic. Official support for networking between players has come through the notion of partnership, applying to both public–private and interagency relationships of service provision (Seddon et al. 2005). As Song and Miskel (2005) have noted in relation to the formation of literacy policies and programs, the field is no longer dominated by state education departments but is characterized by both proliferation and diversity. To some extent, the preschool years have always been characterized by this diversity; it has represented a chance for the shaping of a young citizen before the dominant institution of schooling begins its socializing work. The churches, charities, and community movements we have included in the landscape have, in many cases, long histories of provision. The reemergence of the notion of 'holistic' provision of early childhood services (Haddad 2001) has encouraged recognition of the role of community-based organizations while at the same time, in many cases, drawing them into expanding networks.

Digital technology and networking plays many roles in creating various affordances and opportunities for major, and also minor, players in the field of early learning. We have seen that parents can assume roles as cultural producers, commentators, and commercial operators. By linking to existing networks, some of these entrepreneurial individuals then become co-opted by larger entities to support their programs and enterprises. At the same time, both public and private service providers are actively recruiting parents to their networks, either to provide support for young children's learning and development or, while promising to do so, simultaneously selling them something different.

However, while the players and games are proliferating, the types of knowledge and practice being circulated are far less diverse. From the recurrences of particular ideas about childhood, education, literacy, and parents' roles through texts and images encountered in very many contexts and sites, both local and virtual, we can see that recycling is a key process within the discursive field. The efficiency of networking technologies just makes these ideas more ubiquitous.

The idea that children move through discrete stages crosses into nearly every discourse of childhood and is appropriated by a wide range of players promoting a very diverse array of goods and services to parents and carers. Its appeal can be understood in relation to the notion that, for each stage of childhood, there are developmental tasks that need to be supported through the provision of appropriate experiences and resources. Thinking back to our four common sites—the mall, the church, the library, and the clinic—each one has some form of gate-keeping of stages of development (to greater and lesser degrees). Pediatric clinics, for instance, monitor key stages of development and intervene when there are signs of delay in certain areas.

While past analyses have identified the existence of a singular 'developmental discourse' (Howley et al. 1999; Walkerdine 1984), what we are seeing is that the idea of stages of childhood has broken free from its home in developmental psychology and is no longer inextricably linked to its theoretical origins. The core of the idea—the series of stages—is always present. However, how the stages are defined, and the advice as to what parents should be doing at various stages, varies greatly from context to context.

As with so much mediated cultural production (Zengotta 2005), advice and information on stages of development has been defined and remixed into different forms or genres. The Internet, for instance, offers architectures of participation (Sheridan and Rowsell 2010) for charting a child's developmental stage. Numerous parent participants talked about receiving regular updates on their child's development from chat rooms, online communities, and listservs that distribute automatic updates on each stage of development. Books and parent magazines also chart stages of development and yardsticks. From our analysis, the signifier 'stages of childhood' may be considered a kind of 'immutable mobile' (Latour 1987a), that is, a formation that holds its shape as it circulates. To do this successfully, it needs to be stripped of much that previously anchored it in a particular theoretical location.

We have looked at discursive flows in commercial spaces and how these flows circulate. In commercial chains such as Toys R Us and Kmart, we interpreted how and when commercial providers take up cognitive models and theories of development. An example is Toys R Us taking up multiple intelligence as a guiding principle for differentiating their product lines. Through some triangulation, we interpreted texts disseminated by Toys R Us in which they connect multiple intelligences and different learning styles such as visual or kinesthetic learners with specific lines in their preschool interactive products. We then observed Toys R Us retail spaces for patterns and process with these product lines and attended to parents' references to product lines such as Leapfrog vis à vis their role in their children's development. Such textured, braided research has offered us a multifocal perspective of the discursive landscape, connecting texts, artifacts, practices, and spaces.

The 'Baby Literacy' Discourse

Emerging as the new central character in current story lines of early literacy is the infant/toddler as the ideal subject for the literacy work of carers. The discursive formation which we have termed 'baby literacy' draws from available discourses of infant development weaving these threads with liberal humanist notions of reading for pleasure. Sponsorship of major social institutions and/or powerful and charismatic figureheads is necessary for any discourse to go mainstream (Brandt 1998). The involvement of government health providers in the promotion of reading to infants has been a key mechanism in the universalizing of the 'baby literacy' discourse. The resources available to these services include a large trained workforce, access to parents from before their infants are born, a well-established and growing digital information system, and political support for health promotion. These resources are powerful enablers for the process of circulating knowledge and practice. The embrace of partnership models of service provision by many governments (Malin and Morrow 2007; Seddon et al. 2005) means that health services are also allying with other agents to extend the networks through which the 'baby literacy' discourse can circulate. A case in point is the Little Big Book Club program in which a child health service partners with municipal libraries and commercial publishers (see Chapter 4).

A key feature of the 'baby literacy' discourse, as it is mobilized by health services and their allies, is its employment of theories of infant development to provide both a rationale for and a process by which babies can be engaged in reading. The concept of attachment, drawing new support from interpretations of medical research findings, has reemerged as central to current views of healthy infant development (Hertzman and Boyce 2010). Reading to babies is being promoted as a bonding process, claimed to enable the child to form a secure attachment with the parent (Bus and IJvendoorn 1995). The practice is depicted as bringing carer and child physically together through their shared gaze on the book.

In the 'baby literacy' discourse, parents are positioned not just as the mediators of literacy for their very young children but as educable subjects. Explicit advice on how to manage a proper reading session with a baby or toddler has been a feature of multiple events we have witnessed and texts we have collected including Baby Bounce library sessions, articles in parenting magazines, downloadable fact sheets, parenting courses run by health services, and in the wording of stories written to be read to infants (e.g., Linke 2006). This advice also explicitly or implicitly identifies wrong practices such as choosing books that fail to attract babies' attention, using a dull speaking voice, and holding the child too tightly or not tightly enough. In this, 'baby literacy' is like attachment itself—a social program that gains power from representing itself as natural (Rose 1990; Tyler 1993). At the same time as the practice is often referred to as 'simple', this level of specification suggests that it cannot be left to chance. Pulling this discourse into tension is an additional thread, seldom explicitly named. The institution of schooling, where the present infant will one day be located, makes formal assessment the test and means of comparison of literacy performance. This thread could be called 'failure'.

In a contemporary twist, fathers are being brought under the umbrella of care provider rather than being positioned as backstage support workers. Once, visual images of reading to children mainly featured a mother and a child. In our data set the happy threesome of two parents, a child, and a book was commonly seen, and even images of a father and child without mother were not unusual. The 'baby literacy' discourse is in this respect part of a broader discourse of shared parenting associated with the promotion of father involvement and the extension of the notion of attachment to the male parent (Brookes 2002; King 2001). The promotion of father involvement overall, and particularly in literacy, is linked to concerns about boys' educational underperformance relative to girls (Hodgetts 2008). Theories of role modeling as the means of socialization, promoted in books popular with many parents in this study, underlie the claim that the positive participation of male role models is vital to boys' healthy development (Odih 2002). In the promotion of fathers as key figures in 'baby literacy' practices, literacy and health agendas align through a shared view of causes and solutions to problems in boys' development.

The 'Edutainment' Discourse

Another discursive formation which we have traced through our data is the 'edutainment' discourse. In delineating the features of this discursive formation, we have drawn on the work of analysts of the commercial culture of early childhood (Beder 2009; Luke 1996; MacNaughton and Hughes 2005; Seiter 1995). Following Buckingham and Scanlon (2001) we have defined 'edutainment' as a hybrid construct bringing notions of 'learning' and 'fun' into an indissoluble partnership promoted as essential for young children's development and understood to be facilitated by the child's interaction with material and, increasingly, virtual objects. Psychological theories of child development which emphasize the importance of 'stimulation' and the child's manipulation of objects as a means of learning about the properties of the world have been mobilized in support of the 'edutainment' program (Seiter 1995).

Our survey of multiple sites, objects, and texts has demonstrated that this discourse continues to have primacy in the landscape of early childhood.

The idea of early learning as fun finds its most obvious physical location in the aisles stacked high with boxes portraying infants and toddlers holding, pressing, pushing, and gazing at primary colored plastic objects. Baby computers are represented in a similar way to the old mechanical activity boards; similar text describes the fun-learning benefits and specific skills claimed to result such as coordination, alphabet recognition, etc. Through our geosemiotic analysis of commercial sites, we have come to similar conclusions as those made nearly two decades ago. Supermarket aisles and warehouse toy stores are indeed 'a spatial representation of the rules and boundaries of childhood socialization' (Seiter 1995, 208).

The notion of child–carer attachment is muted or absent from texts promoting edutainment. While it is implied that purchasing edutainment objects or online experiences is an act of care on the part of the parent consumer, portrayals of the child with the object frequently leave out not only the parent figure but the domestic environment. If shown at all, parents are onlookers enjoying their child's absorption in the object-mediated play experience. Unlike the case of the 'baby literacy' discourse, the parent's mediation of the practice is not represented as essential or integral.

Another way in which the 'edutainment' discursive formation differs from the 'baby literacy' discourse is in the dynamic and malleable nature of the objects that are presented as the focus of practice. In depictions of carers reading to babies, the object is a conventional book which is held open and still in the conventional manner. Depictions of toy objects on the other hand, show them as mobile, multisensory, and designed to be used by a child without adult mediation. To complicate matters, these characteristics were also found in book objects. Some books for babies and toddlers may have wheels for pushing along; they may have hooters or buzzers to make sound effects; they may light up or glow in the dark for visual effect. We argue that such book objects actually have meaning within a different discourse from the conventional books which feature in portrayals of shared family reading. They are promoted for the child to use in play potentially without adult mediation; they show the 'edutainment' discourse interweaving with the 'baby literacy' discourse in ways that may subvert the attachment message.

CIVIC AND COMMERCIAL SPACES AND RESOURCES

The importance, and the problematic nature, of the distinction between 'civic' and 'commercial' players and networks in resourcing early learning is a key theme of this study. Outside the domestic spaces of the home, the *civic* spaces of the community library and health clinic (Australia) and hospital or pediatric clinic (United States), and the *commercial* spaces of the shopping mall as a whole—as well as its specific sites such as department stores, bookshops, and toy stores—are significant locations in the early learning landscape. They are zones of resource production and distribution and of encounter between parents and ideas and resources for supporting their children's early learning.

One of the key distinctions between the civic and commercial modes of operation is that the public service mission of civic institutions requires them to provide services at low or no cost to citizens. Rates and taxes provide the revenue which is then redistributed via services. These services potentially provide a vital resource base for families with limited economic capital. Thus it is truly disturbing that services offered free or for low cost by civic organizations were, we found, generally *not* as easy to access as commercially produced and distributed resources. There were several reasons for this. Each region had relatively higher numbers of commercial outlets than civic outlets, and civic organizations were often located in areas that were physically harder for parents to reach, especially when accompanied by small children. In addition, commercial outlets (e.g., shopping malls owned by global companies) often had in place regulations that restricted the display and circulation of 'community' notices, pamphlets, and other information about available resources.

Civic organizations are aware that they are in competition with commercial entities to reach parents with their preferred messages about young children's learning and development. That is evident not just in the ways that civic workers refer to commercial products and services (such as a Play Coordinator shuddering at the influence of *Super Nanny*) but in the redevelopment of civic spaces to mirror the affordances and aesthetic of commercial spaces. Civic institutions are also adopting marketing techniques from the commercial world. For their part, commercially owned organizations claim to provide environments that support public life (the mall as town square) and goods and services that enable people's health and well-being. However, the case of the 'disappearing information booth' (see Chapter 3) demonstrates that civic motives are actually seen as a threat by commercial operations. Gumtree Plaza, despite offering a vast and diverse array of shops and some leisure activities, could never be considered a 'one-stop shop' for early childhood resources since it was in competition, not partnership, with local civic services.

To complicate matters further, some institutions that were once fully public have split their operations into civic and commercial branches. This blurring of the commercial and the civic is a feature of neoliberal societies in which governments look to private–public partnerships to fund institutions such as hospitals and schools that were formerly understood as existing to serve the common good. This is the case with government media corporations such as the BBC (Scanlon and Buckingham 2004). The ABC Shop in Gumtree Plaza, and its online equivalent, has no evident civic service function. Indeed, our researcher was unable to gain any advice or support from shop staff when inquiring into its early literacy program Reading Eggs.

In some locations, both kinds of resources and services were limited. In some cases, this was a matter of distance from a major commercial and civic center, as with the two small Australian country towns, Deepwater and Geraldine. In rural areas, services are often managing with infrastructure developed in the first period of civic growth, when local populations had become established to the extent that capital and resources were available to build local institutions such as churches and schools. In Deepwater, the library was housed in an old institute building, and its small size limited the kinds of uses to which it could be put. In Geraldine, there was not even this level of infrastructure since the area had been late to develop this kind of concentrated civic capital. Successive waves of migrants had invested in their agricultural holdings, eventually attracting rural industries and grocery stores to set up shop along the main street. These ethnic communities also networked outside of their local area in order to develop sufficient human and economic capital to eventually build important institutions such as churches and temples at locations reasonably convenient to their dispersed groups. Strikingly, it was the town's agricultural significance that eventually attracted some social resourcing from outside in the form of a community worker employed by a government department whose main mission was agriculture. Even then, only a major flood had alerted these authorities to the problem of communicating civic information to a multiethnic population, many of whose members had experienced restrictions to their education owing to poverty or war in their first homelands. This individual became an important language and literacy sponsor for this community.

In some places, the relative impoverishment of resourcing was less visible. The continuous nature of suburban hinterlands to major cities, spreading out along main roads, makes differences less immediately apparent. While Falcon Rise was only a few kilometers from Gumtree Plaza, this area of low-cost subsidized housing was mainly home to families on welfare, many of whom could not afford to run a car. The main arterial road was always very busy and represented a serious risk and obstacle to pedestrian access. Local low-rents shops did not include a well-stocked newsagent, let alone a bookstore, although second-hand children's books could be found at local charity shops. If these residents had wanted to access the Gumtree Municipal Library, not only would they have to get themselves, their children, and their bags and prams onto a bus but, after alighting at Gumtree Plaza, they would then have to navigate a vast shopping mall car park and a major highway to reach the library on foot. Meanwhile, in the US, even owning a car would not entitle a resident of a neighboring housing estate to access the very well-stocked Greystone Library, leading one of our participants to use the term 'library envy', half jokingly explaining her decision to relocate to the town proper.

From another perspective, one can look at a particular kind of resource in terms of its availability in different geographic and institutional contexts. Parenting magazines are an interesting case. These magazines are an established means of promoting ideas about child development and how this should be resourced through parents' provision of suitable opportunities to young children (Seiter 1995). Since they are produced by corporate publishing houses and sold in commercial outlets, they may be considered a commercial resource which requires parents' financial capital to possess. However, library managers may choose to stock parenting magazines within their collections and make these available to the community, thus transforming them into a civic resource. Magazines can be also be accessed through social networks as long as at least one member has the financial capital to purchase the resource (borrowing restrictions make it less likely that library stocks will be shared in this way).

Of all our sites and places, the two newsagents at Gumtree Plaza together carried the largest range of parenting magazine titles. Browsing of these titles was well tolerated by vendors. Across the road, the Gumtree Council Library also stocked many of these titles and offered them for borrowing free. In theory, poverty should not prevent Midborough parents from accessing the ideas about child development and parenting promoted through these texts. However, we know that residents of the poorer parts of Midborough, such as Falcon Rise, were not on the library register. Meanwhile in Greystone, the high street newsagent showed a couple of parenting magazines in a glassed-in counter display, but none were available for browsing or immediate sale. Customers had to subscribe to a title in order to purchase. Around the corner at the impressively well-stocked Greystone Library, just one parenting magazine title was available for borrowing. In this affluent university town, if you did not have money for purchasing parenting magazines, accessing them was difficult. Back in Deepwater, the local grocery store stocked many titles of interest to local people including magazines devoted to craft, animal husbandry, and motor sports. To buy a parenting magazine however, you would need to drive 20 kilometers to the nearest suburban mall. The tiny local library did not have space to stock them.

Exposure is a factor in the creation of demand for products. Seeing parenting magazines displayed at local shops, on the shelves of libraries, and in the houses of friends makes it more likely that one will see these objects as part of shared culture and thus desirable. Residents of Midborough traveling through both commercial and civic spaces designed for parents and young children had lots of opportunities to be exposed to these products. Those with the cultural capital to understand the role of a library did not even have to pay for their use; they could read the library's magazines for free while having a coffee at the library's café. The library's position of actively engaging in competition with the nearby commercial hub created this opportunity. In Greystone, however, just walking through the civic and commercial spaces did not provide this kind of exposure to parenting magazines. Thus, parents had to be much more insiders of an educated literate culture to know of the existence of these products and how to access them.

Parents Crossing Discourses, Spaces, and Networks

Our research has involved a wide range of participants whose social locations include working-class, middle-class and affluent upper-middle-class parents as well as Black, White, established, and immigrant families. There are families that proudly call themselves 'country people', those who are metropolitan types, and others very much at home in the sprawling suburbs. Predictably and in support of other research, there are indeed geographies of opportunity (Harwood 2007) that permit greater affordances for families related to location and capital. These play out differently according to regional and sociocultural context. In our North American site, social geographies charted racialized zones with a particular town street marking the border between the African American and White American neighborhoods. The affordances of the community center in which supplementary literacy and educational activities were held in old-fashioned classroom type spaces contrasted sharply with the spacious internal areas, contemporary fittings, and large collections of the downtown library. The Greystone children's librarian spoke in a muted tactful way about the difficulties posed by certain kinds of children treating the library like a playground and their solution of employing male security wardens. Meanwhile on the Black side of 'Deverington Street', a sign in the playground listed all the kinds of behavior that would be subject to disciplinary action.

Parents living in and near Deepwater, the small Australian country town, didn't mention attending any story reading sessions at their local library. The local librarian explained there was no room in their tiny historic institute building to host a group of children while still providing services to other clients. The mobile library bus turned round just a few kilometers down the road because Deepwater was not in the council district of Northborough. Meanwhile, a few kilometers away in Geraldine, home to successive generations of migrant agricultural workers, many parents were either working in the gardens until sundown or out of town at other jobs, leaving young children in the care of their grandparents. Attendees at the kindergarten playgroup were mainly English speaking, and very little information about children's education or parenting was provided in home languages.

Thus while it would be reasonable to say that parents *in general* are inundated with information and networking opportunities in relation to their young children's learning and development, it is important to acknowledge variations and continuing inequities in degrees of choice, awareness, and access. For working-class families, there were more *institutionally mandated* models of what constitutes good parenting and meeting literacy needs provided by government agencies with specific agendas to target problematic populations, whereas middle-class parents had access to a greater range of providers and discourses.

At times in the project, researchers intervened into these geographies of opportunity, becoming part of the networks of resourcing for families. This was the case in Geraldine, where an introduction to an agricultural project coordinator provided an opportunity to meet with a group of local Southeast Asian community members. As the agricultural project had funded an interpreter, communication was facilitated, and the topic of children's early learning and literacy development was discussed with these mainly older women (and two grandfathers). On finding that the community members did not recognize the Little Big Book Club logo or bag and so were not aware of the Vietnamese language resources available for free, the researcher undertook to investigate options for providing the group with the resources. She approached the librarian at Gumtree Municipal Library in Midborough who kindly handed over a dozen bags complete with books and CD ROM. Additionally, a university librarian recommended children's books with minimal text and rich illustrations. Bearing these materials, the researcher met again with the community group who showed great interest, particularly in the idea of telling stories in first language while showing picture books to children.

From the perspective of parents whose access to information and resources is not greatly restricted by economic, cultural, or linguistic capital, or by geographic location, there is potentially a bewildering amount and variety of information, advice, and materials to sift through in their attempts to foster a child's development. While parents face what can seem a formless cloud of information (Johnson-Eilola 1997) we have found that they find paths through this terrain by actively mediating the ideas they encounter with their own personal experiences. Parents venture into a range of local and global, digital and real spaces and places to find information and these resources to meet their child's particular needs, often at the same time encountering service and information providers' views of what children require for optimal learning and development. The sheer amount of information, and differential access to information, makes forging parental identities complicated and at times fraught with tensions. Across these social networks and informational hubs, parents cobble together an identity of a concerned and 'good' parent (Nichols, Nixon, and Rowsell 2009). Given the pervasiveness of social pressures on parents to produce their young children as happy now and successful in the future, together with the complexities of families' lives, it is not surprising that parents draw on a diversity of resources and information in their repertoire of parenting practices.

As previously pointed out, this rapid and dynamic proliferation of networks, and the texts and artifacts circulating through them, has enabled the recycling and redistribution of a limited number of discourses of childhood, parenting, and literacy. So while there may appear to be endless choice and variety, it is still possible to discover that the specific needs of the family or the child are not addressed, particularly by mainstream agencies, propelling some parents into adopting the role of 'detective' to seek out hidden networks. Triggers evident from parents' stories included having a child with some kind of exceptionality (such as Asperger's Syndrome or giftedness) or committing to an exceptional kind of parenting practice (such as a monolingual mother raising her child to be fluently multilingual). These triggers powerfully influence how parents shape their philosophy and practices of parenting for early learning. Some of these parents whose networking has been prompted by imposed or embraced exceptionality become information brokers and even 'sponsors of literacy' (Brandt 2001) of a particular kind, in their own right.

Parents are also the shapers of young children's spaces, and our geo-semiotic analysis revealed the significance of domestic spaces in parents' designs for their children's early learning. Spaces in the home designated for literacy and learning became a theme across interviews and home visits in the two suburban communities of Greystone and Midborough. Parents also arranged for resources to come to their homes from elsewhere, either bringing these back from their travels to local neighborhoods and further afield or by using the Internet to access and order materials. Many parent participants talked about children's development in terms of maximizing time and space for this to occur, taking into account the many other demands on their availability. Fostering independent learning in the home, using 'edutainment' type resources enabled mothers and at-home fathers to fulfill domestic and professional tasks, while at the same time setting their mind at ease that their child was learning. This mode of educational supervision could also be extended to the mobile space of the car. Whether it was putting on an educational DVD while driving to activities or having children read a text while watching Dora the Explorer, suburban parents consistently attempted to make the most of child-care windows for development.

Perhaps a lynchpin to the diverse, eclectic landscape of early childhood information stand personal stories and lived histories which differentiate one parent's story from another. Through analyzing these stories we have seen that parenting habituses take shape from a mixture of dispositions carried from their own childhoods and experiences of being parented as much as they do from dominant discourses of childhood and education. For instance, the dominance of the notion of normative stages of development means there is capital in having a child ahead of the curve, and conversely, there is judgment when a child's growth departs from norms. These subtle and subjective experiences of parenting draw out tensions that arose in our data, and these tensions show how powerful a dominant, almost autonomous model of a 'good' parenting can be for participants in our study. As a result, as important as it has been to analyze corporate, community-based, religious, online networks, so too is it important to acknowledge the role of parent habitus and personal stories and histories to explain their parenting philosophy in relation to children's early learning.

AN ACTOR-NETWORK APPROACH TO RESEARCHING
AND RESOURCING EARLY LEARNING

In this study we set out to track diverse pathways which we could imagine parents taking in their search for advice, assistance, and resources to support their young children's early learning in the preschool years. We drew boundaries around three geographic regions and within each physically drove and walked, looking at signs and noticeboards, entering shops, taking away pamphlets, photographing displays, speaking with nurses, librarians, pastors, and many others. We joined playgroups, sat in on story reading sessions, rode a mobile library bus, and attended new mothers' classes. We considered the ways in which material spaces signified connections with virtual spaces, noting Internet access points and recording URLs seen in signs, packaging, and handouts. Mothers, fathers, grandparents, and community workers spoke to us about the resources they sought, used, and passed on and where they found them. They told us about connections with family and friends locally and further afield and the ideas and practices which circulated through their social networks. We went to many of the places they told us about which often took us outside of our original geographic boundaries or into cyberspace.

While we began with tentative notions of the applicability of actor-network theory to our field of study, this three-year process of investigation and analysis has left us with a much firmer view of its value. Importantly, a network orientation is *inclusive*. All nodes in a network count; all pathways are a means for the passage of knowledge and practice. Taking this perspective led us to appreciate the roles of often overlooked early learning sponsors such as local church groups and community organizations. An actor-network is also inclusive of the material and virtual, the human and nonhuman (Murdoch 1998). This approach encouraged us to attend to every kind of thing that might be circulating through networks. As literacy researchers, we were used to analyzing texts, talk, and certain kinds of practice. Actor-network theory encouraged us to pay close attention to material things, such as the book objects that traveled in and out of shops, libraries, and homes, as well as to immaterial things such as discourses which constructed certain kinds of practice as proper.

Relatedly, actor-network theory is inclusive of every kind of networking process (Law 1999). Networking has generally been considered in terms of either face-to-face social connections or digital information linkages. However, when material things are included in a consideration of what is circulating, we then need to consider physical modes of circulation such as public transport and postal networks. When we walked through, or imagined, pathways to physically access particular places where resources could be found, we were engaged in a networking process.

A network orientation is *dynamic*. It recognizes new connections being formed and attends to changes in the movements of people, information, and other resources. Over the three years of the project, we realized that health services were becoming increasingly active in the promotion, and resourcing, of early literacy. We saw community nurses advising mothers to read to babies and referring them to associated online resources, and we listened as the nurses spoke about their movements conducting home visits. This phenomenon highlighted the significance of networking infrastructure—well developed in the community health system—when governments seek to maximize the reach of their messages about parental involvement in early learning.

Because ANT encompasses multiple kinds of entities and networking processes, it is compatible with a multiliteracies orientation (New London Group 1996). It is also able to manage the idea that texts *transform* as they pass through different kinds of networks. A pdf downloaded from a webpage can be printed out and then handed to someone; a television program can be recorded as a DVD, sold in a shop and played in a car; a piece of advice can be given verbally and then passed on via Facebook. These transformations may be planned by a producer in order to maximize the circulation of a product or program. Nichols' study of the Six Thinking Hats (de Bono 1985) showed how this 'technology for creating thinking subjects' had been taken up by corporations, solo entrepreneurs, educational systems, and individual practitioners including in early years classrooms (2006, 174). The design of the 'hats' built in their transformability across modalities and contexts by making them available in multiple formats including wall poster, copy-free handout, website, and scripts for enactment. We have found that the early learning field offers many opportunities for such transformations. This is partly owing to the nature of young children as creatures who apprehend the world through their senses in the years before formal literacy training equips them to decode print language. Thus programs for early learning tend to exploit multiple modalities, such as Baby Bounce and its equivalents which operate through touch, visual image, rhythm, and music in orienting infants to language. The song may become the mobile element of such a program, traveling home in the embodied memory of parent and child.

For us as researchers, thinking of ourselves as actor-networks has encouraged us to attend to our own networking processes. This was particularly evident as we sought ways to connect with those parents who did not appear at the 'usual' early childhood sites such as playgroups and libraries. We found ourselves at football practice, visiting a charity preschool for homeless children, volunteering a research assistant for weekly sessions at a church-run African Women's Day, and on the phone to ethnic association officers. At times, other actor-networks transformed us into resources by accessing our literacy knowledge, or used us to acquire resources, such as when a researcher brought back children's books to the country town of Geraldine for members of the Southeast Asian community. Some connections took much time to secure, as our requests circulated through both formal and informal approval processes. Not all our attempts to get ourselves connected into networks or to get information about the project into circulation were successful despite time, persistence and financial support.

The actor-network approach to thinking about early learning can be contrasted with a currently popular model for service provision, the 'one-stop shop'. Governments in many parts of the world are investing in the centralization and integration of services for young children and their families. The concept of a 'one-stop shop' appears in many plans and statements issuing from government departments (Laurance 2007; Coorey 2008). Recurring in these descriptions is the notion that families want all their information, advice, and services to be provided in just one place, along with the assumption that differences between service providers can be addressed by providing a localized coordinating management.

Our analysis suggests that there are significant problems both theoretically and practically with the idea of a single geographically located magnet to which parents will be drawn by their need for resources. This is not to say that bringing together services such as child care and kindergarten under the one roof will not be appreciated by families. The problem is when the 'one-stop shop' model becomes associated with the idea that information, advice, and resources are located 'in' the 'shop', and the role of parents is to come and get it. This can reinforce the assumption of a one-way flow of knowledge, denying parents and children agency in circulating knowledge through networks. Paradoxically, these state-run family service 'shops' generally do not offer items for purchase as does the mall or supermarket. Indeed, as we have discussed in Chapter 4, the dominant discourses of early learning promoted by health and education institutions are in tension with the kinds of messages promoted by commercial providers of so-called edutainment products. Therefore, the networking activities of commercial providers and the uptake of commercial resources by parents are not considered in the 'one-stop shop' model.

The dynamic field of early learning is not going to get simpler. It is a zone of intensive cultural production, proliferating players, and multiple networks. Those who work with families and young children might find it helpful to think of themselves as actor-networks. This would mean considering how they make connections with families and other service providers. It would mean reflecting on what kinds of things—both material and immaterial—are put into motion through their networking practices, and whether these things are designed to be transformed as they circulate. It would mean thinking about the early learning resources families may be producing or accessing in other places and what might need to change so that these could be enabled to circulate into playgroups, kindergartens, preschools, and clinics. We hope that some of what this book object carries—ways of thinking and insights into early learning in different spaces—will break away and be circulated in, and transformed through, your networks.

Author Biographies

Sue Nichols is a Senior Lecturer in Education at the University of South Australia, specialising in literacy education and practitioner inquiry. Her research interests include family involvement in education, early childhood literacy, gender, and inclusive education. She utilises ethnography, discourse analysis, case study approaches and network analysis to develop multi-layered analyses of events and interactions. Her work has been published as chapters in edited books including *Travel Notes from the New Literacy Studies*, the *Handbook of Research in Early Childhood and Gender and Early Learning Environments* and in numerous scholarly journals.

Helen Nixon is an Associate Professor of Education in the Children and Youth Research Centre at Queensland University of Technology in Brisbane, Australia. Her research interests include young people's relationships with place, their meaning-making using new media, and the implications of the changing landscape of communication for literacy curriculum and pedagogy in schools. Current projects focus on how mandated literacy assessment changes teachers' work and how teachers address the changing literacy demands of learning inside and outside school.

Sophia Rainbird is a Senior Postdoctoral Research Fellow at the Appleton Institute, Central Queensland University. Her research spans early learning, home and belonging, migrants, refugees and asylum seekers, risk and safety, organisational culture, and social impacts. Much of her research has been conducted using ethnographic research techniques amongst young families from diverse ethnic and religious backgrounds. The interface of service provision to culturally and linguistically diverse (CALD) people has also been a significant aspect throughout her work. Sophia has numerous academic articles, papers and reports published in educational and interdisciplinary fields.

Jennifer Rowsell is a Canada Research Chair in Multiliteracies at Brock University in Canada. She has published in the fields of New Literacy

Studies and multimodality. She is most noted for her books with Kate Pahl, *Literacy and Education: Understanding New Literacy Studies in the Classroom, Travel Notes From the New Literacy Studies: Instances of Practice,* and *Artifactual Literacies: Every Object Tells A Story.* Her current research involves multimodal, design-based work with teenagers; investigating digital reading epistemologies; and, exploring the nature and process of modal learning.

Bibliography

Abboud, S. K., and J. Kim. 2006. *Top of the Class: How Asian Parents Raise High Achievers*. New York: Berkley Publishing Group.

ACP MAGAZINES. 1997–2008. 'Magazine titles', Section 'Bounty's New Mother Bag'. http://www.acp.com.au/Publication.aspx?id=43b6fb8e-3f4f-4d78–98f1–59a12d467b35&mag=Bounty's+New+Mother+Bag [accessed 7 August 2008].

ACP MAGAZINES. 2007/2008. *Mother & Baby*. Free Sample Copy. Sydney, Australia.

ACP MAGAZINES. 2008. *Little Kids*. Free Sample Copy. Sydney, Australia.

American Psychiatric Association. 2000. *Diagnostic and Statistical Manual of Mental Disorders*. 4th ed. Revised. Washington: APA.

Anderson, J., A. Anderson, J. Lynch, and J. Shapiro. 2003. Storybook reading in a multicultural society: Critical perspectives. In *On Reading Books to Children: Parents and Teachers*, edited by A. van Kleek, S. Stahl, and E. Bauer. Mahwah, NJ: Lawrence Erlbaum.

Andi, S. 2011. How the Early Years Learning Framework can help shift pervasive beliefs of the social and emotional capabilities of infants and toddlers. *Contemporary Issues in Early Childhood* 12 (1):4–10.

Appadurai, A. 1990. Disjuncture and difference in the global cultural economy. *Theory, Culture and Society* 7 (2): 295–310.

Arzarello, F., and Paola, D. 2007. Semiotic games: The role of the teacher. In *Proceedings of the 31st Conference of the International Group for the Psychology of Mathematics Education*, Vol. 2, edited by J. H. Woo, H. C. Lew, K. S. Park, and D. Y. Seo, Morelia, Mexico pp 17–24.

Australian Bureau of Statistics. 2006. Census Quickstats. Canberra: Government of Australia. Released 26th July 2007.

Australian Bureau of Statistics. 2009. Childhood Education and Care, Australia June 2008 (Reissue) Released 23rd October 2009 http://www.abs.gov.au/ausstats/abs@.nsf/mf/4402.0

Backes, N. 1997. Reading the shopping mall city. *Journal of Popular Culture* 31 (3): 1–17.

Baerenholdt, J. O., and N. Aarsaether. 2002. Coping strategies, social capital and space *European Urban and Regional Studies* 9 (2): 151–166.

Ball, S., and C. Vincent. 2005. The 'childcare champion'? New labour, social justice and the childcare market. *British Educational Research Journal* 31 (5): 557–570.

Barlow, J., J. Parsons, and S. Stewart-Brown. 2005. Preventing emotional and behavioural problems: The effectiveness of parenting programmes with children less than 3 years of age. *Child: Care Health and Development* 31 (1): 33–42.

Bartlett, T., and S. Gray. 2009. Authors won't say mum on Americanisation. *Brisbane Times*, 6 October 2011.

Baxter, J., and D. Smart. 2010. *Fathering in Australia among Couple Families with Young Children*. Canberra: Australian Institute of Family Studies.

Bearne, E. 2009. Multimodality, literacy and texts: Developing a discourse. *Journal of Early Childhood Literacy* 9 (2): 156.

Beder, S. 2009. *This Little Kiddy Went to Market: The Corporate Capture of Childhood*. Sydney: University of New South Wales Press.

Bennet, K. K., D. J. Weigel, and S. S. Martin. 2002. Children's acquisition of early literacy skills: Examining family contributions. *Early Childhood Research Quarterly* 17:295–317.

Berlin, C., S. Wise, and G. Soriano. 2008. Engaging fathers in child and family services: Participation, perceptions and good practice; Stronger Families and Communities Strategy, 2004–2009. Canberra: Commonwealth of Australia.

Bill and Melinda Gates Foundation. 2005. *Investing in Children: An Early Learning Strategy for Washington State*. Seattle: Bill and Melinda Gates Foundation.

Bloch, M., and T. Popkewitz. 2000, 2005. Constructing the parent, teacher and child: Discourses of development. In *The Politics of Early Childhood Education*, edited by L. D. Soto, 7–32. New York: Peter Lang.

Bourdieu, P. 1984. *Distinction: A Social Critique of the Judgement of Taste*. Cambridge, MA: Harvard University Press.

Boylan, A. 1979. Sunday schools and changing evangelical views of children in the 1820s. *Church History* 49 (3): 320–333.

Brandt, D. 1998. Sponsors of literacy. *College Composition and Communication* 49:165–185.

Brandt, D. 2001. *Literacy in American Lives*. Cambridge: Cambridge University Press.

Brandt, D., and K. Clinton. 2006. Afterword to *Travel Notes and the New Literacy Studies: Instances of Practice* in *Travel Notes and the New Literacy Studies*, edited by K. Pahl and J. Rowsell. Clevedon, UK: Multilingual Matters.

Brantlinger, E. 2003. *Dividing Classes: How the middle class negotiates and rationalizes school advantage* New York: Routledge Falmer.

British Educational Research Association Early Years Special Interest Group. 2003. *Early Years Research: Pedagogy, Curriculum and Adult Roles, Training and Professionalism*. [CITY?]: BERA.

Brookes, S. 2002. Reaching fathers. *Literacy Today* 32 (September): 7–9.

Brusdal, R. 2005. Good and bad consumption—Parents and children's consumption. In *Children and Youth Emerging and Transforming Societies, International Conference*. Oslo, Norway.

Buckingham, D., and M. Scanlon. 2001. Parental pedagogies: An analysis of British 'edutainment' magazines for young children. *Journal of Early Childhood Literacy* 1 (3): 281–299.

Buckingham, D., and M. Scanlon. 2003. Interactivity and pedagogy in 'edu-tainment' software. *Informing Technology, Education and Society* 4 (2): 107–126.

Bulanda, R. E. 2004. Parental involvement with children: The influence of gender ideologies. *Journal of Marriage and Family* 66 (1): 40–45

Burman, E. 1994. *Deconstructing Developmental Pyschology*. London: Routledge.

Bus, A. & M. H. Van IJzendoorn. 1995. Mothers reading to their 3-year-olds: The role of mother-child attachment security in becoming literate' *Reading Research Quarterly* 30(4) 998–1015.

Busse Design USA, Inc. 2000. Case Study: LeapFrog—Corporate Communications Site. http://www.bussedesign.com/bussedesign_before_4–2009/pdfs/bdu_cs_leapfrog.pdf [accessed 28 October 2010].

Caldwell, B. 1991. Educare: New product, new future. *Developmental and Behavioural Pediatrics* 12 (3): 199–205.

Callon, M. 1986. Some elements of sociology of translation: Domestication of the scallops and the fishermen of St Brieuc Bay. In *Power, Action and Belief: A New Sociology of Knowledge*, edited by J. Law. London, Boston: Routledge & Kegan Paul.

Caputo, V. 2007. She's from a 'good family': Performing childcare and motherhood in a Canadian private school setting. *Childhood* 14 (2): 173–192.

Carbone, S., A. Fraser, R. Ramburuth, and L. Nelms. 2004. *Breaking Cycles, Building Futures: Promoting Inclusion of Vulnerable Families in Antenatal and Universal Early Childhood Services*. Melbourne: Department of Human Services.

Cardini, A. 2006. An analysis of the rhetoric and practice of educational partnerships in the UK: An arena of complexities, tensions and power. *Journal of Education Policy* 21 (4): 393–415.

Carrington, V. 2003. 'I'm in a bad mood. Let's go shopping': Interactive dolls, consumer culture and a 'glocalized' model of literacy. *Journal of Early Childhood Literacy* 3 (1): 83–98.

Chan, K., and J. McNeal. 2007. Chinese children's perception of personal and commercial communication: An urban-rural comparison. *Asian Journal of Communication* 17 (1): 97–116

Chiasson, W. 2010. LeapFrog Enterprises, Inc. Chief Executive Officer and President's 2009 Annual Report and 2010 Proxy Statement. http://media.corporate-ir.net/media_files/irol/13/131670/LF2010/HTML2/default.htm [accessed June 9, 2010].

Children Youth and Women's Health Service. 2005. Family Home Visiting Service Outline. Government of South Australia http://www.cyh.com/library/CYWHS_FHV_Service_Outline.pdf

Children, Youth and Women's Health Service. 2007. *Welcome to Your New Baby* Adelaide: Government of South Australia

Chin, E. 1993. Not of whole cloth made: The consumer environment of children. *Children's Environments* 10 (1): 90–109.

Clarke, J. 2001. Using actor-network theories for the study of literacy events and practices in global and local settings. In *International Literacy Conference*. Cape Town, SA?.

Cook, D. T. 2003. Spatial biographies of children's consumption: Market spaces of childhood in the 1930s and beyond. *Journal of Consumer Culture* 3 (2): 147–169.

Cook, D. T. 2004. Beyond either/or. *Journal of Consumer Culture* 4 (2):147–153.

Cook, D. T. 2008. Commercial enculturation: Moving beyond consumer socialization. Paper presented at the *3rd Child and Teen Consumption Conference*. Norwegian Centre for Child Research, Trondheim, Norway.

Cook-Gumperz, J. 1987. *The Social Construction of Literacy*. Cambridge: Cambridge University Press.

Cooke, K. 2004. *Kid Wrangling: The real guide to caring for babies, toddlers and little kids* Berkeley CA: Ten Speed Press.

Coorey, P. 2008. One-stop shop for mums: Rudd unveils centres to support working families. *Sydney Morning Herald* 17th April 2008.

Cope, B., and M. Kalantzis, eds. 2000. *Multiliteracies: Literacy Learning and the Design of Social Futures*. Melbourne: Macmillan.

Coyne, M., J. Kame'enui, D. Simmons, and B. Harn. 2004. Beginning reading intervention as inoculation or insulin: First-grade reading performance of strong responders to kindergarten intervention. *Journal of Learning Disabilities* 37:90.

Cross, G. 2002. Valves of desire: A historian's perspective on parents, children and marketing. *The Journal of Consumer Research* 29 (3): 441–447.

Curtis, P. 2008. Government agrees to rethink early years curriculum. *The Guardian*, 30 June 2008.

David, M. 1993. *Parents, Gender and Educational Reform*. Cambridge: Polity Press.

de Bono, E. 1985. *Six Thinking Hats: An Essential Approach to Business Management*. New York: Little, Brown, & Company.

De Certeau, M. 1984. *The Practice of Everyday Life*. Berkeley: University of California Press.

Department of Family and Community Services. 2005. Stronger Families and Communities Strategy Overview Booklet. Canberra: Government of Australia.

Department for Children Schools and Families. 2008. *Statutory Framework for the Early Years Foundation Stage* Nottingham: DCSF Publications.

Department for Education and Skills. 2004. *Five Year Strategy for Children and Learners*. London: HM Government.

Diamant-Cohen, B. 2004. Mother Goose on the loose: Applying brain research to early childhood programs in the public library. *Learning Exchange* 43 (1): 41–46.

Dickie, J. and M. McDonald 2011. Literacy in church and family sites through the eyes of Samoan children in New Zealand. *Literacy*. 45(1) 25—31.

Donzelot, J. 1979. *The Policing of Families*. New York: Pantheon Books.

Doucet, A. 2000. 'There's a huge gulf between me as a male carer and women': gender, domestic responsibility, and the community as an institutional arena. *Community Work and Family* 3 (2): 163–184.

Doucet, E. 2010. Ten tips for tracking trends. *American Libraries*. Blog post 5th November 2010. Dyson, A. H. 1993. *Social Worlds of Children Learning to Read and Write*. New York: Teachers College Press.

Edwards, M.L.K. 2004. We're decent people: Constructing and managing family identity in rural working-class communities. *Journal of Marriage and Family* 66 (2): 515–529.

Emap Australia. 2007. Promoting the use of commercial discharge packs to encourage breastfeeding. Submission to the House of Representatives Standing Committee on Health and Ageing Inquiry into Breastfeeding. Submission 180. Canberra: Australian Government.

Fallows, C., and S. Collier. 2004. *A Commonsense Guide for Australian Parents*. Sydney: Murdoch Books.

Fairclough, N. 1992. *Discourse and Social Change*. London: Polity.

Fairclough, N. 2003. *Analysing Discourse: Textual Analysis for Social Research*. London: Routledge.

Fenwick, T., and R. Edwards. 2010. *Actor-Network Theory in Education*. Abingdon & New York: Routledge.

Fernback, J. 2007. Selling ourselves? Profitable surveillance and online communities. *Critical Discourse Studies* 4 (3): 311–330.

First Five Nebraska. 2011. Why are the first five years are important? http://www.firstfivenebraska.com/why-the-first-five-years/ [accessed 27 July 2011].

Foucault, M. 1969. *The Archaeology of Knowledge*. New York: Random House.

Foucault, M. 1975. *The Birth of the Clinic: An Archaeology of Medical Perception*. New York: Vintage Books.

Foucault, M. 1990. *The History of Sexuality: Volume 1*. Translated by R. Hurley. London: Penguin.

Gagen, E. A. 2010. Disciplinary domains: Searching out different ways of doing children's research. *Children's Geographies* 8 (2): 213–214.

Garland, D., and M. Darcy. 2009. Working together? The Salvation Army and the Job Network. *Organization* 16 (5): 755–774

Gilman, M. 2007. Fighting poverty with faith: Reflections on ten years of charitable choice. *The Journal of Gender, Race and Justice* 10 (3): 395–438.

Goldberg, S. 2005. *Ready to Learn: How to Help your Preschooler Succeed.* Oxford, New York: Oxford University Press.

Goodall, G. 2003. *The Social Goal Model of Library Behaviour.* London, ON: Facetation.

Goode, S. 2000. McIntyre makes early learning profitable. *Insight on the News* 16 (12): 36–39.

Goodman, A. 2006. The story of David Olds and the nurse home visiting program. Robert Wood Johnson Foundation.

Goss, J. 1993. *The "Magic of the Mall": An Analysis of Form, Function and Meaning in the Contemporary Retail Built Environment.* London: Blackwell Publishers.

Graff, H. 1991. *The Legacies of Literacy: Continuities and Contradictions in Western Culture.* Bloomington: Indiana University Press.

Gram, M. 2004. The future world champions? Ideals for upbringing represented in contemporary European advertisements. *Childhood* 11 (3): 319–337.

Gregory, E. 2008. *Learning to Read in a New Language.* Los Angeles, London: Sage.

Gregory, E., and A. Williams. 2000. *City Literacies: Learning to Read Across Generations and Cultures.* London, New York: Routledge.

Haddad, L. 2001. An integrated approach to early childhood education and care policy: A preliminary study. In *The International Conference on Early Childhood Education and Care: International Policy Issues.* Stockholm, Sweden.

Halfon, N., M. Regalado, and K. T. McLearn. 2003. Building a bridge from birth to school: Improving developmental and behavioural health services for young children. The Commonwealth Fund.

Hamilton, M. 2010. Unruly practices: What a sociology of translations can offer to educational policy analysis. *Educational Philosophy and Theory* 4 (1): 1–21.

Haney, M. R. 2002. Name writing: A window into emergent literacy skills of young children. *Early Childhood Education Journal* 30(2): 101–105

Hartley, D. 2009. Personalisation: the nostalgic revival of child-centred education? *Journal of Education Policy* 24(4) 423–434.

Harwood, S. A. 2007. Geographies of opportunity for whom? Neighborhood improvement programs as regulators of neighborhood activism. Journal of Planning Education and Research 26(3): 261–271.

Heath, S.B. 1982. What no bedtime story means: Narrative skills at home & school. *Language and Society 11* (1):49–76.

Heath, S. B. 1983. *Ways with Words: Language life and work in communities and classrooms.* Cambridge: Cambridge University Press.Herzman, C. and T. Boyce. 2010. How experience gets under the skin to create gradients in developmental health. *Annual Review of Public Health* 31: 329–347.

Hewer, L. A., and D. Whyatt. 2006. Improving the implementation of an early literacy program by child health nurses through addressing local training and cultural needs. *Contemporary Nurse 23* (1):111–119.

High, P., M. Hopmann, L. LaGasse, R. Sege, J. Moran, C. Guiterrez, and S. Becker. 1999. Child-centered literacy orientation: A form of social capital? *Pediatrics* 103 (4) 811.

High, P. C., L. LaGasse, S. Becker, I. Ahlgren, and A. Gardner. 2000. Literacy promotion in primary care pediatrics: can we make a difference? *Pediatrics* 105 (4): 927–934.

Hill, S., and S. Nichols. 2006. Emergent literacy: Symbols at work. In *Handbook of Research on the Education of Young Children,* edited by B. Spodek and O. Saracho. Mahwah, NJ: Lawrence Erlbaum.

Hirsh-Pask, K., R. Golinkoff, and D. Eyer. 2003. *Einstein Never Used Flashcards: How Our Children Really Learn and Why They Need to Play More and Memorize Less.* Emmaus, PA: Rodale.

Hodgetts, K. 2008. Underperformance or 'getting it right'? Constructions of gender and achievement in the Australian inquiry into boys' education. *British Journal of Sociology of Education* 29 (5): 465–477.

Hoffman, D. M. 2009. How (not) to feel: Culture and the politics of emotion in the American parenting advice literature. *Discourse: Studies in the Cultural Politics of Education* 30 (1): 15–31.

Holloway, S. 1998. Local childcare cultures: Moral geographies of mothering and the social organisation of pre-school education. *Journal of Feminist Geography* 5 (1): 29–53.

Hollway, W. 2006. Family figures in 20th century British 'Psy' discourses. *Theory and Psychology* 16 (4):443—464.

Holt, J., and P. Farenga. 2003. *Teach Your Own: The John Holt Book Of Homeschooling*. New Caledonia: Da Capo Press.

Howley, A., L. Spatig, and C. Howley. 1999. Developmentalism deconstructed. In *Rethinking Intelligence: Confronting Psychological Assumptions about Teaching and Learning*, edited by J.K.L. Villaverde. New York, London: Routledge.

Hula, R., C. Jackson-Elmoore, and L. Reese. 2007. Mixing God's work and the public business: A framework for the analysis of faith-based service delivery. *The Review of Policy Research* 24 (1): 67–89.

Inda, J. X. 2005. *Anthropologies of Modernity: Foucault, Governmentality and Politics*. London: John Wiley & Sons.

International Reading Association (2008) Making the most of reading tests. Newark DE: IRA.

Jalongo, M. R., B. S. Fennimore, J. Pattnaik, D. M. Laverick, J. Brewster, and M. Mutuku. 2004. Blended perspectives: A global vision for high-quality early childhood education. *Early Childhood Education Journal* 32 (3): 143–155.

Janes, H., and H. Kermani. 2001. Caregivers' story reading to young children in family literacy programs: Pleasure or punishment? *Journal of Adolescent & Adult Literacy* 44 (5): 458–466.

Jianghong, L., A. D'Angiulli, and G. Kendall. 2007. The Early Development Index and children from culturally and linguistically diverse backgrounds. *Early Years* 27 (3): 221–235.

Johnson-Eilola, J. 1997. Living on the surface: Learning in the age of global communication networks. In *Page to Screen: Taking Literacy into the Electronic Age*, edited by I. Snyder, 185–210. Sydney: Allen & Unwin.

Jutila, C., J. Wideman, and P. Verbal. 2006. *Children's Ministry in the 21st Century*. Loveland, CO: Group Publishing.

Karas, D. 2011. Public libraries fight to stay relevant in digital age. *The Christian Science Monitor* (June).

Kaverley, K., and J. Kostelc. 2008. *Focus on Fathering*. St. Louis MO: Parents as Teachers National Center.

Kellner, D. 1995. *Media Culture: Cultural Studies, Identity and Politics Between the Modern and the Postmodern*. London, New York: Routledge.

Kidspot. Buddy's Bright Ideas. http://www.kidspot.com.au/sponsor/sultana-bran+30.htm [accessed 11 November 2011].

King, A. 2001. Engaging fathers in group work: Creating cooperative environments. *Developing Practice: The Child, Youth and Family Work Journal* 1 (Winter): 30–37.

Kizman, H. J., D. L. Olds, R. E Cole, C. A. Hanks, E. A. Anson, K. J. Arcoleo, D. W. Luckey, M. D. Knudtson, C. R. Henderson, and J. R. Holmberg. 2010. Enduring effects of prenatal and infancy home visiting by nurses on children: Follow-up of a randomized trial among children age 12 years. *Archives of Pediatrics & Adolescent Medicine* 164 (5): 412–418.

Klass, P. 2002. Pediatrics by the book: Pediatricians and literacy promotion. *Pediatrics* 110 (5): 989–995.

Kress, G. 2000a. Design and transformation: New theories of meaning. In *Multiliteracies: Literacy Learning and the Design of Social Futures*, edited by B. Cope and M. Kalantzis. Melbourne: Macmillan.

Kress, G. 2000b. Multimodality. In *Multiliteracies: Literacy Learning and the Design of Social Futures*, edited by B. Cope and M. Kalantzis. Melbourne: Macmillan.

Kress, G., and T. van Leeuwen. 1996. *Reading Images: The Grammar of Visual Design*. London, New York: Routledge.

Kress, G., and T. van Leeuwen, 2001. *Multimodal Discourse: The Modes and Media of Contemporary Communication*. London: Arnold.

Kuo, A. A., T. M. Franke, M. Regalado, and N. Halfon. 2004. Parent report of reading to young children. *Pediatrics* 113 (6): 1944–1951.

Kwan, C. and S. S. Nam. 2004. Utilizing parental observations and computer technology in developing a child-screening instrument in Singapore. *International Journal of Early Years Education* 12 (2).

Lancaster, J., and British and Foreign Society. 1816/1994. *Manual of the System of Teaching*. Bristol: Thoemmes Press.

Lareau, A. 1989. *Home Advantage: Social Class and Parental Intervention in Elementary Education*. London, New York: Falmer Press.

Latour, B. 1987a. *Science in Action*. Cambridge, MA: Harvard University Press.

Latour, B. 1987b. The powers of association. In *Power, Action and Belief: A New Sociology of Knowledge*, edited by J. Law. London: Routledge.

Latour, B. 1993. *We Have Never Been Modern*. Translated by C. Porter. New York: Harvester Wheatsheaf.

Latour, B. 1996. On actor-network theory: A few clarifications plus more than a few complications. English version in *Soziale Welt* 47:369–381. Available http://www.bruno-latour.fr/sites/default/files/P-67%20ACTOR-NETWORK.pdf [accessed 14 Dec 2011].

Laurance, J. 2007. GP surgeries to become 'one-stop shop' for patients. *The Independent*. UK, 6 February.

Law, J. 1992. Notes on the theory of the actor network: Ordering, strategy and heterogeneity. Published by the Centre for Science Studies, Lancaster University. http://www.comp.lancs.ac.uk/sociology/papers/Law-Notes-on-ANT.pdf [accessed 9 July 2005]

Law, J. 1999. After ANT: Complexity, naming and topology. In *Actor Network Theory and After*, edited by J. Law and J. Hassard. Oxford: Blackwell Publishing.

Law, J. 2003. Materialities, spatialities, globalities. Published by the Centre for Science Studies, Lancaster University. http://www.comp.lancs.ac.uk/sociology/papers/Law-Heatherington-Materialities-Spatialities-Globalities.pdf [accessed 9 July 2005].

Law, J. 2007. Actor network theory and material semiotics. 25 April 2007. http://www.heterogeneities.net/publications/Law2007ANTandMaterialSemiotics.pdf [accessed 26 October 2011].

Lawhon, T., and J. B. Cobb. 2002. Routines that build emergent literacy skills in infants, toddlers and preschoolers. *Early Childhood Education Journal* 30 (2): 113–118.

Leach, P. 1988. *Baby and Child*. Fort Lauderdale FL: Michael Joseph Ltd.

LeapFrog Enterprises, Inc. 2001–2010. Learning Path. Demo. http://www.leapfrog.com/en_au/landingpages/demo_page.html [accessed 9 June 2010].

Learning Ladder. 'About Us'. http://www.learningladder.com.au/aboutus.cfm [accessed 7 November 2011].

Lefebvre, H. 1976. *The Survival of Capitalism: Reproduction of the Relations of Production.* Translated by F. Bryant. New York: St. Martin's Press.

Lemke, J. L. 2000. Across the scales of time: Artifacts, activities and meanings in ecosocial systems. *Mind, Culture, and Activity* 7 (4): 273–290.

Levi-Strauss, C. 1966. *The Savage Mind.* Chicago: University of Chicago Press.

Lewis, T. E. 2009. Education and the immunization paradigm. *Studies in the Philosophy of Education* 28:485–498.

Lindmark, D. 2003. Reading cultures, christianization, and secularization: Universalism and particularism in the Swedish history of literacy. *Interchange* 34 (2): 197–217.

Linke, P. 2006. *Right from the Start . . . Loving Reading With Your Baby.* Adelaide, SA: Parenting SA/Child, Youth and Women's Health Services. 2ⁿᵈ ed.

Linn, S. 2005. *Consuming Kids: Protecting Our Children from the Onslaught of Marketing and Advertising.* New York: Anchor Books.

Luke, A., and C. Luke. 2001. Adolescence lost/childhood regained: On early intervention and the emergence of the techno-subject *Journal of Early Childhood Literacy* 1(1) 91–120

Luke, A., and C. Luke. 2000. A situated perspective on cultural globalization. In *Globalization and Education: Critical Perspectives*, edited by N. Burbules and C. A. Torres. New York: Routledge.

Luke, C. 1989. *Pedagogy Printing and Protestantism: The Discourse on Childhood.* Albany: State University Press of New York.

Luke, C., ed. 1996. *Feminisms and Pedagogies of Everyday Life.* Albany: State University of New York Press.

Lury, C. (1996). *Consumer Culture.* Oxford: Polity Press.

Luther, M. 1530/1967. A sermon on keeping children in school. *Luther's Works*, vol. 46. Philadelphia: Fortress Press, 213–257.

MacGillivray, L., A. Ardell, and M. Curwen. 2009. Libraries, churches, and schools: The literate lives of mothers and children in a homeless shelter. *Urban Education* 45 (2): 221–245.

MacNaughton, G., and P. Hughes. 2005. Take the money and run? Toys, consumerism, and capitalism in early childhood conferences. In *The Politics of Early Childhood Education*, edited by L. Diaz Soto. New York: Peter Lang.

Madge, C., and H. O'Connor. 2006. Parenting gone wired: Empowerment of new mothers on the Internet? *Social and Cultural Geography* 7 (2): 199–220.

Malin, N., and G. Morrow 2007. Models of interprofessional working within a Sure Start 'Trailblazer' programme. *Journal of Interprofessional Care* 21 (4): 445–457.

Manguel, A. 2007. *The Library at Night.* Toronto: Vintage Canada.

Mannion, G., R. Ivanic, and the LfFE Research Group. 2007. Mapping literacy practices: Theory, methodology, methods. *International Journal of Qualitative Research in Education* 20 (1): 15–30

Manzo, J. 2005. Social control and the management of 'personal' space in shopping malls. *Space and Culture* 8 (1): 83–97.

Marcus, G. E. 1998. *Ethnography through Thick and Thin.* Princeton: Princeton University Press.

Marsh, J. 2006. Global, local/public, private: young children's engagement in digital literacy practices in the home. In *Travel Notes from the New Literacy Studies*, edited by K. Pahl and J. Rowsell. Clevedon UK: Multilingual Matters Ltd.

Marsh, J. 2008. Out-of-school play in online virtual worlds and the implications for literacy learning. Paper presented at the Centre for Studies in Literacy, Policy and Learning Cultures, University of South Australia, July 2008.

Massey, D. 2000. The conceptualization of place. In *A Place in the World? Places, Cultures and Globalization*, edited by D. Massey and P. Jess. New York: Oxford University Press.

Massey, D. 2005. *For Space*. London: Sage.

McNaughton, S. 2002. On making early interventions problematic: A response to Luke and Luke. *Journal of Early Childhood Literacy* 2 (1): 97–103.

Moll, L. C., C. Amanti, D. Neff, and N. Gonzalez. 1992. Funds of knowledge for teaching: Using a qualitative approach to connect homes and classrooms. *Theory Into Practice* 31 (2): 133–141.

Monaghan, E, J. 2005. *Learning to Read and Write in Colonial America* Amherst MA: University of Massachusetts Press.

Morgan, R. 1993. Transitions from English to cultural studies. *New Education* 15 (1): 21–48.

Mulcahy, D. 2010. Assembling the accomplished teacher: The performativity and politics of professional teaching standards. *Educational Philosophy and Theory* 43 (December): S94–113.

Murdoch, J. 1998. The spaces of actor-network theory. *Geoforum* 29 (4): 357–374.

Nadesan, M. H. 2002. Engineering the entrepreneurial infant. *Cultural Studies* 16 (3): 401–432.

Needleman, R., and M. Silverstein. 2004. Pediatric interventions to support reading aloud: How good is the evidence? *Journal of Developmental and Behavioural Pediatrics* 25 (5): 352–363.

Needleman, R., K. Toker, B. Dreyer, P. Klass, and A. Mendelsohn. 2005. Effectiveness of a primary care intervention to support reading aloud: A multicenter evaluation. *Ambulatory Pediatrics* 4 (5): 209–215.

Neuman, S., and D. Celano. 2001. Access to print in low-income and middle-income communities: An ecological study of four neighbourhoods. *Reading Research Quarterly* 36 (1): 8–26.

Neuman, S., and D. Celano. 2010. *Executive Summary (2010): Evaluation of Every Child Ready to Read 1st Edition*. http://www.everychildreadytoread. org/project-history%09/executive-summary-2010-evaluation-every-child-ready-read-1st-edition [accessed 9 August 2011].

New London Group. 1996. A pedagogy of multiliteracies. *Harvard Educational Review* 60 (1): 66–92.

Nichols, S. 2000. Unsettling the bedtime story: Parents' reports of home literacy practices. *Contemporary Issues in Early Childhood* 1 (3): 315–328.

Nichols, S. 2002. Parents' construction of their children as gendered, literate subjects: A critical discourse analysis. *Journal of Early Childhood Literacy* 2 (2): 123–144.

Nichols, S. 2006. From boardroom to classroom: Tracing a discourse on thinking across internet texts and classroom practice. In *Travel Notes from the New Literacy Studies*, edited by K. Pahl and J. Rowell, 173–194. London: Routledge.

Nichols, S. 2009. Fathers in educational research. Paper presented at the *Gender and Education Conference*, London, March 25–27.

Nichols, S. 2011. Young children's literacy in the activity space of the library: A geosemiotic investigation. *Journal of Early Childhood Literacy* 11 (2): 164–189.

Nichols, S., H. Nixon, and J. Rowsell. 2009. The "good" parent in relation to early childhood literacy: Symbolic terrain and lived practice. *Literacy* 43 (2): 65–74.

Nichols, S., H. Nixon, and J. Rowsell. 2011. Researching early childhood literacy in place. *Journal of Early Childhood Literacy* 11 (2): 107–113.

Nixon, H. 1998. Fun and games are serious business. In *Digital Diversions: Youth Culture in the Age of Multimedia*, edited by J. Sefton-Green. London: University College London Press.

Nixon, H. 2011. 'From bricks to clicks': Hybrid commercial spaces in the landscape of early literacy and learning. *Journal of Early Childhood Literacy* 11 (2): 114–140.

Nord, C. W., J. Lennon, B. Liu, and K. Chandler. 1999. *Home Literacy Activities and Signs of Children's Emerging Literacy, 1993–1999*. National Center for Education Statistics, US Department of Education.

Odih, P. 2002. Mentors and role models: Masculinity and the educational 'under-achievement' of young Afro-Caribbean males. Race Ethnicity and Education 5(1) 91–105.

Organisation for Economic Cooperation and Development. 2001 *Starting Strong: Early childhood education and care*. Paris: OECD.

Ortlipp, M., L. Arthur, and C. Woodrow. 2011. Discourses of the early years learning framework: Constructing the early childhood professional. *Contemporary Issues in Early Childhood* 12 (1): 56–70.

Oklahoma Champions for Early Opportunities. 2011. State Group of Business & Community Leaders Promotes Investment in Early Learning. http://www.facebook.com/note.php?note_id=204240402920364 [accessed 12 August 2011].

Oser, C. 2006. Babies and libraries: Serving the youngest patrons of a community. *Library Student Journal* (September).

Parenting SA. Various dates. *Parent Easy Guides*. Adelaide: Government of South Australia. http://www.parenting.sa.gov.au/pegs/peg_category.asp?peg_category_id=9#peg80 [access 20 Aug 2008].

Parenting SA. 2010. *Why Stories are Important. Parent Easy Guide 57*. Adelaide: Government of South Australia.

Peers, C. 2011. The Australian Early Development Index: Reshaping family–child relationships in early childhood education. *Contemporary Issues in Early Childhood* 12 (2): 134–147.

Peterson, G. 2011. Let's connect: Living breathing examples. *E-Connect* Issue 43 http://www.salvationarmy.org.au/e-connect-issue-43.html?s=0 Accessed online 16th December 2011.Pianta, R., M. Kraft-Sayre, S. Rimm-Kaufman, N. Gercke, and T. Higgins. 2001. Collaboration in building partnerships between families and schools: The National Centre for Early Development and Learning's kindergarten transition intervention. *Early Childhood Research Quarterly* 16 (1): 117–132.

Plowman, L., J. McPake, and C. Stephen. 2008. Just picking it up? Young children learning with technology at home. *Cambridge Journal of Education* 38 (3): 303–319.

Prosser, J. 2008. Introducing Visual Methods. Southampton: ESRC National Centre for Research Methods.

Puchner, L. D. 1995. Literacy links: Issues in the relationship between early childhood development, health, women, families and literacy. *International Journal of Educational Development* 15 (3): 307.

Raising Arizona Kids. 2011. *Doctor's Prescription: Reading*. http://rakschoolsetc.wordpress.com/tag/improving-reading-skills/ [accessed 8 January 2011].

Pyjama Foundation, The. (http://www.thepyjamafoundation.com/about_us.htm [accessed 15 November 2011]).

Reay, D. 1998. *Class Work: Mothers' Involvement in Their Children's Primary Schooling*. London: UCL Press.

Reese, L. A. 2004. A matter of faith: urban congregations and economic development. *Economic Development Quarterly*, 18(1), 50–66.

Richter, L. 2004. *The Importance of Caregiver-Child Interactions for the Survival and Healthy Development of Young Children: A Review*. Geneva, Switzerland: World Health Organization, Department of Child and Adolescent Health and Development.

Ricouer, P. 1980. On Narrative. *Critical Inquiry* 7(1) 169–190.

Riley, D. 1983. *War in the Nursery: Theories of the Child and Mother*. London: Virago.

Roditti, M. G. 2005. Understanding communities of neglectful parents: Child caregiving networks and child neglect. *Child Welfare* 84 (2): 277–298.

Rose, N. 1990. *Governing the Soul: The Shaping of the Private Self.* New York: Routledge.

Rowsell, J., and S. Nichols 2009. Time-space travel: Fostering parenting identities through movement across neighbourhood hubs. Paper given at the American Educational Research Association Conference, San Diego, April 13–17.

Ruby, M. 2008. Hasanat and Qur'an reading in Britain. In *Learning to Read in a New Language*, edited by E. Gregory. Los Angeles, London, New Delhi, Singapore: Sage.

Rundman, D. 2009. Ministry to the Sippy-cup Set. *Lutheran Partners* 25 (4). http://www.elca.org/Growing-In-Faith/Vocation/Lutheran-Partners/Complete-Issue/090708/090708_06.aspx [accessed 20 October 2011].

Salamon, A. 2011. How the early years learning framework can help shift pervasive beliefs of social and emotional capabilities of infants and toddlers. *Contemporary Issues in Early Childhood* 12 (1): 4–10.

Salcedo, R. 2003. When the global meets the local at the mall. *American Behavioral Scientist* 46 (8): 1084–1103.

Salvation Army, The. First Steps. http://www.salvationarmy.org.au/children/first-steps.html [accessed 15 November 2011].

Salvation Army, The. 2010. Tasmania Division gains funding for parenting support scheme. *E-Connect* Issue 17. http://www.salvationarmy.org.au/e-connect-issue-17.html [accessed 15 November 2011].

Sarkadi, A., and S. Bremberg. 2005. Socially unbiased parenting support on the Internet: A cross-sectional study of users of a large Swedish parenting website. *Child: Care, Health & Development* 31 (1): 43–52.

Saulnier, K. M., and C. Rowland, 1985. Missing links: An empirical investigation of network variables in high-risk families. *Family Relations* 34:557–560.

Scanlon, M., and D. Buckingham. 2004. Home learning and the educational marketplace. *Oxford Review of Education* 30 (2): 287–303.

Scharer, K. 2005. An internet discussion board for parents of mentally ill young children. *Journal of Child and Adolescent Psychiatric Nursing* 18 (1):17–25.

Schneider, R. and P. Burke. 1999. Multiple attachment relationships within families: Mothers and fathers with two young children. *Developmental Psychology* 35(2) 436—441.

Scollon, R., and S. Scollon. 2003. *Discourse in Place: Language in the Material World.* London: Routledge.

Seddon, T., S. Billett, and A. Clemans. 2005. Navigating social partnerships: Central agencies—local networks. *British Journal of Educational Studies* 26 (5): 567–584.

Seiter, E. 1995. *Sold Separately: Parents and Children in Consumer Culture.* New Brunswick: Rutgers University Press.

Sheller, M., and J. Urry. 2006. The new mobilities paradigm. *Environment and Planning A* 38 (2): 207–226.

Sheridan, M. P., and J. Rowsell. 2010. *Design Literacies: Learning and Innovation in the Digital Age.* London: Routledge

Smeyers, P. 2008. Child-rearing: On government intervention and the discourse of experts. *Educational Philosophy and Theory* 40 (6): 719–738.

Smythe, S. 2009. The good mother: A critical discourse analysis of literacy advice to mothers in the 20th century. Dissertation, University of British Columbia, Vancouver BC.

Song, M., and C. Miskel. 2005. Who are the influentials? A cross-state social network analysis of the reading policy domain. *Educational Administration Quarterly* 41 (1): 7–48.

Soja, E. 2010. *Seeking Spatial Justice*. Minneapolis: University of Minnesota Press.

Steward, E. P. 1995. *Beginning Writers in the Zone of Proximal Development*. London, Lawrence Erlbaum.

Sulzby, E., and W. Teale. 1986. *Emergent Literacy: Writing and Reading*. Norwood, NJ: Ablex.

Teel, C. 2007. Spirituality in the Christian nursery: Toddler, family and church family. Doctoral dissertation. United Theological Seminary, Dayton, Ohio.

Terman, L. 1914. *The Hygiene of the School Child*. [publisher] In T. E. Lewis. 2009. Education and the immunization paradigm. *Studies in the Philosophy of Education* 28:485–498.

Thompson, A. 2011. How Kidspot got started (then sold for $10 million more than Myspace). http://www.getstarted.com.au/Blog/Blog/July-2011/How-Kidspot-got-started-sold-for-more-than-myspace.aspx [accessed 11 November 2011].

Thomson, P. 2002. *Schooling the Rustbelt Kids: Making the Difference in Changing Times*. Allen & Unwin: Crows Nest, NSW.

Toys"R"Us, Inc. 2010. *Toys"R"Us Toy Guide for Differently Abled Kids*. http://www.disabled-world.com/entertainment/games/toy-guide.php#ixzz1czE5VNYk [accessed 6 November 2011].

Trelease, J. 2006. *The Read-Aloud Handbook*. 6th ed. New York: Penguin Books.

Trushell, J. 1998. Juliet makes her mark. *Reading* April:29–32.

Tyler, D. 1993. Making better children. In *Child and Citizen: Genealogies of Schooling and Subjectivity*, edited by D. Meredyth and D. Tyler. Nathan, Qld: Griffith University Press.

US Departments of Education and Health and Human Services. 2010. *Promoting Early Learning for Success in School and in Life*. Federal Budget Paper. http://www.ed.gov/sites/default/files/2011-budget-promoting-early-learning.pdf [accessed 28 Nov 2011].

Vera, E., and T. Schupp. 2006. Network analysis in comparative social sciences. *Comparative Education* 42 (3): 405–429.

Vernon, D. 2005. *Having a Great Birth in Australia*. Canberra: Australian College of Midwives.

Viseu, A., A. Clement, J. Aspinall, and T. L. Kennedy. 2006. The interplay of public and private spaces in Internet access. *Information, Communication and Society* 9 (5): 633–656.

Volk, D. 2008. Julializ and Bible Readings in the United States. In *Learning to Read in a New Language: Making Sense of Words and Worlds*, edited by E. Gregory. London: Sage.

Volling, B., N. McElwain, P. Notaro, and C. Herrera. 2002. Parents' emotional availability and infant emotional competence: Predictors of parent-infant attachment and emerging self-regulation. *Journal of Family Psychology* 16(4) 447–465.

Walkerdine, V. 1984. Developmental psychology and the child-centred pedagogy. In *Changing the Subject: Psychology, Social Regulation and Subjectivity*, edited by J. Henriques, W. Holloway, C. Urwin, C. Venn, and V. Walkerdine. London: Methuen.

Walkerdine, V. 1988. *The Mastery of Reason*. London: Routledge.

Walkerdine, V., and H. Lucey. 1989. *Democracy in the Kitchen*. London: Virago.

Wallace, C. 2008. Literacy and identity: A view from the bridge in two multicultural London schools. *Journal of Language, Identity & Education* 7 (1): 61–80.

Wang, G. 2003. 'Net-Moms'—a new place and a new identity: parenting discussion forums on the Internet in China. *Provincial China* 8 (1): 78–88.

Ward, A., and L. Wason-Elam. 2005. Reading beyond school: Literacies in a neighbourhood library. *Canadian Journal of Education* 28 (1): 92–108.

Webber, R., and D. Boromeo. 2005. The sole parent family: Family support networks. *Australian Journal of Social Issues* 40 (2): 269–283.

Weitzman, C. C., L. Roy, T. Walls, and R. Tomlin. 2004. More evidence for Reach Out and Read: A home-based study. *Pediatrics* 113 (5): 1248–1253.

Westfield Corporation. 2008. Westfield BrandSpace. http://westfield.com/corporate/property-portfolio/australia/brand-space/ [accessed 11 Oct 2008].

Whalley, M., and Pen Green Centre Team. 2001. *Involving Parents in their Children's Learning*. London: Paul Chapman.

Woodhead, M. 2006. Changing perspectives on early childhood: Theory, research and policy. *International Journal of Equity and Innovation in Early Childhood* 4 (2): 1–43.

Woods, A., and R. Henderson. 2008. The early intervention solution: Enabling or constraining literacy. *Journal of Early Childhood Literacy* 8 (3): 251–268.

Woollet, A., and A. Phoenix. 1996. Motherhood as pedagogy: Developmental psychology and the accounts of mothers of young children. In *Feminisms and Pedagogies of Everyday Life*, edited by C. Luke. Albany: State University of New York Press.

Wynne-Jones, J. 2011. Philip Pullman leads day of protests at planned closure of libraries. *The Telegraph*, 20 September.

Zengotta, T. 2005. *Mediated: How the Media Shapes Your World*. London: Bloomsbury.

Zuckerman, B., and N. Halfon. 2003. School readiness: An idea whose time has arrived. *Pediatrics* 111 (6):1433–1436.

Zuckerman, B.,,and S. Parker. 1995. Preventive pediatrics: New models of providing needed health services. *Pediatrics* 95 (5): 758–762.

Index